YOU&YOUR
CAT

YOU&YOUR CAT

DAVID TAYLOR B.V.M.S. F.R.C.V.S.

DORLING KINDERSLEY · LONDON

Project editor	Judith More
Art editor	Carole Ash
Assistant designer	Tina Vaughan
Assistant editor	Janice Lacock
Senior art editor	Peter Luff
Managing editor	Alan Buckingham

First published in Great Britain in 1986 by
Dorling Kindersley Publishers Limited,
9 Henrietta Street, London WC2E 8PS.
First published in paperback in 1987 by
Dorling Kindersley Limited
ninth impression 1997

British Library Cataloguing in Publication Data

Taylor, David, 1934–
You and your cat,
1. Cats
I. Title
636.8'083 SF447
ISBN 0-86318-085-X (hardback)
ISBN 0-7513-0272-4 (paperback)

Printed in Hong Kong by Wing King Tong

Contents

INTRODUCTION

The human race can be roughly divided into two categories: *ailurophiles* and *ailurophobes* — cat lovers and the underprivileged. The appreciation of cats is engraved deep in the human soul, and is of ancient origin. Cats have had great significance for humans over the centuries. They have been worshipped and feared, cherished as good omens and massacred for being agents of the devil.

When did cats first become pets?

The first tamed cats were used for pest control in ancient Egypt, probably around 3,000 BC, and came to be loved as household companions and worshipped as gods. The Egyptians were impressed by these supremely successful hunters — with their strength, agility, cunning and lethal purpose — and began to treat them as sacred. The name for these household gods was "miw". Owners went into mourning when "miw" died, the cat was embalmed, placed in a wooden coffin, and taken to the Great Temple of Bast (the cat god) at Bubastis. The ancient Egyptians mummified their dead pets in vast numbers, and studies of these mummies have helped scientists to prove that *Felis libyca* was the original domestic species (see *Origins of the cat*, pp. 41–2). Cats were domesticated in the Far East in ancient times too, but at a later date than in Egypt. Some authorities put domestication at 2,000 BC in China, others place it as late as AD 400.

From Egypt, domestic cats spread to Italy and then slowly throughout Europe, gaining "worshippers" in many lands. But by the Middle Ages cats' fortunes had changed. The Christian church disliked their connections with pagan cults, and waged a campaign against them. Perhaps because of the inscrutable, knowing ways of the animal, the superstitious believed that witches could assume the feline form. This belief had unfortunate consequences — cats were often burnt alive by Christians, who believed them to be agents of the devil. But slowly, the unpopularity of cats faded as their usefulness was realized again, and by the eighteenth century they were once more a familiar sight in many households. During the nineteenth century they became very popular, and by the end of the century the early pedigree breeds were exhibited at the first cat shows (see *Showing*, p. 178).

1554 engraving of a cat's execution (above)
In pagan religions, cats were often deified. As part of the campaign to rid Europe of pagan cults, the Christian church denounced cats as agents of the devil. As a result, thousands of cats were executed in the Middle Ages. In Protestant England cats were associated with heresy — in this engraving the cat is dressed as a Catholic priest.

Roman mosaic of a domestic tabby (top)
Cats were first brought to Italy from Egypt before the birth of Christ. In classical times, the followers of Diana revered cats.

Ancient Egyptian statuette (right)
Cats were worshipped as gods in ancient Egypt. This bronze figure was probably used for religious ceremonies.

What is the value of a cat as a pet?

Cats are inexpensive to buy — you can obtain a non-pedigree from a friend or a humane society for nothing, and even a pedigree kitten from a breeder, with a few rare and expensive exceptions, will only cost the equivalent of a couple of days' pay for the average citizen. And cats cost very little to feed and care for compared to other popular pets such as dogs or ponies.

Although cheap to acquire and cheap to run in monetary terms, a cat is worth its weight in gold to its new owner. It will provide amusement and companionship, as well as adding a touch of style and elegance to your home. A cat can be fitted into the smallest apartment, and is an excellent pet for a working owner as it doesn't require 24-hour attention. Elderly folk benefit from the companionship of a cat, and young people can learn a lot by having a feline pet of their own to care for. The stewardship of a cat isn't difficult: your cat won't make the exercise demands of a dog, and it doesn't need a battery of costly technical equipment, such as that required for aquarium fishes.

Building a good relationship with your cat

Unlike dogs, cats don't take lightly to being "owned" — their individuality is never up for grabs. For a good relationship with your cat you shouldn't treat it as a possession, instead try to see it as a sojourner in your household, choosing to spend its time with you and asking nothing in return apart from a modest supply of food and drink (see *Feeding*, pp. 154—65).

A cat's affection has to be won — unlike a dog, it won't remain with a poor owner out of a misguided sense of loyalty. On the other hand, a cat will recognize an understanding, appreciative owner and respond with affection and respect. In order to get the best out of your feline friend you must understand its nature and behave towards your household companion accordingly.

The nature of the cat

The cat is in essence a perfect animal — one of nature's designs that works supremely well: it looks good, functions precisely, owes nothing to anyone, gives much and demands little. Quintessentially

A companion in old age (left)
Cats make excellent pets for senior citizens: they provide undemanding companionship and are easy to care for. And they may even be good for the health — stroking one is said to be an effective way of lowering blood pressure.

Cats and children (above)
Children appreciate the amusement and affectionate contact that a cat provides. And under a parent's guidance, a child can learn to become a responsible pet owner.

aware, it is always finely "tuned-in" to the world about it. All felines have the stamp of innate aristocracy. The domestic cat's family tree boasts the most cunning, subtle, dangerous, handsome and valiant mammals on this planet. Your pet is quite docile compared to a puma, but unlike other domesticated animals such as the dog, it has an independent streak that smacks of its wild past. Indeed, the cat was tamed much later than other domestic beasts. Its inclination is never to fawn or creep — if you want an obedient servant as a pet you shouldn't choose a cat; pick a dog instead.

Although the dog and the cat are both classical carnivores, the cat is more adapted to the role of hunter. In general, wild dogs hunt in packs, whilst cats, with the exception of some lion prides, venture out on the chase singly. Like its wild "cousins", the domesticated cat is a beast who walks alone, and this individuality makes the cat a particularly suitable pet, in my view, for the individualistic sort of human being.

A close association with man has resulted in a wide gulf between the modern dog's physique and that of its wild roots, a wolf-like

The "cat nap" (above)
Cats are often seen stretching
and yawning. Originators of the
"cat nap", they sleep, albeit in
short bursts, more than any other
mammal.

Raising the hackles (right)
This characteristic feline behaviour is an "on-guard" reaction
to a potential threat, whether
it be an unexplained noise or
aggression from another cat. It
may be accompanied by hissing.

Battling cats (opposite)
Displays of feline aggression
usually involve disputes over
territory. Here, one cat has
indicated its submission by lying
on its back.

ancestor. This isn't the case with cats, where even the show-bench
Longhair or Siamese remains close in physique and spirit to its
origins. Just beneath the skin of your slumbering fireside ginger tom
the ocelot elegantly reclines, and in the face of your tabby queen,
gazing intently at the sparrow on your lawn, you can see the eye of the
tiger. Indeed, one of the many satisfactions that can be derived from
the presence of a cat in a household is being able to observe the rich
variety of behaviours that are the primeval essence of the perfect,
polished warrior. In fact, it was the cat's basic predatory nature that
first led to its relationship with man. After man had turned from
hunter to grower and gatherer of food, the cat's prowess as a vermin
catcher was put to use, resulting in its domestication.

The feline hunting technique is a marvel of stealth and subtlety (see
Understanding your cat, pp. 190−1). In the domestic cat hunting
isn't necessarily related to hunger − rather it is a kind of sport or
game. One aspect of feline behaviour that many people find hard to

understand is their seeming cruelty; they cite the cat that doesn't kill its prey outright, preferring to play with its luckless victim before adminstering the death bite. However, human morality can't be applied to non-humans — such a cat is merely polishing its skills, and this instinctive behaviour shouldn't be punished. Besides, many humans have double standards when it comes to the great hunter — applauding their cat's ability to rid the house of vermin, but criticising it when it catches birds.

As a hunter, your pet has good eyesight (see *Anatomy*, pp. 28—30), and much of its day is spent in keen observation of the world. If it is in "active mode", perhaps hunting prey, it will lurk in places where it can't be seen: behind bushes, trees or half-open doors, or in long grass. On the other hand, if it is on "auto-pilot", taking one of its famous naps, it will choose a vantage point where it is safe from attack: outdoors, this may be a wall, roof or outhouse; indoors, where it feels more secure, it may choose a chair or bed. Even when it is dozing, it is still receiving sensory messages, and is able to spring into action at the slightest hint of danger. Thus, it is still "on watch", ready to defend its territory against intruders.

The watchful beast (left)
Outdoors, the cat's equivalent of a deckchair is a vantage point like a sunny wall. Even when a cat appears to be asleep, its body is still receiving messages, and if it senses danger it is ready to react very quickly.

Surveying territory (right)
An opening in a shed gives these two cats a perfect vantage point for keeping an eye on their property. If there are two or more cats in a household, they will generally see their territory as communal, and mutually defend their boundaries.

Stalking prey (below)
Most cats' favourite form of relaxation is hunting prey. Long grass is a popular location for this as it affords the cat some cover.

The cat has a sense of curiosity that is boundless. What is the motivation for this? Why does it bother to investigate an empty paper bag, the inside of a cupboard or a garden shed? Part of the explanation is that it is always on the look-out for food, for prey to hunt, or for a warm place to curl up and take a nap. The other half of the story is that, by nature, the cat is an explorer, with a strong interest in the world about it. For example, a bold feline may wander into the house of a cat-less neighbour, and if it is welcomed, it will adopt it as a "holiday home" and visit when you are out. Unfortunately, this natural trait doesn't always bring the cat benefits and, as the saying goes, curiosity can kill the cat. As a responsible owner, you should therefore safeguard your pet from potential dangers it is unaware of, just as a parent protects a child. But don't be over-protective — the supreme individualist doesn't appreciate mollycoddling.

Caring for a cat requires an understanding and appreciation of its basic nature. If you read the information and follow the advice given in this "owner's manual" you and your cat should enjoy a long and happy friendship.

A head for heights (left)
*One of the cat's most
vital assets is its
wonderful sense of
balance. This enables it
to walk safely across the
narrowest ledges.*

Seeking food (left)
*An inquisitive cat will
soon spot a potential
meal. With its innate
combination of
initiative and
determination, it won't
be long before this cat
has worked out a way
of reaching the
goldfish.*

***Exploring containers
(right)***
*Any sort of container,
from a small jar like this
to a large box, is an open
invitation for a cat to
investigate. Make sure
that anything in your
home that your cat
might decide to climb
into is safe.*

CAT ANATOMY

The cat is basically a predator, and its elegant, athletic body has evolved to match that purpose. As shown in this chapter, its neat skeleton, powerful muscles, short digestive system, acute senses and sharp teeth are all those of a carnivore. And the physical feature that appeals most to humans — its glorious coat — is designed to keep it warm and dry while out hunting, and is coloured so that it is hidden from its prey. Information on the feline reproductive system is given in the *Breeding* chapter (see p. 203). Further anatomical information is provided in the *Health Care* chapter (see pp. 225, 231, 251, 257, 259 and 260).

The basic design of the cat

Like us, the cat is a mammal, and therefore it shares some common features: a skeleton, all the usual organs and tissues, muscles and a circulatory system. But whereas we are omnivores, the cat is a carnivore, so it has various modifications that are essential to make it an efficient hunting animal.

The internal organs

The cat's heart, lungs, kidneys and other organs work and are designed in much the same way as those of other mammals.

The brain

As a hunter, the parts of the cat's brain associated with the senses are well-developed. However, the frontal lobe development (the "seat" of intelligence) is much simpler in a cat than in a primate such as an ape or human being.

The digestive tract

Since the cat is the most highly developed carnivore, its alimentary canal is designed for meat-eating alone, with a shorter intestinal tract than that of omnivores like dogs or humans. However, the intestines of the domestic cat are longer than those of its wild relatives, probably because of its more varied, often less carnivorous, diet.

The skeleton

Size apart, the cat's "multi-purpose" skeletal design is very similar to ours. However, aside from the fact that we have adapted to walk on two legs, there are two significant differences between a cat and a human skeleton.

First, a cat's spine or backbone contains more bones than ours, partly due to the tail. The spine is made up of vertebrae of various types: it has 7 *cervical* or neck, 13 *thoracic* or chest, 7

The flexible backbone
The characteristic arching of a cat's back is only possible because its vertebrae are greater in number and more loosely connected than ours.

lumbar or back, 3 *sacral* or hip, and 14–28 caudal or tail vertebrae. (The tail-less Manx cat has a minimum of 3 caudal vertebrae.) And these vertebrae are less tightly connected than ours, making the cat's spine extremely flexible. It is this feature that enables it to arch its back into a "U" shape, or twist and turn its body so that it can squeeze through the tiniest gaps.

Second, the cat lacks a clavicle or collarbone; instead, it has a very much reduced scrap of clavicle tissue buried in the breast muscle. This is because a collarbone would broaden the chest, thus reducing the cat's ability to get through narrow gaps, and limiting the length of its stride. This design "modification" is possible because a cat doesn't need a forearm that can be lifted outwards.

The head

A cat has a hunter's head, with a large, powerful mouth, eyes that work well in dim light (see p. 28) and efficient ears. Its teeth are those of a carnivore, with large canine or fang teeth for biting, and blade-like molars, known as *carnassial* teeth, that are adapted for shearing flesh. To power its bite, the cat has short, strong jaws activated by very sturdy bundles of muscles. The design of the skull includes space for the ample jaw and neck muscles, and strengthened arches of bone that reinforce all the points on the skull which are likely to be under strain when the cat bites.

The cat's skull also houses well-developed ear bone anatomy, including large, round auditory *bullae* (echo chambers) that produce a sensitivity to sounds of certain frequencies, particularly the high-pitched, rustling noises made by small rodents or birds.

THE HUMAN BACKBONE

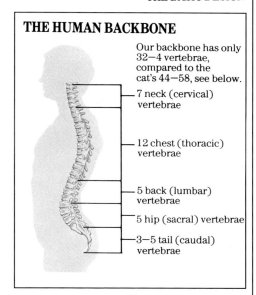

Our backbone has only 32—4 vertebrae, compared to the cat's 44—58, see below.

7 neck (cervical) vertebrae

12 chest (thoracic) vertebrae

5 back (lumbar) vertebrae

5 hip (sacral) vertebrae

3—5 tail (caudal) vertebrae

THE DOMESTIC CAT'S SKELETAL ANATOMY

The cat's skeleton is more flexible than ours because of two important differences: the vertebrae in its spine are more loosely connected and greater in number, and it doesn't have a collarbone.

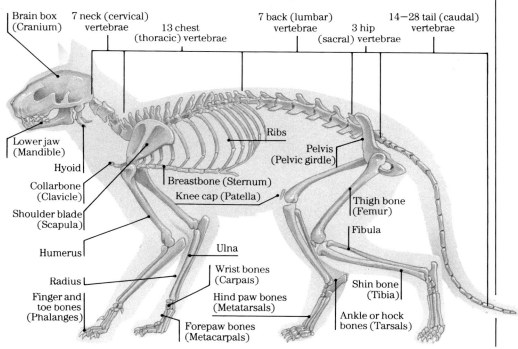

Brain box (Cranium)

7 neck (cervical) vertebrae

13 chest (thoracic) vertebrae

7 back (lumbar) vertebrae

3 hip (sacral) vertebrae

14—28 tail (caudal) vertebrae

Lower jaw (Mandible)

Hyoid

Collarbone (Clavicle)

Shoulder blade (Scapula)

Humerus

Radius

Finger and toe bones (Phalanges)

Ribs

Pelvis (Pelvic girdle)

Breastbone (Sternum)

Knee cap (Patella)

Ulna

Wrist bones (Carpals)

Hind paw bones (Metatarsals)

Forepaw bones (Metacarpals)

Thigh bone (Femur)

Fibula

Shin bone (Tibia)

Ankle or hock bones (Tarsals)

The muscles

The musculature of the cat is designed to complement its flexible hunter's skeleton, providing maximum power where it is most needed. Thus, the cat has very strong jaw, leg and back muscles in order to help it to chase and kill successfully. Like its wild relatives, the domestic cat uses its skeleton and muscle combination in such a way that very little energy is expended when it is walking (see p. 21). It therefore conserves its strength for the hunt.

Size and shape

Unlike dogs, domestic cats are much of a muchness when it comes to size and shape. However, there are three basic variations in body type, as shown in the diagram on the right. An average adult domestic cat is about 30 cms high at the shoulder and 45 cms from head to tail base, with a further 30 cms of tail.

Weight

An average adult domestic cat weighs between 2.75 and 5.5 kilograms. However, heavyweight felines occasionally hit the headlines; the heaviest domestic cat on record topped 18 kilograms. By comparison, the smallest of the wild cats, the Rusty Spotted Cat of India and Ceylon, rarely exceeds 1.25 kilograms in weight.

Unlike humans, cats usually manage to stay in trim without having to spend time working out in the gymnasium or jogging around the park. It is thought that the stretching that all cats indulge in may provide all the exercise necessary in order to keep them fighting fit.

A complete lack of conventional exercise and gross over-feeding by doting humans will eventually produce obesity. However, in cats this condition doesn't seem to lead to the detrimental effects of ill-health or curtailment of lifespan that generally occurs in dogs or humans.

VARIATIONS IN SHAPE

There are three basic body conformations in the cat: the cobby, flat-faced sort, the muscular kind, and the thin, narrow-faced type.

Cobby body type
Solidly built cats have short, thick legs, broad shoulders and rump, and a short, rounded head.

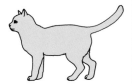

Muscular body type
Cats that are muscular in build have medium-length legs, shoulders and rump that are neither wide nor narrow, and a medium-long, slightly rounded head.

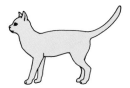

Lithe body type
Lightly built cats have long, slim legs, narrow shoulders and rump, and a long, narrow, wedge-shaped head.

Why doesn't the body shape and size of cats differ as much as that of dogs?
The domestic cat has a less varied genetic make-up (see p. 200) than the dog, and it has only been selectively bred (a process which develops the more extreme genetic mutations) for just over 100 years, compared to several thousand years of breeding programmes for dogs.

Movement

Like any hunter, a cat needs to be fast, agile and silent in its movements. Its skeletal development, muscles and limbs must therefore suit this purpose.

Walking

The way that a cat walks combines maximum economy of effort with minimum expenditure of energy. Its walking pattern is basically diagonal, with the step of a forefoot always followed by that of the diagonally opposite foot. Thus, the pattern goes: left hindfoot, right forefoot, right hindfoot, left forefoot, as shown below. A cat's centre of gravity is nearer to its head than its tail, so its forelimbs support its body while its hind legs carry out the main propulsion.

Running

As runners, cats are short-distance specialists rather than stayers. And their legs are therefore designed for short bursts of speed. When a cat runs, its limbs aren't just extended and then planted on the ground, they are extended completely in the air, and then brought downwards and backwards at speed (see p. 23). And the cat's highly flexible spine allows its rear end to continue moving forward, even while its forelimbs are on the ground. So rather than speeding up by increasing the number of times its feet make contact with the ground, the cat moves faster by stretching its trunk fully and thus lengthening its stride. As the speed increases the overlap between right and left feet on landing is steadily reduced. Thus with each of these "cycles" of limb movements the time involved remains constant (about half a second), but the distance per cycle increases steadily.

Domestic cats cover about three times their own length per cycle at full tilt — a speed of about 31 miles per hour. Their wild "cousin" the cheetah is the fastest feline, with a reputed top speed of 70 miles per hour.

Climbing

The strong thrust of a cat's back and hindleg muscles enable it to climb upwards very efficiently. It reaches forward with its forelimbs, seeking a grip with its hooked and extended claws. A climb generally begins with a leap in order to gain height quickly. However, once up, a cat isn't very well equipped for coming down: its claws curve the wrong way, and it can't use the powerful muscles in its hind quarters to hold back the weight of its body. This is why cats often get stuck up trees. A cat will descend a tree tentatively, often letting itself down backwards by holding onto the trunk with its claws and slowly "backpedalling" with its hind legs — a very undignified process.

Walking
When a cat walks, its hindfoot moves first, followed by the diagonally opposite forefoot, then the other hindfoot, and finally the last forefoot.

Jumping

As with climbing, the strong muscles of the hind quarters and back provide a cat with jumping power. First, it crouches, tipping back its pelvis and bending the three joints of the hip, knee and ankle. These joints have little or no lateral mobility, and are designed to take strong forces acting only in one direction — down the length of the body. When the muscles contract, the hip, knee and ankle joints are rapidly extended, propelling the body sharply forwards.

The design of the limbs

A cat's limb bones, like those of other carnivores, are similar to human ones. In most mammals the limb segments decrease in length, with the longest nearest the trunk and the shortest nearest the toes. Thus, the thighbone (*femur*) is longer than the shinbone (*tibia*), which is longer than the foot. But in running animals there is a tendency for the reverse system to be adopted: the feet are longer, and the bones closer to the chest are relatively shorter. As the cat needs to be able to run very fast over short distances, this principle applies to its limb bones. However, it is modified because a cat needs to use its feet for other purposes, such as catching prey.

Trotting
The speed with which the hindfeet move increases, so they are in motion at the same time as the diagonally opposite forefeet.

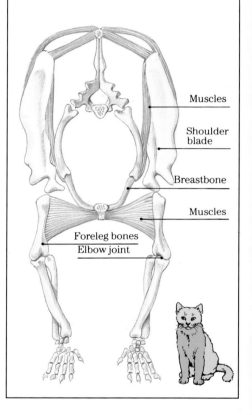

LIMB STRUCTURE

Unlike us, the cat is a quadruped, and its forelimbs are therefore significantly different from our arms. Its narrow chest and lack of a collarbone enable it to twist and turn more freely than a biped, and give it a longer stride.

Muscles

Shoulder blade

Breastbone

Muscles

Foreleg bones
Elbow joint

The feet

Unlike some carnivores, which possess "plantigrade" feet, cats have "digitigrade" feet. In plantigrade animals the body's weight is borne by a series of bones (the equivalent of the human finger and hand bones) placed flat on the ground. But the digitigrade cat walks on the ends of its fingers. This design is excellent for running, and can be compared with the athlete who sprints along on the tips of his or her toes.

Feline feet are regularly subjected to the shock of travelling at speed and of landing from heights. To help them withstand this, the bones are strapped tightly together by ligamentous tissue, and the wrist and ankle bones are arranged so that there is little possibility of lateral movement.

The pads of a domestic cat's feet are made of modified skin covering a dense cushion of connective tissue, making them harder than normal skin. The function of these hard pads is threefold: to act as shock absorbers, devices for binding the "toe" bones together, and also braking aids.

All cats can make rapid turns when running at high speed, and the most brilliant exponent of this manoeuvre is undoubtedly the cheetah. This animal has the advantage of possessing unique longitudinal ridges on the pads of its feet, rather like the tread on a car tyre. Other cats, including domestic ones, don't have these special ridges, and therefore run on "bald tyres".

Running
At a gallop, the cat pushes forward from both back feet at once, landing on one front foot and transferring its weight to the other.

Climbing
A cat's climb starts with a jump, then using its claws as "crampons" it moves upward powered by its strong leg muscles.

Balance

Cats have a better sense of balance than us. This is because the nerve messages from their eyes to their muscles and joints work extremely fast. Also, a cat uses its tail for balance very much in the same way that a tightrope walker uses a long pole as a counterweight. For example, if it is walking along a narrow wall or fence and decides to peer over in one direction, thereby shifting its centre of gravity, it will automatically move its tail in the other direction, re-establishing its body's centre of gravity and keeping it from falling off. The tail is also used as a counterweight when changing direction suddenly at high speed.

The righting reflex

When a cat falls through the air, its eyes and vestibular apparatus (a complex organ found within the inner ear) transmit information to its brain on the position of its head in relation to the ground. As the head changes position, crystals and liquid inside the vestibular organ are affected, and this movement is detected by sensitive hairs in contact with them. In fractions of a second, the brain receives the signal and sends nerve commands to the head to put it "square" with the ground, the rest of the body aligns with the head, and the cat reaches *terra firma* perfectly prepared for landing.

When a kitten is born, its vestibular apparatus is fully developed, but because its eyes haven't opened it can't see. Since perfect balance requires a combination of eye and inner ear messages, a kitten's righting reflex isn't operational until its eyes open.

Falling
A cat can fall from a height without hurting itself because, more often than not, its excellent righting reflex (see above) enables it to land on its feet.

Teeth

The main functions of a hunter's teeth are killing and "carving up" its prey. The classic feline kill uses the fang or canine teeth to break the victim's neck by inserting them into the space between two adjacent cervical vertebrae and forcing the bones apart. Some scientists claim that the size, shape and distance apart of the canines of various cat species are designed with the neck skeleton measurements of their prey in mind. In other words, your cat's fangs are made to measure for a particular collarsize of house-mouse!

When your cat makes this precise bite to the neck, it seeks for the right spot to drive its fangs in. A cat will know whether or not they are in the right place because it can "feel" with its teeth, having abundant receptor nerves around them.

The teeth of a carnivore
The domestic cat's fearsome dentistry is specially designed to cope with its carnivorous eating habits (see below).

THE STRUCTURE OF THE TEETH

Cats' teeth are constructed from dentine and enamel, like ours. However, the shapes and functions of the various teeth differ from those of humans because the cat's mouth is specially designed for meat-eating, whereas ours is tailored to suit our omnivorous diet.

A cat's molars can only be used for slicing — no grinding-type chewing is possible. The *carnassial* teeth (the last premolar in the upper jaw and the first molar in the lower jaw) are adapted for shearing flesh. They are larger than the molars, and shaped like narrow, pyramidal blades.

The arrangement of a cat's teeth

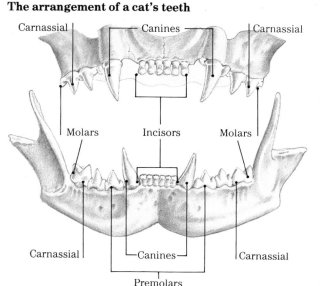

The cat's coat

Apart from the Sphynx (see p. 111), all members of the cat family share a glorious feature — their fur. The major purpose of this is to provide insulation against cold, heat and wet; it is basically a roof for the cat's body.

Coat colour and pattern

Selective breeding from natural mutations has led to the development of a wide range of coat colours in pedigree domestic cats that aren't seen in the wild felines.

The tiger-striped "mackerel" tabby has the basic feline coat pattern. In fact, every cat is a "masked" tabby (see p. 202). The purpose of this marking is to disguise the cat from its prey by making it appear to have no definite form, so that the prey

Colouring and camouflage in the wild
The leopard's coat (above) is perfectly matched to its habitat, disguising it from its prey.

The domestic cat's coat
The pet cat in its own back garden (right) is as well-camouflaged as its wild "cousin" shown above.

COAT LENGTHS AND DENSITY

There are three types of hair in a cat's coat: the topcoat or guard hairs (coloured orange), and two kinds of undercoat hairs, the bristly awn hairs (coloured brown), and the soft, curly down hairs (coloured blue).

The Sphynx
An unusual mutation, the Sphynx is practically hairless, with no guard or awn hairs, only a sparse covering of down hairs on the face, tail and legs.

The American Wirehair
This wirehaired cat has guard, down and awn hairs. All three types are short and very curly, and some hairs may be coiled in spirals. The awn hairs look like a shepherd's crook.

The Cornish Rex
This curly coated mutation has no guard hairs, only very short, curly awn and down hairs. These are about the same length, and are very difficult to tell apart.

The Longhair
The very long guard hairs (up to 12.5 cm) in the Longhair, coupled with its plentiful, long down hairs, make its coat extremely full and dense. This breed has no awn hairs.

The Maine Coon
This cat's coat is very similar to that of non-pedigree longhaired cats. It has long guard and down hairs like the Longhair and the Angora, but they are shaggier and more uneven in distribution. There are no awn hairs.

The British Shorthair
The average length of the guard hairs in a British Shorthair is 4.5 cm. The shorter awn hairs are sparse and only moderately curly. This breed has no down hairs.

The Devon Rex
Unlike the Cornish, this Rex has guard, down and awn hairs. However, the guard and awn types are almost like the down. All three are very short and curly. Whisker hairs are short or non-existent.

The Angora
Like the Longhair, the Angora has very long guard and down hairs, but they are finer and silkier, and the down hairs are less profuse. There are no awn hairs.

confuses it with the background. In addition to the disruptive effect of the pattern, camouflage is also provided by the colour of the fur. Thus in wild cats coat colour is linked to habitat: sandy coloured cats come from semi-desert regions, dark grey or brown spotted cats come from forested areas, and striped cats come from prairies or jungles.

A secondary function of colour and marking in cats is as a signalling device. For example, markings around a cat's face will highlight expressions of the mouth, eyes or ears; thus dark lines around a cat's mouth will emphasize the open-mouthed threat of the snarl. And marks on a mother's tail tip are used as a "follow-me" banner for her cubs.

A cat's habitat affects its coat type. For example, in cold, mountainous regions cats develop long, thick hair and oily, waterproof topcoats as a form of protection. Another factor that affects the coat is natural mutation, as in the curly coated Rex.

The eyes

Although the inner organs of the cat don't differ greatly from the basic mammalian design, its sense organs, including its eyes, are more specialized, incorporating modifications essential to a hunter.

The power of a cat's eyes

Cats can't see any better than human beings in total darkness, but their eyes are adapted to work well in the dimmest light. The feline eye has to gather and process every scrap of light that is available. Its retina isn't proportionately larger than ours, but it receives unusually high amounts of light in comparison to ours because the cornea, pupil-hole and lens are much larger. As a result, the lens and cornea lie relatively closer to the retina, so in order to focus the light sharply, their curvature has been increased. Another advantage of this design is that the cat's eyeball is rounder and shorter than ours, giving it a wider angle of view than us (see p. 30).

The ability to "see" in the dark

Humans lack the special light-conserving mechanism built into cat's eyes (and those of some other animals), known as the *tapetum lucidum*. This reflective structure lies behind the retina, and is composed of up to 15 layers of special glittering cells which act as a very efficient mirror.

The cat's eyes at night
In the dark, a cat's eyes have a characteristic green or gold shine. This effect occurs because the cat's pupils are wide open, and so light is reflected back off the tapetum lucidum.

HOW A CAT'S EYE WORKS

The eye functions very much like a camera. Light passes through a movable aperture (the pupil hole in the iris) which controls the amount of light that enters, and is focused by a lens. Unlike a camera, where the lens moves backwards or forwards to change focus, the lens in a cat's eye focuses by changing shape when tugged by muscles. Finally, the light falls on the retina (the eye's equivalent to film) which sends impulses to the interpretation centres of the brain via the optic nerve.

Like our retina, a cat's contains two kinds of receptor cells: rods and cones. Rods provide good night vision and sensitivity to low light, and cones give resolving power. A cat's eye contains relatively more rods and fewer cones than a human's. It is therefore more efficient at low light levels, but lacks detailed resolving power.

The structure of the eye

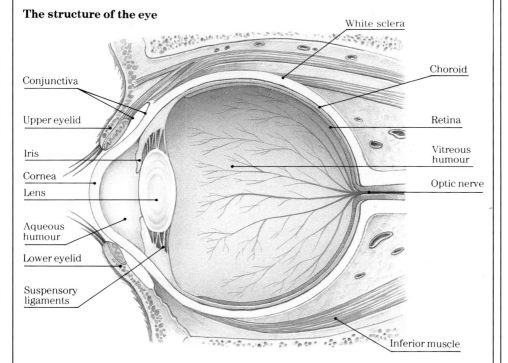

White sclera

Choroid

Conjunctiva

Upper eyelid

Retina

Iris

Vitreous humour

Cornea

Lens

Optic nerve

Aqueous humour

Lower eyelid

Suspensory ligaments

Inferior muscle

The effect of light on the pupil

The cat's slit pupils enable it to protect the retina from strong light. Of course, total closure of the pupil would be pointless, as the eyelids can do that if necessary. So when the pupil is contracted to its maximum, it only closes completely in the middle, leaving a tiny pinhole orifice at each end.

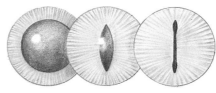

Pupil in darkness

Pupil in medium-bright light

Pupil in bright sunlight

FIELDS OF VISION

When the fields of vision of two eyes overlap, a stereoscopic effect is created. Our eyes' fields overlap far more than cats' do, whilst dogs' overlap less.

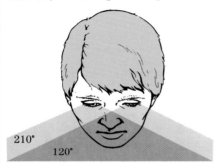

How much can a human see?
A human has a visual field of 210 degrees, of which 120 is binocular overlap.

How much can a cat see?
A cat has a total visual field of 285 degrees, of which 130 degrees is binocular overlap.

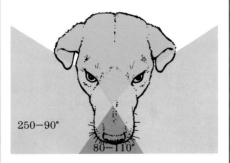

How much can a dog see?
A dog has a total visual field of 250–90 degrees, of which 80–110 is binocular overlap.

The strengths and weaknesses of a cat's vision

Like us, a cat has binocular vision. This means that parts of the fields of vision of each of its two eyes overlap, as shown in the diagram on the left. This overlap is essential for a stereoscopic effect — one eye working alone with a field of vision which doesn't overlap the field of the other eye can't receive three-dimensional impressions.

Binocular vision is very important for a hunting animal like the cat because it needs to be able to judge range accurately in order to gauge the distance to its target. The distance judgement of a cat isn't quite as good as that of a human, but it is better than that of a dog. Our visual field isn't as extensive as that of a cat, but we make up for this by the far more extensive eye movements permitted by the large area of white sclera which surrounds the human iris.

Focusing ability

When an eye focuses on an object the shape of its lens is changed by tiny muscles behind the iris (a process known as "accommodation"). When these muscles contract, the lens bows and objects near to it come into focus; when they relax the lens flattens and objects further away are focused on. Unlike many animals, the cat's power of accommodation is almost as well developed as ours.

Can cats see colours?

At one time, it was thought that cats were colour-blind, and could only see in shades of black, grey and white. But now this belief has been disproved as cats have been trained to discriminate between colours, although this takes a long time. Many scientists think that cats don't pay attention to colours — that although they can see them, they don't attach any significance to them.

The ears

Sharp eyesight is only one string to a hunter's bow; an acute sense of hearing is very important too. Cat and man are about equal in the ability to locate the position of sounds, discriminating with around 75 percent accuracy between two sounds separated by an angle of five degrees. Like us, a cat uses the elaborate shape of its outer ear to pick up variations in the quality of sound, and these variations help it to pinpoint the position of its target.

A cat's skull contains two large echo chambers (*bullae*) which give the animal a high sensitivity to sounds on particular frequencies, such as high-pitched noises of the sort made by small prey animals.

At high frequencies a cat's hearing, like that of dogs, is far more acute than ours. A cat can hear sounds up to two octaves higher than the highest note that we can hear, and, more surprisingly, it can hear sounds about half an octave higher than the highest note that a dog can detect. In addition, the cat has great powers of discrimination between notes in the high frequency range; a cat in its prime can discriminate a fifth to a tenth of a tone difference between two notes.

Like ours, a cat's sensitivity to high notes is reduced with age. This reduction in acuity may begin as early as three years of age, and is very marked by the time the cat is four-and-a-half years old.

HOW A CAT'S EAR WORKS

Sound waves are gathered by the funnel-shaped outer ear and channelled down to the ear drum. This membrane vibrates like a drum skin, and moves a series of three tiny bones lying in the middle ear. In turn, these pass on the movement to the inner ear's entrance (the "oval window"). Beyond this, the sound waves reach the cochlea, a system of coiled, fluid-filled chambers. Within these chambers lies the sensitive Organ of Corti, which translates the waves into electrical impulses and sends them along the auditory nerve to the brain.

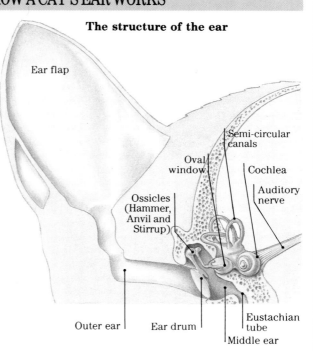

The structure of the ear

Ear flap

Semi-circular canals

Oval window

Cochlea

Auditory nerve

Ossicles (Hammer, Anvil and Stirrup)

Outer ear

Ear drum

Eustachian tube

Middle ear

The senses of smell and taste

One of the reasons that colour doesn't particularly matter to cats (see p. 30) is that smell and taste play a more important role for them than they do for us.

The nose and smell

In some long-nosed animals, where the lining to the nasal membrane is folded in such away that its surface area is greatly enlarged, the sense of smell is extremely well-developed. For example, a long-nosed fox terrier possesses about 147 million specialized nerve endings in its nose. In contrast, a cat has around 19 million nerve endings, and we get by with a mere five million.

The cat's nose is particularly sensitive to odours that contain nitrogen compounds. This ability enables a cat to reject rancid or slightly "off" food as these release chemicals rich in nitrogen.

Cats and catnip

It is surprising how entranced cats are by catnip *(nepeta cataria)*. Watch your cat as it savours this particular bit of herbage, and you will see that it almost makes love to the stuff. In fact, its behaviour is identical to that displayed by a male cat (tom) in the presence of a female cat (queen) who is on heat (in oestrus). The scent of catnip probably excites cats because it contains a chemical called trans-nepetalactone,

HOW THE ORGANS OF SMELL AND TASTE WORK

Behind its hairless tip, the cat's nose, like ours, is lined by mucus membrane. Deep in the nasal passageways, part of this lining is filled with nerve-endings.

How taste and smell are sensed

When molecules are carried by the air and deposited on the membrane they trigger the nerve-endings, which send signals via nerve fibres to the olfactory centre in the brain. Taste sensations picked up by taste buds on the tongue are also sent to this centre.

Jacobson's organ

Cats have a sense we lack. It is midway between taste and smell, and has its own receptor: Jacobson's organ.

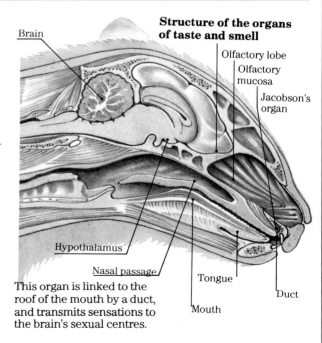

Structure of the organs of taste and smell

Brain
Olfactory lobe
Olfactory mucosa
Jacobson's organ
Hypothalamus
Nasal passage
Tongue
Mouth
Duct

This organ is linked to the roof of the mouth by a duct, and transmits sensations to the brain's sexual centres.

which is closely related to a substance excreted by the queen, usually in urine. I have seen wild cats react in the same way to catnip. The plant also affects queens and neutered males, but not as strongly as toms. Another herb, valerian, can produce this effect.

Flehming
This cat is making the characteristic lip-curling grimace that brings certain scents into contact with Jacobson's organ.

Flehming

Many carnivores, including some cats, make a strange lip-curling, nose-wrinkling grimace known as "flehming". This is thought to bring the chemicals of some odours, probably sexual ones, in contact with a structure called Jacobson's organ, found in the roof of many mammal's mouths, including that of the cat. This organ is very small and poorly developed in domestic cats, so "flehming" is less obvious than in cat species like the lion or tiger.

The tongue and taste

Cats tend to be fussier, "faddier" eaters than dogs, who will more readily share a human diet, including sweet things. Dogs have "sweet" receptors in their taste buds, whereas cats, as pure carnivores, don't. Scientists have studied the nerves in the tongues of both animals, and found channels that run from the dog's tongue to its brain associated with the transmission of "sweet" messages. But no such sweet-sensitive nerve pathways have been found in the cat. The main reason for the lack of a sweet tooth is that a carnivore has no need for it, but it also may be self-protective as sugars don't agree with many felines, producing digestive upsets.

Day-old kittens have a well-developed sense of taste but, like us, as cats grow older the acuity diminishes. A temporary reduction in this sense, with accompanying loss of appetite, can be a side-effect of upper respiratory disease (see p. 229).

The rasp-like upper surface of a cat's tongue is formed by hundreds of backward-pointing small protruberances (papillae) constructed of virtually the same substance as fingernails. This substance doesn't have a taste function. In the big cats it helps in abrading flesh from the bones of carcasses, and in small felines, like the domestic cat, it helps in self-grooming.

The cat's tongue
This is very long and flexible (see p. 163). The abrasive papillae at the centre are used for grooming. The taste buds are sited at the tip, sides and base.

Vallate (cup-shaped) papillae — carry taste buds

Filiform (hooked) abrasive papillae — carry no taste buds

Fungiform (mushroom-shaped) papillae — carry taste buds

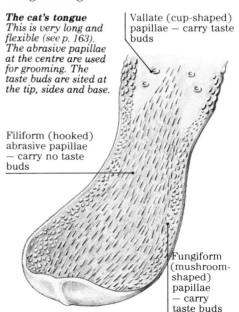

Other special features of the cat

Like the main "design features" covered in the previous pages, other special feline characteristics are linked to the cat's role as a hunter and carnivore.

The skin glands

There are three main types of skin gland: sebaceous, eccrine and apocrine. Sebaceous glands are located near the hair follicles, and they secrete sebum which forms a waterproof film on the hairs. Unlike us, cats don't have eccrine (watery sweat-producing) glands over their entire body, only on the pads of their feet. They have apocrine sweat glands (the type that produce a milky fluid) all over, but because of the coat these aren't very useful for cooling purposes. The main function of the apocrine glands in a feline is to produce a scent that is used as a signal; the cat rubs its body against objects to leave its scent and mark its territory.

Do cats sweat?

Cats have very few eccrine glands and can't therefore "sweat like horses, perspire like men or glow like ladies". And because their apocrine glands don't help them to cool down, you might think that they would have a problem coping in hot weather. As an alternative to sweating, in order to lose heat cats radiate it from their body surfaces (these are much larger in relation to their bulk than those of bigger creatures like man), and, occasionally, they pant.

The gullet

The whole of a cat's gullet wall contains muscles capable of facilitating regurgitation, enabling it to bring back excess or unsuitable food easily. This facility is used for rejecting relatively indigestible portions of a carcass. Occasionally, too, it is used as a means of carrying food back to cubs or kittens. In contrast, in humans these muscles are only found in the upper part of the gullet, and so voluntary vomiting isn't easily achieved.

The intestines

The intestines of the cat are approximately four times the length of its body — much shorter than those of omnivores like dogs or humans, but longer than those of other carnivores. This is probably because it has had to adapt to a much more varied diet as a result of its association with mankind.

The carpal pad

A slightly mysterious special feature of the cat is the single carpal pad which lies behind and above the other pads on the feet, and doesn't come into contact with the ground. This pad doesn't play a part in normal locomotion, but it is thought to have a role as an anti-skidding device when the cat lands after a jump.

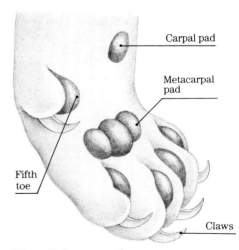

Carpal pad

Metacarpal pad

Fifth toe

Claws

The cat's forepaw pads
The carpal pad is found on the forepaws only, and is thought to work as an anti-skidding device.

THE CAT'S PURR

This unique feline feature (tigers, cheetahs, pumas and ocelots also purr) is interpreted by humans as meaning that their cat is communicating its contentment, but cats can purr when they are sick or even terminally ill, though never when they are asleep. It was long thought that purring was caused by vibration of blood in a large vein in the chest cavity. However, it has now been proved to be the product of regular, rapid, alternating contractions of muscles in the larynx and the diaphragm.

Purring isn't just an auditory phenomenon, it can also be felt as a vibration. When kittens are newly born, they are blind, they have no sense of smell, and their ears are undeveloped. Therefore, their main reaction is to the purring vibrations of their mother, which act as a homing device.

What are whiskers for?

Cats possess specialized hairs in the form of whiskers, the function of which isn't fully understood. They are thought to be something to do with touch, and removing them can distinctly disturb a cat for some time. The theory is that in the dark, a cat's whiskers act as immensely sensitive and rapid-acting antennae — the cat uses them to identify things it can't see. Also, some scientists think that the cat may bend some or all of its whiskers downwards to guide it when jumping or bounding over uneven ground at night.

The lifespan of pet cats

The average lifespan of the domestic cat is about 15 years. It isn't uncommon to find individuals which pass this figure, but few achieve the ripe old age of 20. The record stands for a tabby called "Puss" who attained 36 years and one day, although there is an unsubstantiated claim that a cat lived to the age of 43! It isn't easy to equate any particular period of a cat's life with the corresponding one in a human. The common practice of multiplying the cat's age by a figure (often said to be seven), and saying that there is a human equivalent isn't satisfactory. The most accurate table of equivalent ages would look something like this:

Cat	Man
1 year	16 years
2 years	24 years
3 years	28 years
4 years	32 years
8 years	48 years
12 years	64 years
15 years	76 years
20 years	96 years

The nine lives myth

It is often said that cats have nine lives, but although this is technically impossible, is it true in spirit? Is a cat more tenacious of life than other animals? The saying may have arisen as a result of people noticing how cats manage to endure all sorts of accidents, indignities and upsets, and still come out smiling. Nine has always been one of the mystical numbers, and it may be that this myth came about because of the general aura of mystery and magic that has always surrounded felines. Certainly, I've found that, compared with dogs, cats lead charmed lives, but this is probably due to their righting reflexes and good sense of balance (see p. 24) rather than any supernatural powers.

THE ORIGINS OF THE CAT

Although your pet will often give the impression that it is the only cat in the world, in fact it is just one of 500 million or so members of the domesticated species. In addition to these numerous "brothers and sisters", your pet has 35 different sorts of wild "cousin", some of which can be found in any zoo or circus. The lion, tiger, leopard and puma, although under threat in some natural habitats, are common in captivity. However, other species of wild cat are less well-known — you probably haven't heard of or seen the domestic cat's closest relation, the African wild cat *(Felis silvestris libyca)*. And some wild felines, such as the Iriomote cat which is only found on one island near Japan, are very rare.

The forerunners of the cat

Your fireside pet is a member of the great family of *Felidae*, the supreme hunters among terrestrial carnivores. These sophisticated assassins, who specialize in locating, catching and killing vegetarian creatures, all had their beginnings in the late Cretaceous Period, which took place 65 million years ago.

The earliest ancestors of the cat

The mammals which witnessed the extinction of the dinosaurs were small, long-nosed and insect-eating. Some of their present-day descendants such as the solenodon (a long-nosed mammal, that resembles a large shrew, and is found in Cuba and Haiti) probably look very similar to these first mammals. Others evolved into peaceful herbivores. And a third group, the creodonts, developed an appetite for feeding on their insectivorous and herbivorous brethren.

The creodonts

The earliest carnivorous mammals were known as creodonts, and had long bodies and short limbs with clawed feet. Their powerful jaws were equipped with 44

THE EVOLUTION OF THE CAT

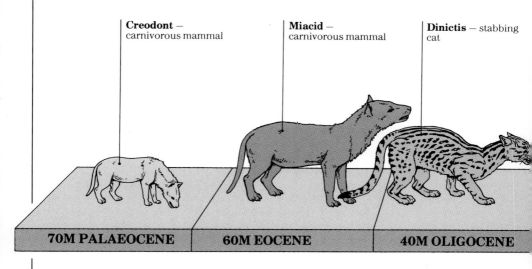

Creodont – carnivorous mammal

Miacid – carnivorous mammal

Dinictis – stabbing cat

70M PALAEOCENE

60M EOCENE

40M OLIGOCENE

Creodonts
The first carnivorous small mammals were short in limb and brain power. They began to die out at the end of the Eocene Period, 60 million years ago, and were extinct by the start of the Pliocene Period 12 million years ago.

Miacids
These brighter, more efficient carnivores evolved from the creodonts. Miacids are thought to have been the forerunners of today's carnivorous animals, including the cat.

Dinictis
A "halfway house" between a civet and a cat in appearance, this animal was long in the leg and tail, and was about the size of a small civet. Unlike a true cat, it was a plantigrade (placing all of its foot bones on the ground when walking).

teeth: 33 molars, three incisors, one fang or canine tooth, and seven grinding teeth. They didn't have much in the way of a brain, but then neither did their prey, and so, although they weren't very efficient hunters, they survived.

The creodonts evolved into a wide number of more formidable predators, some as big as lions. However, by the end of the Eocene Period, 60 million years ago, most branches of the creodont family went into decline, and all of them were extinct by the start of the Pliocene Period 12 million years ago.

The miacids
Before the creodont family became extinct, one of its earliest members had evolved into a new and very important group of creatures called the miacids, from which all the modern terrestrial carnivores are thought to have sprung. These small, forest-dwelling creatures had bigger brains than the creodonts, and possessed about 40 teeth. Four of the cheek teeth, known as carnassials, were specially modified in shape for shearing flesh: they had a cutting blade and a notch which held the flesh against the sharp edge. Competition for scant food resources from the brighter, more efficient miacids may have played an important part in the disappearance of the creodonts.

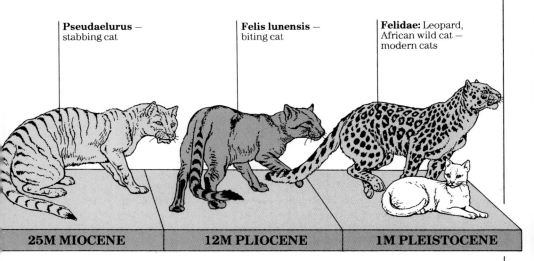

Pseudaelurus – stabbing cat

Felis lunensis – biting cat

Felidae: Leopard, African wild cat – modern cats

25M MIOCENE

12M PLIOCENE

1M PLEISTOCENE

Pseudaelurus
By this stage, animals that looked quite like some of today's cats had appeared. This animal had long limbs and five-toed feet, and walked almost in digitigrade fashion (on the tips of its toes) like the modern cat. Its teeth were those of a true cat.

Felis
During the Pliocene Period the first true cats were seen. Felis lunensis (Martelli's wild cat) was similar in size to the small modern wild cats.

Felidae
By this stage, modern felines had evolved. They comprise the great cats (including the leopard), the cheetah, and the small cats (including the African wild cat, the probable ancestor of the domestic cat).

The first cats

From the early mammals known as the miacids (see pp. 38—9) a number of creatures evolved. One of the earliest of these was the *Proailurus*. This animal was about the size of a fox, with long limbs and tail, and a mixture of civet and cat-like features. During the Pliocene Period, 12 million years ago, animals began to appear that were more and more like true cats and less and less like civets. Some developed exaggerated canine teeth, and sabre-toothed tigers and lions may have evolved from them.

The sabre-toothed cats

Animals with exaggerated canine teeth were widespread throughout Europe, Asia and the Americas during the Pleistocene Period, one million years ago. They used their dramatic dental work for scavenging among the carcasses of dead herbivores or for killing thick-skinned animals like elephants and rhinos. The last of these cats, *Smilodon*, became extinct around 14,500 years ago.

Early true cats

The first true cats were found at the beginning of the Pliocene Period, 12 million years ago. Six million years later, at the beginning of the Pleistocene Period, the world was full of cats: lions, lynx and giant cheetahs roamed the forests of Europe, Asia and China. By the middle and late Pleistocene, half-a-million years ago, cave lions and leopards had spread throughout Europe, giant tigers were found in China, and giant jaguars padded across North America. And smaller feline species such as the manul and Martelli's wild cat were found right across Europe. Martelli's cat is extinct now, but the manul still exists. The great family of cats colonized every land mass except for the Polar regions, Australasia, and some small islands.

The manul
Slightly larger than the domestic cat, this longhaired feline first came into existence around 2 million BC, and is still found today in Asiatic Russia, Tibet, China, Iran and Afghanistan.

The domestic cat's closest relations

Martelli's wild cat, which became extinct in the mid-Pleistocene Period, may well have been a direct ancestor of the modern small wild cats. One of these, *Felis silvestris*, had made its appearance by the end of the Second Ice Age, 600,000 years ago, and possibly by the end of the First Ice Age, 900,000 years ago. *Felis silvestris* soon spread over Europe, Asia and Africa, developing into three main types: the forest wild cat (*Felis silvestris*), the African wild cat (*Felis silvestris libyca*) and the Asiatic desert cat (*Felis silvestris ornata*).

It is from one of these types, the African wild cat (though the Asiatic wild cat may have played a part) that today's domestic cat is thought to be descended.

MODERN SMALL WILD CATS

Cat	Habitat	Temperament
The forest wild cat 	Found in Spain, Portugal, France, Italy, Greece, Yugoslavia, Czechoslovakia, Poland, Russia and Scotland. *Felis silvestris* had almost disappeared from Britain by the mid-nineteenth century. The call-up of gamekeepers in 1914 saved the cats left in the Scottish Highlands.	The forest wild cat shuns contact with man, and when captured is virtually impossible to tame. This cat's fierce, misanthropic temperament makes it an unlikely candidate for the primary source of the domestic cat's lineage.
The African wild cat 	Found in the hills of Majorca, Corsica, Sardinia, Sicily, Crete, Morocco, Tunisia and Israel, *Felis silvestris libyca* inhabits almost any kind of terrain: forest or scrub, rocky or sandy plain, mountains or flat country.	Like its forest relative, the African wild cat is nocturnal, and therefore although it isn't rare, it is hardly ever seen by man. But unlike the forest wild cat, it often lives close to human settlements, and its kittens are easily reared and tamed in captivity.
The Asiatic desert cat 	Found in India, Pakistan, Iran and Asiatic Russia. Although commonly seen on open plains, *Felis silvestris ornata* doesn't sleep outdoors, preferring to make its den in old buildings, hollow trees or badger setts.	The Asiatic desert cat, like the African wild cat, isn't averse to close contact with humans.

What does the African wild cat look like?

Slightly larger than the domestic cat, the African wild cat has a coat colour that varies with habitat. It ranges from pale sepia in animals from desert areas, through shades of grey-brown, to a colour that is almost that of charcoal in animals that live in forested areas. Markings may be scanty and almost invisible, or deep red-brown with darker red-brown patches on the face and chest area, and undulating stripes running down the sides of the body. The forelegs and thighs are usually ringed with broad lines of dark fur, and the black-tipped tail has 3—4 dark red-brown rings along it. The back of the ears may be brown, dark grey or sandy red.

Vital statistics of the African wild cat

Height	36 cm at shoulder
Length	60 cm head to tail base
Tail	30 cm long
Weight	5—5.5 kg
Food	Small animals e.g. birds
Gestation	50—60 days
Litter	2—5 kittens

THE "FAMILY TREE" OF THE CAT

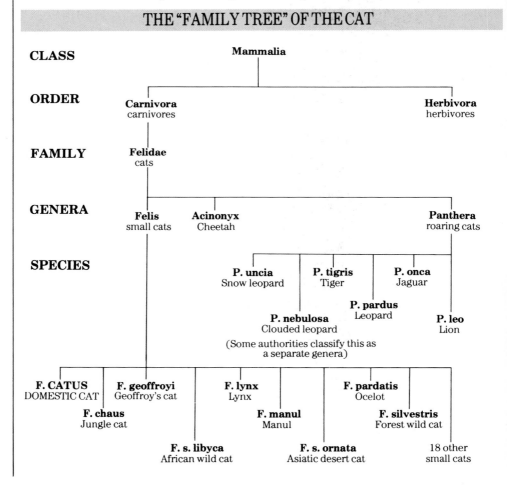

CLASS — Mammalia

ORDER — Carnivora (carnivores) ... Herbivora (herbivores)

FAMILY — Felidae (cats)

GENERA — Felis (small cats) ... Acinonyx (Cheetah) ... Panthera (roaring cats)

SPECIES

P. uncia — Snow leopard
P. tigris — Tiger
P. onca — Jaguar
P. pardus — Leopard
P. nebulosa — Clouded leopard (Some authorities classify this as a separate genera)
P. leo — Lion

F. CATUS — DOMESTIC CAT
F. geoffroyi — Geoffroy's cat
F. lynx — Lynx
F. pardatis — Ocelot
F. chaus — Jungle cat
F. manul — Manul
F. silvestris — Forest wild cat
F. s. libyca — African wild cat
F. s. ornata — Asiatic desert cat
18 other small cats

The cat's biological niche

Cats fill a very precise biological role. They are total carnivores who, by preying on the prolific vegetarians of the animal kingdom, act as one of nature's control mechanisms. They fit perfectly into the balance of living things, weeding out the weakest representatives of their prey and cutting back overproduction.

Cats occur on every continent but one, and they have existed in most parts of the world at one time or another. (The locations of some well-known cats are shown below.) However, because of a shortage of prey animals and the advent of man they have been driven out of some areas.

The cat in Australia

Australia is a curious exception to the general pattern of ecological balance between prolific prey and controlling predators. It possesses animals of all types (albeit marsupial), except for a great predator. Some people believe that there is an Australian big cat, an animal as elusive and mysterious as the yeti or the Loch Ness monster. The Queensland lion (a tawny, puma-like creature with a pouch) has been sighted, but never killed or captured.

The role of the domestic cat

So wild cats have a precise ecological role, but what is the niche of the 500 million or so domestic cats? Apart from their important role as rodent operatives, they provide companionship for humans. In return they get bed and board, and so they survive as a species.

WHERE ARE CATS FOUND?

Habitat	Cat	Area
Savannah (open sandy plains, steppes)	African wild cat	Africa, Mediterranean,
	Asiatic desert cat	Indian subcontinent, China
	Cheetah	Africa, Iran
	Jaguar	S. America
	Lion	Africa, India
	Manul	S. America
	Ocelot	Southern U.S., S. America
Forest	African wild cat	Africa, Mediterranean
	Forest wild cat	Scotland, Europe, Russia
	Lynx	Europe, Asia, N. America
Jungle	Jaguar	S. America
	Tiger	Indian subcontinent
	Jungle cat	Middle East, Asia, Indian subcontinent, China
High sierra (mountains)	Mountain cat	S. America
	Snow leopard	Indian subcontinent, China, Russia
Desert	Asiatic desert cat	Indian subcontinent, China
Open grass- and shrubland	Geoffroy's cat	S. America
	Manul	S. America
	Ocelot	Southern U.S., S. America

The domestication process

The bones of the African wild cat *(Felis silvestris libyca)* have been found in the caves lived in by ancient man. Our ancestors may simply have hunted, killed and eaten these cats, but it is also quite possible that they raised and tamed wild kittens and used them to control pests.

By 3,000 BC in Egypt, when agriculture was well-established, tabbies with very similar markings to those of the African wild cat were employed to protect grain stores from the ravages of rodents. These feline guardians became so valuable to the Egyptians that they regarded them as gods (see p. 6). The basic non-pedigree domestic cat is a descendant of this Egyptian stock.

The spread of the shorthaired cat
Tame tabbies from Egypt were imported into Italy by Phoenician traders, and became established there long before the

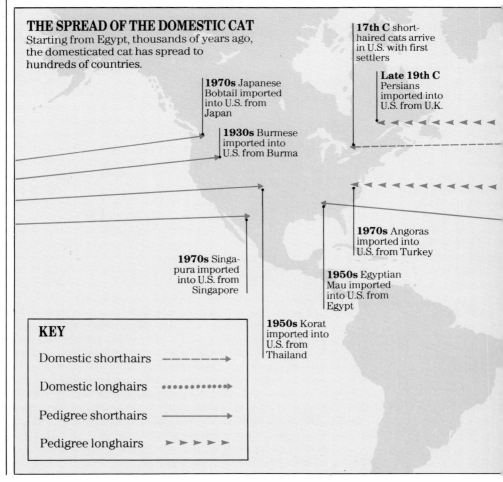

THE SPREAD OF THE DOMESTIC CAT
Starting from Egypt, thousands of years ago, the domesticated cat has spread to hundreds of countries.

17th C short-haired cats arrive in U.S. with first settlers

Late 19th C Persians imported into U.S. from U.K.

1970s Japanese Bobtail imported into U.S. from Japan

1930s Burmese imported into U.S. from Burma

1970s Angoras imported into U.S. from Turkey

1970s Singapura imported into U.S. from Singapore

1950s Egyptian Mau imported into U.S. from Egypt

1950s Korat imported into U.S. from Thailand

KEY

Domestic shorthairs   – – – – –→

Domestic longhairs   •••••••••••➤

Pedigree shorthairs   ————→

Pedigree longhairs   ➤ ➤ ➤ ➤ ➤

birth of Christ. Further progress across Europe was slow, and cats were rare in England up to the tenth century A.D. The first record of domestic cats in the British Isles dates from A.D. 936, when Howel Dda, Prince of South Central Wales, enacted a law for their protection.

The spread of the longhaired cat

Although shorthaired domestic cats are probably descended from the wild cats of Europe and Africa, it is more likely that longhaired types are descended from wild felines in Iran and Afghanistan, which may have developed from the longhaired manul of Central Asia.

The introduction of breeds

The concept of breeds began in the mid-nineteenth century, with the first cat shows (see p. 178). Pedigree cats were developed by breeders from the natural domestic types which had already been in existence for thousands of years. And new breeds have been added to the list over the years as unusual true-breeding cats have been discovered by travelling cat-lovers.

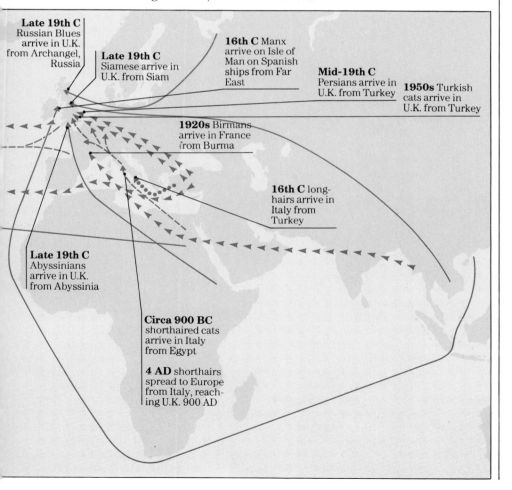

Late 19th C Russian Blues arrive in U.K. from Archangel, Russia

Late 19th C Siamese arrive in U.K. from Siam

16th C Manx arrive on Isle of Man on Spanish ships from Far East

Mid-19th C Persians arrive in U.K. from Turkey

1950s Turkish cats arrive in U.K. from Turkey

1920s Birmans arrive in France from Burma

16th C longhairs arrive in Italy from Turkey

Late 19th C Abyssinians arrive in U.K. from Abyssinia

Circa 900 BC shorthaired cats arrive in Italy from Egypt

4 AD shorthairs spread to Europe from Italy, reaching U.K. 900 AD

CAT BREEDS

There are over a hundred different recognized breeds and colour varieties of pedigree domestic cat. And these breeds can be divided into five basic categories: Persians or Longhairs, other longhaired cats, British Shorthairs, American Shorthairs, and Foreign Shorthairs. But don't feel too disgruntled if you can't find your pride and joy among them. A non-pedigree cat isn't a second-class beast, and all cats share that characteristic feline personality, charm and elegance.

The concept of a pure-bred or pedigree cat began just over one hundred years ago, with the early cat shows (see p. 178). Breeding programmes were started to perpetuate, and even accentuate, the best or most unusual features of certain strains of cat. Today, national associations in each country (the Governing Council of the Cat Fancy in Britain) lay down the standards that pedigree cats are judged by, and register kittens.

LONGHAIRED CATS

Originally, domestic European cats were all shorthaired, so how did longhaired cats arrive on the scene? There are several theories on their origin. Some people regard them as descendants of the European wild cat, which has medium-long hair; others believe that they developed in cold climates, perhaps in Russia, where there was a need for a long coat. But the generally accepted view today is that they probably arose from a spontaneous mutation, and because the original animal was born in an isolated mountainous region, this new feature was perpetuated through inter-breeding.

When were longhaired cats brought to Europe?

Cats with long coats were first imported into Europe in the late sixteenth century. The story is that the Italian traveller, Pietro della Valle, brought them back from Asia Minor. However, today's long-haired pedigree cats are mostly descended from cats brought to Britain from Turkey and Persia in the late nine-teenth century.

What is a Persian or Longhair cat?

Most longhaired cats are of the exotic-looking Longhair type popularly known as Persian. In America these cats are formally classified as Persian, with the colours listed as varieties. However, in Britain they are called Longhairs, and each colour is classified as a separate breed (White Longhair, Black Longhair, for example).

All Longhairs have a cobby (sturdy and rounded) body with a round face and head, short, thick legs, a short nose and large, round eyes. The other feature these cats have in common is an exceptionally full coat. This is known as a double coat because it consists of two types of hair — long, soft, woolly under-coat hairs and slightly longer, coarser guard hairs (these can be as much as 12 cms long in a good show specimen). Longhairs are bred in a large range of colours and coat patterns: from the snowy purity of the White to the deep jet of the Black, and from the hazy, two-colour effect of a lightly tipped Chinchilla to the brightly patched colours of a Tortoiseshell-and-White. Longhairs of show standard are extremely expensive.

How do other longhaired cats differ from Longhairs?

There are several pedigree longhaired cats that aren't of the Persian type. These cats have various origins, but they all come from cold climates where a long coat is useful. In general, their coats aren't as woolly or as full as those of Longhairs — which makes them easier to groom. They differ from Longhairs in other ways, too: they are slimmer, longer in the body and leg, and have narrower faces. Cats in this category range from very oriental-looking animals such as the Balinese, which is basically a longhaired Siamese (see p. 94), to elegant breeds like the Angora, and rugged types such as the Maine Coon.

Advantages and disadvantages of a long coat

The coat of a longhaired cat generally looks very spectacular, and is often extra-long around the head, forming an attractive ruff. However, there is one major disadvantage that goes hand-in-hand with these cats' best feature — moulting. Most longhaired cats moult all year round, and they need regular daily grooming (see p. 170) to prevent their coats from matting.

Longhairs or Persians pages 50–69

The first part of this chapter introduces you to the cats known as Longhairs or Persians. They have been divided into separate categories according to their coat pattern or colour.

Black Longhair (p. 51)

Chinchilla Longhair (p. 56)

Other longhaired cats pages 70–5

This second section covers six different breeds of longhaired pedigree cat — the Birman, the Ragdoll, the Balinese, the Angora, the Turkish and the Maine Coon. None of these six types fall into the Longhair or Persian category.

Lilac-point Balinese (p. 72)

Seal-point Mitted Ragdoll (p. 71)

White Longhair

These decorative cats aren't as difficult to care for as they look. Obviously, daily grooming is essential to keep their coats looking beautiful, but otherwise no special treatment is required.

History Whites were the first longhaired cats to be introduced into Europe — their earliest mention dates from the sixteenth century. At first, they were of the Angora type (see p.73). However, from the mid-nineteenth century Angoras were inter-bred with Persians to produce the contemporary White Longhair. As a result, the Angora became almost extinct.

Temperament All White Longhairs are calm, affectionate cats.

Varieties The White Longhair can be orange-eyed, blue-eyed, or odd-eyed. The blue-eyed type is prone to deafness.

Blue-eyed White Longhair
Many blue-eyed cats inherit deafness. A breeding programme aimed at curing this produced Whites with perfect hearing but orange eyes.

Odd-eyed White
The interbreeding of orange-eyed cats and blue-eyed stock has produced a number of animals which have one orange eye and one blue one.

KEY CHARACTERISTICS *Orange-eyed White Longhair*

Coat The fur should be silky, thick and dense, with a full frill. Colour should be pure white.

Ears Small and round-tipped.

Eyes Large, round, and orange in colour.

Head Round and broad, with full cheeks and a short nose.

Body A cobby, solid type, with a short, bushy tail.

Legs Short and thick.

Feet The paws are large and round.

Black Longhair

A true Black Longhair is comparatively rare; many cats that seem to be black in fact have specks of white or rustiness in their coat. Even when you find a cat with pure jet black fur, you will still have problems as it won't stay attractive for long. Because damp tends to give the coat a brownish tinge and strong sunlight bleaches it, a Black Longhair needs a great deal of grooming and attention, including daily brushing.

History Longhaired black cats have been recorded in Europe as far back as the sixteenth century, and were shown at the first cat shows (see p. 178).

Temperament The Black Longhair is a lively, affectionate cat.

Varieties There are no varieties of Black Longhair.

Assessing a Black Longhair kitten
Don't write off a kitten with specks in its coat; often jet black fur doesn't develop until the cat is more than six months old.

KEY CHARACTERISTICS

Coat The fur should be silky, thick and dense. Colour should be jet black, with no sign of rustiness, white hairs or markings of any kind.

Ears Small and round-tipped.

Eyes Large, round, and copper or dark orange in colour.

Head Round and broad, with full cheeks and a short nose.

Body A solid, cobby type, with a short, bushy tail.

Legs Short and thick.

Feet The paws are large and round.

Cream Longhair

Though a beautiful cat in its own right, the Cream can also be crossbred with the Blue (see p. 54), to produce the stunning Blue-Cream Longhair (see p. 55).

History The breed originally arose from accidental matings between Blue and Red Longhairs, and wasn't initially taken seriously by British breeders. Creams were labelled "Spoiled Oranges" and sold off as pets. However, American breeders recognized their potential and began to develop the line. Today, the Cream's popularity is rising in Britain, and it is almost as popular as the Blue.

Temperament The Cream Longhair is a calm, affectionate cat.

Varieties There are no varieties of Cream Longhair.

Cream Longhair and Blue Longhair kittens
Creams are related to Blues (see p. 54), and kittens in both colours often appear in the same litter.

KEY CHARACTERISTICS

Coat The fur should be silky, thick and dense. Colour can be any even shade from pale to medium cream.

Ears Small and round-tipped.

Body A cobby, solid type, with a short, bushy tail.

Head Broad and round, with full cheeks and a short nose.

Eyes Large, round, and copper in colour.

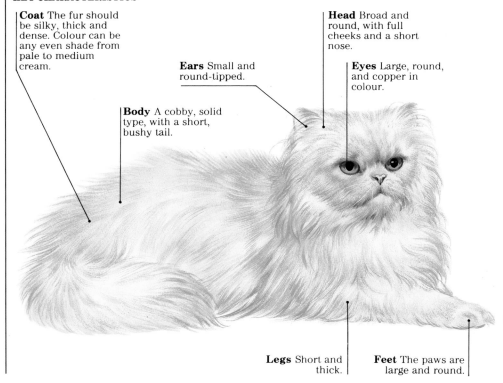

Legs Short and thick.

Feet The paws are large and round.

Red Self Longhair

A true example of this outstanding breed is pure red with no tabby markings. But such perfection is impossible in practice, and the majority of Red Self cats will have some markings, particularly on the face. However, in the best show examples the pattern is largely hidden by the diffusing nature of the longhaired coat.

History Developed in Britain early this century, the Red Self was originally referred to as the Orange. However, because cats with a deep red colouring were most favoured, the name was soon changed to Red.

Temperament Despite its fiery colouring, the Red Self Longhair is a calm, docile and affectionate cat.

Varieties There is only one other variety of Red: the Peke-Face Longhair. As the name suggests, this cat has a face resembling that of a Pekingese dog, with an extremely short, snub nose, a wrinkled muzzle, and an obvious indentation between its copper-coloured eyes.

The Peke-Face sometimes appears as a spontaneous mutant in a litter of Red or Red Tabby kittens, and is deliberately encouraged as a breed in America. As a variety, it is eligible for showing in the U.S. with either a self-coloured or a tabby coat. But the Peke-Face isn't recognized for showing in Britain. The reason for this ban is that most British vets disapprove of its breeding because the squashed face is basically a deformity that can lead to feeding and breathing troubles.

KEY CHARACTERISTICS *Red Self Longhair*

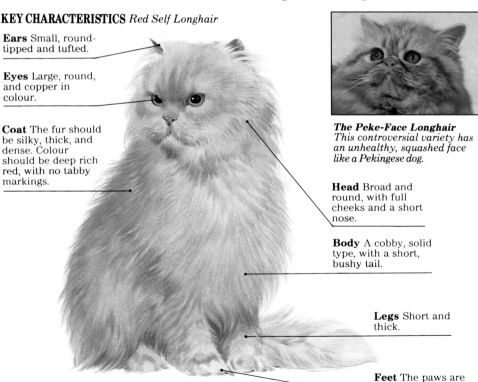

Ears Small, round-tipped and tufted.

Eyes Large, round, and copper in colour.

Coat The fur should be silky, thick, and dense. Colour should be deep rich red, with no tabby markings.

The Peke-Face Longhair
This controversial variety has an unhealthy, squashed face like a Pekingese dog.

Head Broad and round, with full cheeks and a short nose.

Body A cobby, solid type, with a short, bushy tail.

Legs Short and thick.

Feet The paws are large and round

Blue Longhair

The Blue is the most popular of all Longhairs — there are even shows devoted solely to it. Crossed with the Cream, it produces the attractive Blue-Cream (see opposite). Because the Blue is usually nearest in body shape to the accepted show standards for Longhairs, it is used in breeding programmes to improve the type of other colour varieties.

History The Blue is probably the result of crossbreeding Black and White Longhairs. The variety was a star of early cat shows in the late nineteenth century.

Temperament The Blue Longhair is a calm, affectionate cat.

Varieties There are no varieties of Blue Longhair.

Assessing a Blue Longhair kitten
Most Blue kittens are born with faint tabby markings, but these should fade once the kitten is a few months old.

KEY CHARACTERISTICS

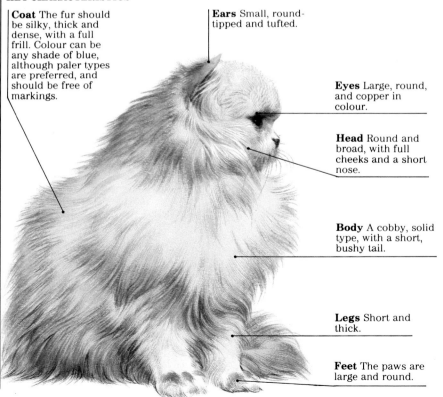

Coat The fur should be silky, thick and dense, with a full frill. Colour can be any shade of blue, although paler types are preferred, and should be free of markings.

Ears Small, round-tipped and tufted.

Eyes Large, round, and copper in colour.

Head Round and broad, with full cheeks and a short nose.

Body A cobby, solid type, with a short, bushy tail.

Legs Short and thick.

Feet The paws are large and round.

Blue-Cream Longhair

The silky coat of this Longhair is a mixture of pastel blue and cream. Because of the way colour genes are inherited (see p. 202), Blue-Creams are almost always female cats.

History The Blue-Cream is a recent cross of two self-coloured cats: the Blue (see p. 54) and the Cream (see p. 52).

Temperament The Blue-Cream Longhair is a quiet, affectionate cat.

Varieties There are no varieties of Blue-Cream Longhair, but different standards for the coat have developed in Britain and the U.S. In America, coats with clearly separated areas of colour are preferred, whilst the British rules demand that the two colours should be intermingled.

The American Blue-Cream Longhair
In the U.S. the blue and cream colours of this variety are separated into patches, rather than intermingled.

KEY CHARACTERISTICS *British variety*

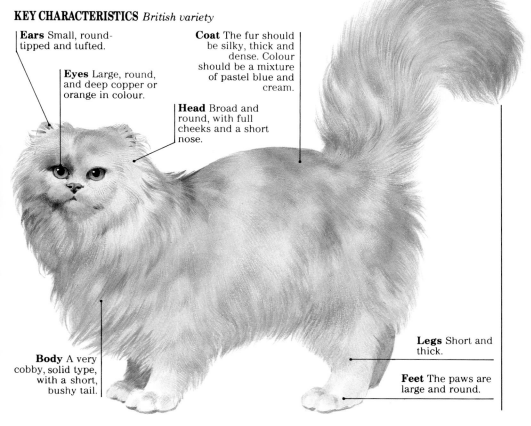

Ears Small, round-tipped and tufted.

Eyes Large, round, and deep copper or orange in colour.

Coat The fur should be silky, thick and dense. Colour should be a mixture of pastel blue and cream.

Head Broad and round, with full cheeks and a short nose.

Body A very cobby, solid type, with a short, bushy tail.

Legs Short and thick.

Feet The paws are large and round.

Chinchilla Longhair

The South American rodent that gives this cat its name has a dark undercoat tipped with white. Perversely, the Chinchilla Longhair has a pure white coat tipped with black. The cat's appearance is deceptive too — although it looks delicate, in fact it tends to be strong and healthy.

History A "man-made" Longhair, the Chinchilla arose from various cross-matings of Longhairs early this century.

Temperament The Chinchilla Longhair is a placid, affectionate cat.

Varieties There is one other variety of Chinchilla Longhair: the green-eyed, slightly darker Shaded Silver. This cat isn't recognized in Britain, but it is used for breeding Chinchillas.

Shaded Silver Longhair
This variety has a white undercoat with black tipping on its sides, face and tail that shades to white.

KEY CHARACTERISTICS *Chinchilla Longhair*

Coat The fur should be silky, thick and dense. Colour should be snowy white, delicately and evenly tipped with black on the back, flanks, ears and tail. This tipping has a sparkling appearance. The chin, ear tufts, stomach and chest should be pure white.

Body Cobby, but finer-boned than most Longhairs, with a short, bushy tail.

Ears Small, round-tipped and tufted.

Eyes Very large, round, and emerald or blue-green in colour.

Head Round and broad, with full cheeks and a short nose.

Feet The paws are large and round.

Legs Short and thick.

Cameo Longhair

This attractive cat has similar coat markings to the Chinchilla, but is tipped with red, cream, tabby or tortie instead of black. The length of tipping depends on the variety: the Shell has short coloured tips on a white coat, giving a hazy effect, the Shaded has longer coloured tips that sparkle against the white, and in the Smoke the tips are so long that the white undercoat isn't visible until the cat moves.

History This breed was developed from Smoke (see p. 58) and Tortoiseshell Longhairs (see p. 62) in the 1950s.

Temperament Cameo Longhairs are placid, affectionate cats.

Varieties There are eight varieties, as shown in the chart on the right.

Varieties	Markings	Eyes
Red Shell Cameo	Short red tips	Copper
Red Shaded Cameo	Longer red tips	Copper
Red Smoke Cameo	Longest red tips	Copper
Cream Shell Cameo	Short cream tips	Copper
Cream Shaded Cameo	Longer cream tips	Copper
Cream Smoke Cameo	Longest cream tips	Copper
Cameo Tortie	Black, red, cream tips	Copper
Cameo Tabby	Cream, red tips	Copper

Tortie Cameo Longhair
This attractive cat has patches of black, red and cream tipping on a white undercoat. The tips on a Tortie Cameo can be of any length.

KEY CHARACTERISTICS *Shaded Cameo Longhair*

Ears Small, round-tipped and tufted.

Eyes Large, round, and copper in colour.

Coat The fur should be silky, thick and dense. Colour should be white, with medium-long red tips.

Head Round and broad, with full cheeks and a short nose.

Body A cobby, solid type, with a short, bushy tail.

Legs Short and thick.

Feet The paws are large and round.

Smoke Longhair

The tipping on a Smoke is so long and dark that the cat appears to be a solid colour. In fact, it has a pale undercoat with dark tips, but this only becomes evident when the cat moves and the pale colour shimmers through.

History Crosses of Chinchilla, Black and Blue Longhairs produced this splendid animal. The Smoke was first recorded in the 1870s at the early British shows.

Temperament The Smoke Longhair is a placid, good-tempered cat.

Varieties There are two varieties of this breed: a black-tipped type that is simply known as the Smoke Longhair, and the Blue Smoke Longhair which has blue tips. All types have orange eyes.

KEY CHARACTERISTICS *Blue Smoke Longhair*

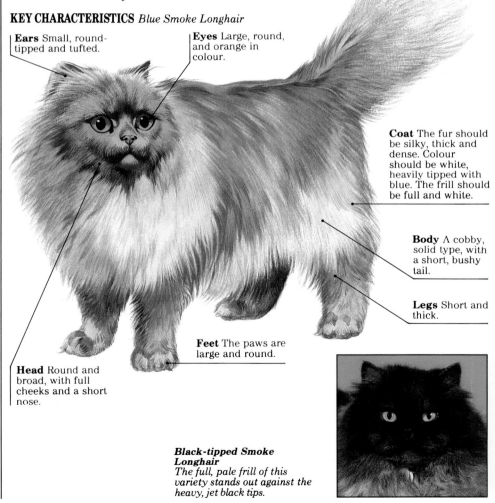

Ears Small, round-tipped and tufted.

Eyes Large, round, and orange in colour.

Coat The fur should be silky, thick and dense. Colour should be white, heavily tipped with blue. The frill should be full and white.

Body A cobby, solid type, with a short, bushy tail.

Legs Short and thick.

Feet The paws are large and round.

Head Round and broad, with full cheeks and a short nose.

Black-tipped Smoke Longhair
The full, pale frill of this variety stands out against the heavy, jet black tips.

Bicolour Longhair

These Longhairs have coats in mixtures of white and a colour. Overall, the colour should predominate, and the underparts should be mostly white.

History Bicolours first appeared in the "Any Other Colours" class. When they were given a class of their own, the rules required the patching to be exactly symmetrical, but the standard has been revised to make any even patching acceptable.

Temperament Bicolour Longhairs are calm, affectionate cats.

Varieties These cats can be any recognized solid colour combined with white; the eye colour should harmonize.

Blue Bicolour Longhair
This variety has a soft grey-blue coat evenly patched in white.

KEY CHARACTERISTICS
Red-and-White Bicolour Longhair

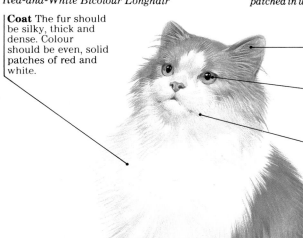

Coat The fur should be silky, thick and dense. Colour should be even, solid patches of red and white.

Ears Small, round-tipped and tufted.

Eyes Large, round, and brilliant copper in colour.

Head Broad and round, with full cheeks and a short nose.

Body A cobby, solid type, with a short, bushy tail.

Legs Short and thick.

Feet The paws are large and round. They are usually white in colour.

Tabby Longhairs

The markings on longhaired tabbies can be either Classic (see below) or Mackerel-patterned (see p. 83). Tabby Longhairs are comparatively rare compared to Shorthairs.

History These cats were first seen on the show benches in the nineteenth century. It has proved very difficult to breed longhaired cats with a pattern of markings that can be clearly seen, matching the show standards set for shorthaired cats.

Temperament Tabby Longhairs are quiet, affectionate, docile cats.

Varieties There are five varieties of Tabby Longhair, as shown in the chart on the right.

Varieties	Coat	Eyes
Red Tabby	Rich copper marked in red	Copper or orange
Brown Tabby	Tawny brown marked in black	Copper or orange
Silver Tabby	Silver-grey marked in black	Green or hazel
Blue Tabby (U.S. only)	Bluish-ivory marked in slate-blue	Copper
Cream Tabby (U.S. only)	Pale cream marked in rich cream	Copper

KEY CHARACTERISTICS *Silver Tabby Longhair*

Coat The fur should be silky, thick and dense. Colour should be silver-grey marked in black in the classic pattern. This consists of butterfly markings on the shoulders, two narrow stripes across the chest, and lines on the forehead that form the letter M.

Head Round and broad, with full cheeks and a short nose.

Eyes Large, round, and green or hazel in colour.

Ears Small and well-tufted.

Body A cobby, solid type, with a short, bushy tail.

Legs Short and thick.

Feet The paws are large and round.

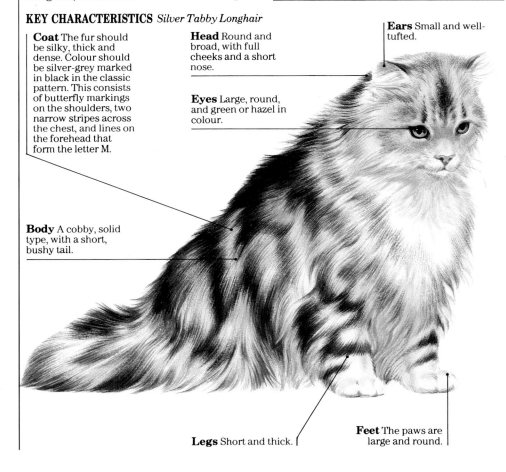

KEY CHARACTERISTICS *Brown Tabby Longhair*

Red Tabby Longhair
Years of careful breeding have produced this striking-looking variety, with rich red markings that stand out well against the bright copper coat.

Blue Tabby Longhair
An attractive cat produced from crosses between Brown Tabbies and self-coloured Blue Longhairs.

Coat The fur should be silky, thick and dense. Colour should be tawny brown, marked in black in a classic pattern.

Ears Small, round-tipped and well-tufted.

Head Round and broad, with full cheeks and a short nose.

Eyes Large, round, and copper or orange in colour.

Body A cobby, solid type, with a short, bushy tail.

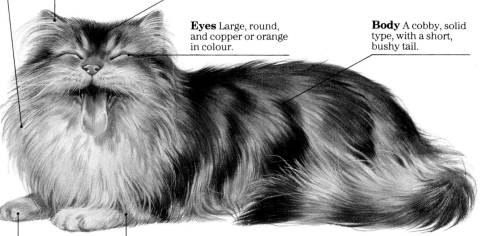

Legs Short and thick.

Feet The paws are large and round.

Tortoiseshell Longhair

Commonly known as the "Tortie", this rare cat is difficult to breed, and so is likely to be more expensive than other Longhairs. Because of the way colour genes work (see p. 202), Torties are always female.

History It is thought that this cat developed as a result of accidental matings between imported longhaired cats and shorthaired non-pedigree tortoiseshells.

Temperament The Tortoiseshell Longhair is a calm, affectionate cat.

Varieties There are no varieties of Tortoiseshell Longhair.

KEY CHARACTERISTICS

Coat The fur should be silky, thick and dense. Colour should be a mixture of rich red, cream and black patches.

Ears Small, round-tipped and well-tufted.

Eyes Large, round, and copper or orange in colour.

Head Round and broad, with full cheeks and a short nose.

Feet The paws are large and round.

Legs Short and thick.

Body A cobby, solid type, with a short, bushy tail.

Special feature: Facial blaze
Torties with a cream or red blaze running from nose to forehead are particularly sought after.

Tortoiseshell-and-White Longhair

This cat is basically a Tortoiseshell (see opposite), with the addition of white patches. The coat's pattern consists of bright, bold patches of colour, and is said to resemble printed cotton. Tortie-and-Whites are always female.

History Like the Tortie, this cat probably developed from matings between Longhairs and non-pedigree tortoiseshell shorthairs.

Temperament The Tortoiseshell-and-White Longhair is a calm, affectionate cat.

Varieties There are no varieties, but the U.S. show standards differ, as shown right.

KEY CHARACTERISTICS *British variety*

Coat The fur should be silky, thick and dense. Colour should be a mixture of red, cream, black and white patches.

Ears Small, round-tipped and well-tufted.

Eyes Large, round, and copper or orange in colour.

Head Round and broad, with full cheeks and a short nose.

American Tortoiseshell-and-White Longhairs
Because this cat's coat is said to resemble printed cotton, it is called a "Calico" in the U.S. The breed looks slightly different in America, as the American show standard calls for a white cat with coloured patches. In contrast, British judges don't like a dominance of white.

Body A cobby, solid type, with a short, bushy tail.

Legs Short and thick.

Feet The paws are large and round.

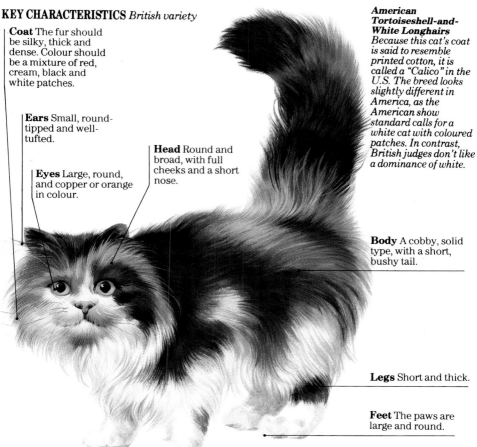

Colourpoint Longhair

As the name suggests, a Colourpoint's mask, ears, legs, feet and tail (the points) are a different shade or colour to the rest of its body. It isn't unusual for a Colourpoint Longhair to be mistaken for a longhaired Siamese, as this breed is found in the Siamese colouring patterns, and has the same distinctive sapphire-blue eyes. However, the Colourpoint is a true Longhair type. It has the characteristic cobby build of the Longhair, with short, thick legs, a broad face and a snub nose, rather than the long, slim body, wedge-shaped head and straight nose of the Siamese.

History The Colourpoint varieties are the result of a long, scientifically based pro-gramme in which Siamese and Longhairs were crossbred to produce a cat which has the body type and coat of a Longhair, with the distinctive point markings of the Siamese.

Temperament A cat with a lot of character, the Colourpoint is more inquisitive and enterprising than most Longhairs. It usually becomes very devoted to its owner, often to the extent of following him or her around in a dog-like fashion.

Varieties The Colourpoint comes in a wide range of colour combinations, as shown in the chart below. Whatever colour its coat is, a Colourpoint's eyes are always bright sapphire-blue.

Varieties	Coat	Markings
Seal	Warm cream	Deep seal-brown
Chocolate	Ivory	Warm brown
Blue	Bluish-white	Slate-blue
Lilac	Magnolia	Pinkish-grey
Red	Creamy white	Orange or red
Cream	Creamy white	Buff-cream
Tortie	Warm cream	Red and cream patches
Blue-Cream	Bluish or creamy white	Blue and mottled cream
Lilac-Cream	Magnolia	Pinkish-grey patched in cream

Colourpoint kittens
These kittens are just beginning to show their point markings. At birth, the markings are hardly visible; they darken as the cat grows, reaching the full shade when it is about 18 months old.

Blue Colourpoint Longhair
This cat has a bluish-white body and slate-blue point markings.

Red Colourpoint Longhair
The creamy white body of this Red contrasts with its orange points and blue eyes.

KEY CHARACTERISTICS *Seal-point Colourpoint Longhair*

Coat This should be thick, silky and dense. Colour should be warm cream with deep seal-brown markings.

Ears Small and round-tipped.

Eyes Large, round, and bright sapphire-blue in colour.

Head Round and broad, with full cheeks and a short nose.

Body A cobby, solid type, with a short, bushy tail.

Legs Short and thick.

Feet The paws are large and round.

Pewter Longhair

This handsome cat has a thick, white coat with delicate black shading over the head, back, flanks, legs and tail. The chin, ear tufts and stomach are white. This shading is similar to the tipping on Chinchillas (see p. 56), but the amount of colour is greater, giving the Pewter a darker look than the Chinchilla.

History The result of Chinchilla, Blue and Black crosses, this cat resembles the old Chinchilla variety, the Shaded Silver (see p. 56), but with orange or copper eyes rather than the Silver's sea-green.

Temperament The Pewter Longhair is a calm, affectionate cat.

Varieties There are no varieties of Pewter Longhair.

Chinchilla tipping
Slightly lighter in colour than the Pewter, this breed is often confused with it, but has less heavy tipping.

Pewter tipping
The Pewter is often confused with the Chinchilla (left), but the tipping is deeper, making the coat darker.

KEY CHARACTERISTICS

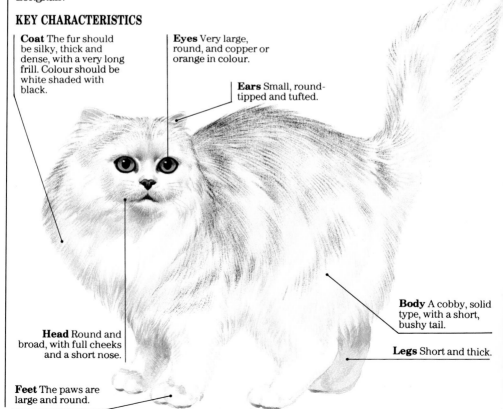

Coat The fur should be silky, thick and dense, with a very long frill. Colour should be white shaded with black.

Eyes Very large, round, and copper or orange in colour.

Ears Small, round-tipped and tufted.

Body A cobby, solid type, with a short, bushy tail.

Legs Short and thick.

Head Round and broad, with full cheeks and a short nose.

Feet The paws are large and round.

Chocolate and Lilac Longhairs

An interior decorator would be tempted to match a colour scheme to the stunning coat and eye colours of these cats. The Chocolate Longhair has rich medium to dark chocolate-brown fur with copper-coloured eyes, whilst the Lilac Longhair's coat is pinkish dove-grey and its eyes are pale orange or copper.

History Both cats are a by-product of the selective breeding programme for Colourpoint Longhairs (see pp. 64–5).

Temperament Like their Colourpoint "relations", Chocolate and Lilac cats are more inquisitive and enterprising than most Longhairs.

Varieties There are no varieties of the Chocolate or the Lilac Longhair.

Chocolate Longhair
A typical Longhair in build, the Chocolate has medium to dark chocolate-brown fur and copper-coloured eyes.

KEY CHARACTERISTICS *Lilac Longhair*

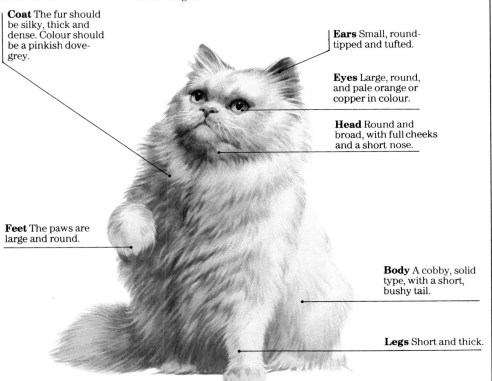

Coat The fur should be silky, thick and dense. Colour should be a pinkish dove-grey.

Ears Small, round-tipped and tufted.

Eyes Large, round, and pale orange or copper in colour.

Head Round and broad, with full cheeks and a short nose.

Feet The paws are large and round.

Body A cobby, solid type, with a short, bushy tail.

Legs Short and thick.

New Longhairs

Experimental breeding programmes have resulted in several new varieties of long-haired cat. None of these are recognized by cat fancy organizations at present, but they may achieve show status in time.

History The Lilac-Cream and the Chocolate-Tortoiseshell Longhair are a side-effect of the breeding programme for Colourpoints (see pp. 64–5), and the Golden Longhairs were developed from Chinchillas (see p. 56).

Temperament Like all Longhairs, these new varieties are affectionate animals. True to their Colourpoint parentage, the Lilac-Cream and the Chocolate-Tortoiseshell are slightly livelier than most Longhairs. Inquisitive and enterprising cats, they usually become very devoted to their owners.

Varieties There are four new Longhairs that may achieve show status in the future, as shown in the chart opposite.

KEY CHARACTERISTICS

Lilac-Cream Longhair

Coat The fur should be silky, thick and dense. Colour should be pinkish-grey and cream intermingled.

Ears Small, round-tipped and tufted.

Eyes Large, round, and copper in colour.

Head Round and broad, with full cheeks and a short nose.

Body A cobby, solid type, with a short, bushy tail.

Legs Short and thick.

Feet The paws are large and round.

Varieties	Coat	Eyes
Lilac-Cream	Pinkish-grey and cream	Copper
Chocolate-Tortoiseshell	Chocolate, red and cream patches	Deep orange or copper
Chinchilla Golden	Light seal-brown tips on rich cream	Green
Shaded Golden	Heavy seal-brown tips on rich cream	Green

Shaded Golden Longhair
A brown-and-cream version of the Shaded Silver (see p.56), the Shaded Golden has long brown tips on a cream undercoat, and green eyes.

KEY CHARACTERISTICS *Chocolate-Tortoiseshell Longhair*

Coat The fur should be silky, thick and dense. Colour should be a mixture of rich chocolate-brown, red and cream patches.

Body A cobby, solid type, with a short, bushy tail.

Head Round and broad, with full cheeks and a short nose.

Ears Small, round-tipped and tufted.

Eyes Large, round, and deep orange or copper in colour.

Legs Short and thick.

Feet The paws are large and round.

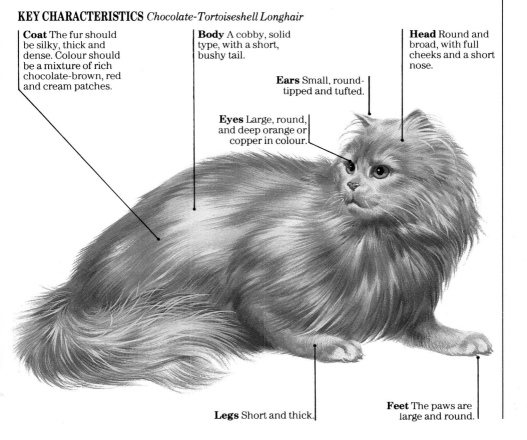

Birman

Longer in build than the typical longhaired cat, with a narrower face, the Birman has a pale gold-coloured body with contrasting mask, ears, head and tail. Its front paws are tipped with white, whilst its back paws have white gloves at the front and white gauntlets at the rear that finish in a point up the back of the legs.

History According to legend, these cats were originally white in colour, with yellow eyes, and were kept in the temples of Burma centuries ago, at a time of war. One day, the High Priest was found dying in front of a golden, sapphire-eyed statue of a goddess. The priest's cat jumped onto this idol, and as the cat touched the goddess the priest's soul passed into it. Miraculously, the cat changed from white to gold, and its yellow eyes turned to sapphire. Its feet, mask, tail and ears darkened, and only the ends of its front paws, which touched its master, remained white. This miracle encouraged the other priests to fight off their enemies, and from that day on, all the temple cats took on the new colouring of the High Priest's cat.

Temperament A gentle, well-behaved cat, the Birman is very sociable; it enjoys the company of humans and is friendly towards other animals.

Varieties There are two varieties of Birman: the Seal-point Birman, a pale beige-gold cat with dark brown point markings; and the Blue-point Birman, a bluish-white cat with blue-grey point markings.

Blue-point Birmans
These cats have slate-blue points on a bluish-white coat.

KEY CHARACTERISTICS *Seal-point Birman*

Coat The fur should be silky and long. Colour should be beige-gold with seal-brown points.

Head Fairly round and broad, with full cheeks and a medium-size nose.

Ears Dark in colour, medium in size, and round-tipped.

Eyes Almost round, slightly slanted, and sapphire-blue in colour.

Body A long, muscular type, with a medium-length tail.

Legs Medium in length.

Feet The paws are large and round. The front pair are gloved in white. The back pair are white at the front, with white gauntlets at the back.

Ragdoll

This large cat, first recognized in 1965 and of Persian origin, gets its name from a unique feature – when held it completely relaxes, becoming as floppy as a ragdoll.
History Developed in California, at present this breed is fairly rare outside the U.S.
Temperament The Ragdoll is said to have a high tolerance of pain. Placid by nature, it can be trained to walk on a lead.
Varieties Ragdolls are bred in three coat patterns: Bi-colour (a pale body with a dark mask, ears and tail, and a white chest, stomach and legs), Colourpoint (a pale body with darker points), and Mitted (as Colour-point, with a white chest, bib, chin and front paw "mittens"). Colours are Seal-point, Chocolate-point, Blue-point, Lilac-point.

Chocolate-point Bi-colour Ragdoll
Ivory-coloured, with a white chest, stomach and legs, and warm brown markings on its mask, ears and tail, this Chocolate-point is shown in a typical Ragdoll pose.

KEY CHARACTERISTICS *Seal-point Bi-Colour Ragdoll*

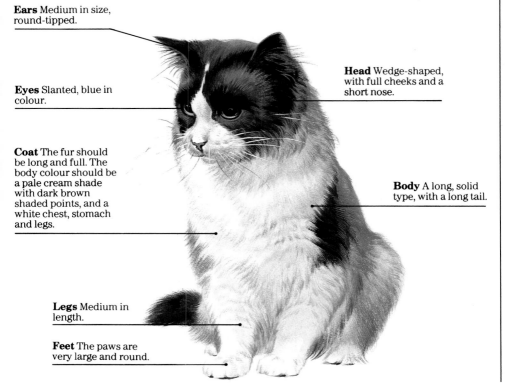

Ears Medium in size, round-tipped.

Eyes Slanted, blue in colour.

Coat The fur should be long and full. The body colour should be a pale cream shade with dark brown shaded points, and a white chest, stomach and legs.

Legs Medium in length.

Feet The paws are very large and round.

Head Wedge-shaped, with full cheeks and a short nose.

Body A long, solid type, with a long tail.

Balinese

Basically a longhaired Siamese (see pp. 94–5), the Balinese has the same long, slim body, wedge-shaped head, and vivid blue eyes. Its soft, ermine-like coat is short in comparison to those of other longhaired cats, and doesn't form a ruff.

History The Balinese appeared as a spontaneous mutation in Siamese litters in the U.S. in the 1950s.

Temperament Like the Siamese, the Balinese loves attention; it is very playful and fond of human company.

Varieties This breed is available in the same colours as the Siamese (see p. 95).

Seal-point Balinese
This variety has a warm cream body with seal-brown markings on the face, ears, tail and legs.

KEY CHARACTERISTICS *Lilac-point Balinese*

Head Wedge-shaped, with a long nose.

Ears Large and pointed.

Eyes Medium in size, slanted, almond-shaped, and sapphire-blue in colour.

Coat The fur should be medium-long. Colour should be magnolia, with pinkish-grey points.

Body A lithe, slim type, with a long tail.

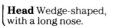

Legs Long and slim, with the forelegs shorter than the hind legs.

Feet The paws are small and oval.

Angora

The slim, long-bodied Angora looks very different from the cobby-bodied, round-faced Longhairs (see pp. 50–69). And because it lacks the Longhair's woolly undercoat, it doesn't have the dramatic "powder-puff" look that makes the Longhair so appealing. However, the Angora is an elegant, attractive cat, and has the advantage that its fine, silky fur is much easier to groom.

History The very first longhaired cats introduced into Europe in the sixteenth century were the Angoras from Ankara in Turkey. This breed almost died out in Europe, though, because of a preference for the Persian type (the ancestors of the contemporary Longhair). But recently Angoras have been introduced directly into the U.S. from Turkey, and today they are being bred again for showing in America. The breed is likely to be recognized for show purposes in Britain in the near future.

Temperament The Angora is a quiet, affectionate, playful cat.

Varieties In addition to the traditional white colouring, the contemporary Angora is produced in several colour varieties, as shown in the chart below.

KEY CHARACTERISTICS *Orange-eyed White Angora*

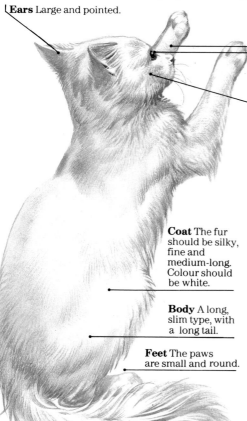

Ears Large and pointed.

Legs Long and slim, with the forelegs slightly shorter than the hind legs.

Eyes Medium in size, slanted, almond-shaped, and orange in colour.

Head Long and wedge-shaped, with a long nose.

Coat The fur should be silky, fine and medium-long. Colour should be white.

Body A long, slim type, with a long tail.

Feet The paws are small and round.

Varieties	Coat	Eyes
White	Pure white	Orange, blue or odd-eyed
Black	Jet black	Orange
Blue	Blue-grey	Orange
Black Smoke	White, black tips	Orange
Blue Smoke	White, blue tips	Orange
Silver Tabby	Silver, black marking	Orange or green
Red Tabby	Red, rich red marking	Orange
Brown Tabby	Brown, black marking	Orange
Blue Tabby	Bluish-ivory, blue marking	Orange
Calico	White, black and red patches	Orange
Bi-colour	Black, blue, red or cream with white	Orange

Turkish cat

During the summer, this longhaired cat loses a great deal of its white and auburn fur, and looks almost shorthaired, but by winter its coat is long and silky again.

History This cat is thought to be a naturally occurring Turkish breed. First imported into Britain in the 1950s, it has been recognized for showing since 1969.

Temperament Unlike most self-respecting cats, this animal actually enjoys playing in the water, and may even swim in shallow, warm pools. The Turkish cat has a lively, affectionate nature.

Varieties There are no recognized varieties, but a Turkish cat with cream markings is being bred in Britain.

Special feature: The swimming cat
In its native Turkey this unique breed swims happily in shallow streams or pools.

KEY CHARACTERISTICS

Coat The fur should be long and silky. Colour should be white, with auburn markings on the face and tail. The tail should be ringed in darker auburn.

Head Short, wedge-shaped, with a long nose.

Ears Large and pointed.

Eyes Round, and amber in colour.

Body A long, muscular type, with a long, full tail.

Legs Medium in length.

Feet The paws are small and round.

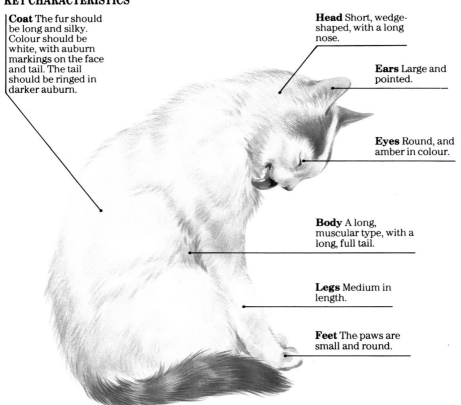

Maine Coon

The heavy, shaggy coat of the Maine Coon is almost shorthaired at the front, but grows very long on its back and stomach.

History This breed was developed from hardy American farm cats, thought to be crosses between early Angoras and non-pedigree shorthairs. It isn't recognized for showing in Britain.

Temperament A gentle, affectionate cat, the Maine Coon makes a good pet. However, unlike most longhaired cats, it isn't suitable for apartment life as it needs plenty of space, and access to a garden or yard. The Maine Coon has a peculiar habit of sleeping in strange positions in the oddest of places. One theory put forward to explain this is that its farm-cat ancestry has accustomed it to sleeping rough. Another unusual feature of the Maine Coon is the attractive, quiet, chirping sound it makes.

Varieties The Maine Coon is found in any coat colour or pattern except for the chocolate, lilac or Siamese point-type patterns. Its eyes should be green, gold or copper in colour. In general, there is no relationship between coat colour and eye colour, although blue-eyed and odd-eyed types are also permitted in Whites.

Not related to the Maine Coon, but very similar in appearance, is the Norwegian Forest Cat. It isn't recognized in Britain, and it is very rare outside Norway.

KEY CHARACTERISTICS *Brown and White Tabby Maine Coon*

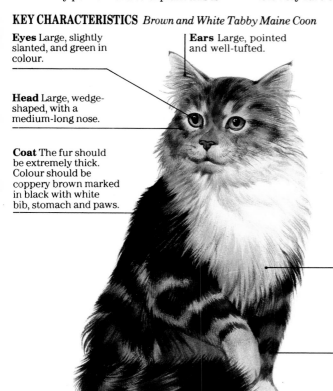

Eyes Large, slightly slanted, and green in colour.

Head Large, wedge-shaped, with a medium-long nose.

Coat The fur should be extremely thick. Colour should be coppery brown marked in black with white bib, stomach and paws.

Ears Large, pointed and well-tufted.

Black Maine Coon
This variety should have shaggy, dense black fur, with no trace of rustiness.

Body A very large, long, muscular type, with a long, flowing tail.

Legs Medium in length.

Feet The paws are large and round.

SHORTHAIRED CATS

Short hair is by far the most common type of coat in both domestic and wild cats. The main reason for this is that the genes for short hair are dominant over those for long hair (see pp. 200—2). This is perfectly sensible on nature's part, because although a long coat looks beautiful, a short one is far more practical.

Where did shorthaired pedigree cats originate?

Shorthaired domestic cats have been around for thousands of years (see pp. 44—5), but pedigree breeds are a relatively new concept; they emerged with the first cat shows, which were held in Britain in the late nineteenth century (see p. 178). Pedigree shorthaired cats can be divided into three basic types: British Shorthair, American Shorthair and Foreign Shorthair.

What is a British Shorthair?

The British Shorthair is a sturdy, healthy cat with a strong, muscular body on short legs, and a short, dense coat. It has a broad, rounded head, with a short, straight nose, and large, round eyes. This Shorthair is bred in a wide range of colours and coat patterns: from the solid-coloured Black to the pure White, and from the subtly tipped Blue Smoke to the strongly patterned Silver Tabby. European Shorthair breeds are identical.

What is an American Shorthair?

Ancestors of the British and European Shorthairs were taken to America with the early settlers, and developed into a slightly different strain of cat. Larger and leaner than the British type, the American Shorthair has slightly longer legs, a more oval head with a square muzzle, a medium-length nose and large, round eyes. Like the British Shorthair, this cat is bred in a wide range of colours and patterns.

What is a Foreign Shorthair?

"Foreign" cats look quite different to the rounded, sturdy British and American Shorthairs. A Foreign-type cat has a wedge-shaped head with slanting eyes and large, pointed ears, a lithe, slim body with long legs, and a very fine, short coat. This category includes a variety of breeds. The quirkily attractive Siamese is the most typical example of a Foreign Shorthair, but the classification also embraces the hairless Sphynx and the elegant Abyssinian.

The advantages of a shorthaired coat

Unlike long hair, a short coat is easy to care for: it is simpler to clean, won't tangle, and is less likely to cause hairballs or blockages (see p. 235) within the cat's digestive system. It also has health advantages, as wounds can be cared for easily, and parasites kept to a minimum.

Apart from a twice-weekly grooming session to remove old hairs in its coat, a shorthaired cat can look after itself. In contrast, a longhaired type depends on a caring owner to look after its coat by giving it daily half-hour grooming sessions.

British Shorthairs pages 78–89

Silver Spotted British Shorthair (p. 85)

The first section of this chapter introduces you to the British pedigree version of the European domestic cat. There are 12 types of British Shorthair covered here, classified according to their coat pattern and colour. This section also includes that odd breed from the Isle of Man, the tailless Manx cat.

American Shorthairs pages 90–3

This section looks at special U.S. breeds. It includes the British Shorthair's "cousin", the American Shorthair, and its curly-haired version, the American Wirehair. It also looks at a new breed from America known as the Exotic. This cat is a cross between the American Shorthair and the Longhair, and is currently just reaching Europe.

American Shaded Silver Shorthair (p. 90)

Foreign Shorthairs pages 94–111

The final part of this chapter looks at a selection of different breeds, all classified as "Foreign". This name can be misleading as it refers to the cat's body type, not its place of origin. Although some Foreigns came from distant lands like Japan or Singapore, others were developed or arose as mutations in Britain and North America.

Cream Tabby Devon Rex (p. 108)   *Blue Burmese* (p. 101)

British White Shorthair

Like the blue-eyed White Longhair (see p. 50), blue-eyed White British Shorthairs tend to be deaf.

History The White was developed in the late nineteenth century when cat shows first started. It was selectively bred from the best street cats.

Temperament The British White is a good-natured, affectionate, intelligent cat.

Varieties There are three varieties: Blue-eyed, Orange-eyed and Odd-eyed.

KEY CHARACTERISTICS
British Blue-eyed White Shorthair

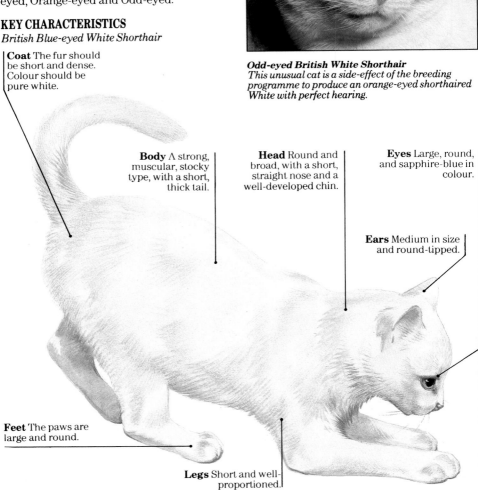

Odd-eyed British White Shorthair
This unusual cat is a side-effect of the breeding programme to produce an orange-eyed shorthaired White with perfect hearing.

Coat The fur should be short and dense. Colour should be pure white.

Body A strong, muscular, stocky type, with a short, thick tail.

Head Round and broad, with a short, straight nose and a well-developed chin.

Eyes Large, round, and sapphire-blue in colour.

Ears Medium in size and round-tipped.

Feet The paws are large and round.

Legs Short and well-proportioned.

British Black Shorthair

An adult British Black should have a glossy coat that is jet black right down to the roots, with no trace of white or rustiness. But a rusty looking kitten shouldn't be written off until it is more than six months old, as the colour may improve.

History The Black was developed in the late nineteenth century when cat shows first started. It was selectively bred from the best street cats.

In the past, black cats have been the victims of superstition. During the Middle Ages black cats were often burnt alive because they were thought to be the familiars of witches. Today, they are still branded as unlucky in some countries, but in others, like Britain, they are regarded as a source of good luck.

Temperament The British Black is a good-natured, affectionate, intelligent cat.

Varieties There are no varieties of British Black Shorthair.

KEY CHARACTERISTICS

Ears Medium in size and round-tipped.

Eyes Large, round, and deep copper, gold or orange in colour.

Coat The fur should be short and dense. Colour should be jet black, with no sign of rustiness.

Legs Short and well-proportioned.

Head Round and broad, with a short, straight nose and a well-developed chin.

Body A strong, muscular, stocky type, with a short, thick tail.

Feet The paws are large and round.

British Cream Shorthair

The British Cream is comparatively rare, and perfect examples are even rarer, as it is very difficult to produce a cat which has the desired even cream colour without any tabby markings. Crossed with British Blues, Creams produce the British Blue-Cream Shorthair (see p. 82).

History When these cats first appeared in Tortoiseshell litters in the late nineteenth century, nobody knew how to breed them other than accidentally. Because of this, the British Cream Shorthair wasn't recognized for showing until the 1920s, by which time a correct breeding programme had been worked out.

Temperament The British Cream is a good-natured, affectionate, intelligent cat.

Varieties There are no varieties of the British Cream Shorthair.

KEY CHARACTERISTICS

Coat The fur should be short and dense. Colour should be an even, soft ivory.

Head Round and broad, with a short, straight nose and a well-developed chin.

Ears Medium in size and round-tipped.

Eyes Large, round, and copper, orange or deep gold in colour.

Body A strong, muscular, stocky type, with a short, thick tail.

Legs Short and well-proportioned.

Feet The paws are large and round.

British Blue Shorthair

The Blue is the most popular British Shorthair. It isn't difficult to guess the reason for this — its plush, blue-grey coat and brilliant, copper- or orange-coloured eyes are particularly striking.

History When shows started in the nineteenth century, the pedigree British Blue was one of the first cats on the show benches. Like other British Shorthairs, it was developed from the best street cats.

Temperament The British Blue Shorthair is a good-natured, affectionate, intelligent cat.

Varieties The French have a variety of Blue called the Chartreux, said to have been bred in a monastery by the Carthusian monks who produced the well-known liqueur, Chartreuse. Opinion differs as to whether this cat is identical to the British Blue or a separate variety. In all British and most North American shows they are classed together, but some American clubs class the Chartreux separately, saying that it has a higher proportion of grey in its grey-blue coloured coat.

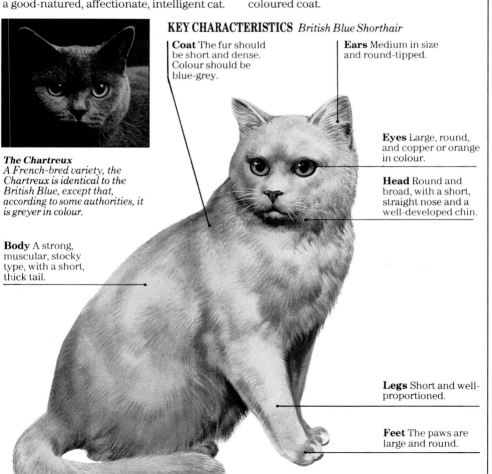

The Chartreux
A French-bred variety, the Chartreux is identical to the British Blue, except that, according to some authorities, it is greyer in colour.

KEY CHARACTERISTICS *British Blue Shorthair*

Coat The fur should be short and dense. Colour should be blue-grey.

Ears Medium in size and round-tipped.

Eyes Large, round, and copper or orange in colour.

Head Round and broad, with a short, straight nose and a well-developed chin.

Body A strong, muscular, stocky type, with a short, thick tail.

Legs Short and well-proportioned.

Feet The paws are large and round.

British Blue-Cream Shorthair

Basically a cross between Blue and Cream British Shorthairs, the Blue-Cream's coat is a softly intermingled mixture of the two colours. The U.K. show standard holds true for British Shorthairs shown in the U.S. As a result, distinguishing between a British and an American Blue-Cream Shorthair (see p. 91) is simple, because on the coat of the latter cat the blue and cream colouring is broken up into patches.

The correct coat pattern doesn't become obvious until the young cats are several months old, and therefore at birth the kittens are often mistaken for pale-coloured British Blues (Blues, Creams and Blue-Creams are often born in the same litter). Because of the way that colour genes are inherited (see p. 202), British Blue-Cream Shorthairs are almost always female.

History Developed from crosses between Blue and Cream British Shorthairs, this cat was first recognized for showing in Britain in the late 1950s.

Temperament The British Blue-Cream Shorthair is a good-natured, affectionate, intelligent cat.

Varieties There are no varieties of British Blue-Cream Shorthair.

KEY CHARACTERISTICS

Head Round and broad, with a short, straight nose and a well-developed chin.

Ears Medium in size and round-tipped.

Eyes Large, round, and copper, orange or deep gold in colour.

Body A strong, muscular, stocky type, with a short, thick tail.

Coat The fur should be short and dense. Colour should be blue and cream inter-mingled, with no sign of tabby markings.

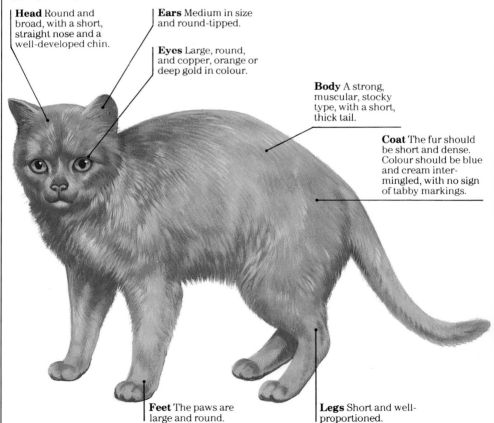

Feet The paws are large and round.

Legs Short and well-proportioned.

British Tabby Shorthair

Despite the dominance of this coat pattern in the cat world, breeding a cat with one of the two correct patterns of pedigree markings (Classic or Mackerel) isn't easy. The Classic has a butterfly shape on the shoulders, from which three stripes run along the spine. There is an oyster-shaped spiral on each flank, and the chest is crossed with two narrow, necklace-like stripes. On the forehead frown marks form the letter M. Both tail and legs are evenly ringed, and the abdomen is spotted. The Mackerel pattern is more striped and less blotchy, and lacks the spiral on the flanks.

British Silver Tabby Shorthair
A striking hazel or green-eyed cat, the Silver Tabby has strong black markings that stand out well against its grey coat.

History The tabby pattern is the original, basic cat coat pattern — tabby cats featured on Egyptian murals, and most new-born kittens have faint tabby markings. The British Shorthair Tabby is a selectively bred version of the best street cats.

Temperament The British Tabby is a good-natured, affectionate, intelligent cat.

Varieties There are three varieties: Brown (black markings on a brown ground, copper, orange or deep gold eyes), Silver (black markings on grey, and green or hazel eyes), and Red (very dark red markings on red, and orange or copper eyes).

KEY CHARACTERISTICS
British Brown Tabby Shorthair (Classic pattern)

Coat The fur should be short and dense. Colour should be rich brown with dense black markings in a classic tabby pattern.

Head Round and broad, with a short, straight nose and a well-developed chin.

Eyes Large, round, and copper or orange in colour.

Ears Medium in size and round-tipped.

Body A strong, muscular, stocky type, with a short, thick tail.

Feet The paws are large and round.

Legs Short and well-proportioned.

British Tortoiseshell Shorthair

Affectionately known as the "Tortie", the British Tortoiseshell Shorthair has a black coat marked with evenly distributed, distinct patches of cream and red. Because of the way that colour genes are inherited (see p. 202), Tortoiseshells are almost always female.

History When shows started in the late nineteenth century, the Tortoiseshell was one of the first cats on the show benches.

Like other British Shorthairs, it was developed from the best street cats.

Temperament The British Tortoiseshell Shorthair is a good-natured, affectionate, intelligent cat.

Varieties There is a variety with white patches: the British Tortoiseshell-and-White Shorthair. This cat has the same coat colourings as the Tortie, with the addition of white patches.

KEY CHARACTERISTICS *British Tortoiseshell Shorthair*

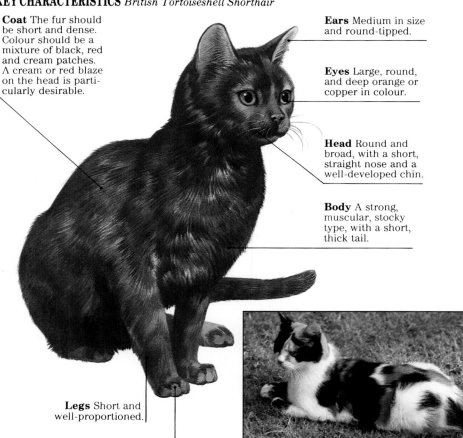

Coat The fur should be short and dense. Colour should be a mixture of black, red and cream patches. A cream or red blaze on the head is particularly desirable.

Ears Medium in size and round-tipped.

Eyes Large, round, and deep orange or copper in colour.

Head Round and broad, with a short, straight nose and a well-developed chin.

Body A strong, muscular, stocky type, with a short, thick tail.

Legs Short and well-proportioned.

Feet The paws are large and round.

British Tortoiseshell-and-White Shorthair
This cat is identical to the Tortie, except it has white patches as well as black, cream and red.

British Spotted Shorthair

The "Spottie" has a striking coat, with a pattern rather like that of a Mackerel Tabby broken up into spots. These dark spots should be as numerous and distinct as possible.

History The Spottie was exhibited at the first shows in the late nineteenth century and was bred from the best street cats.

Temperament The British Spotted is a good-natured, affectionate, intelligent cat.

Varieties The British Spotted Shorthair can be bred in any tabby-type colour combination, but the Silver, Brown and Red varieties are the most popular. The Silver has a pale grey body spotted in black, and green or hazel eyes. The Brown has a pale brown coat with black spots, and copper, orange or deep gold eyes. And the Red is light red spotted in rich red, with deep orange or copper eyes.

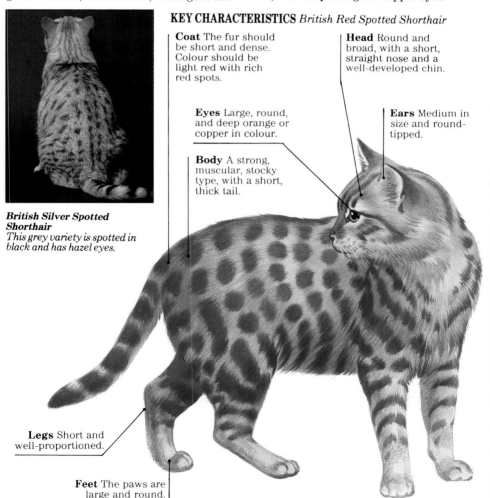

British Silver Spotted Shorthair
This grey variety is spotted in black and has hazel eyes.

KEY CHARACTERISTICS *British Red Spotted Shorthair*

Coat The fur should be short and dense. Colour should be light red with rich red spots.

Head Round and broad, with a short, straight nose and a well-developed chin.

Eyes Large, round, and deep orange or copper in colour.

Ears Medium in size and round-tipped.

Body A strong, muscular, stocky type, with a short, thick tail.

Legs Short and well-proportioned.

Feet The paws are large and round.

British Bicolour Shorthair

Although there are large numbers of pet cats that resemble the Bicolour, the pedigree version isn't very common. It has evenly distributed patches of white on a solid colour.

History Despite being the epitome of the street cat from which British Shorthairs were developed, Bicolours have only been recognized for showing recently.

Temperament The British Bicolour is a good-natured, affectionate, intelligent cat.

Varieties Bicolours are bred in Black-and-White, Blue-and-White, Red-and-White, and Cream-and-White.

KEY CHARACTERISTICS
British Cream-and-White Bicolour Shorthair

Coat The fur should be short and dense. Colour should be cream with white patches.

Body A strong, muscular, stocky type, with a short, thick tail.

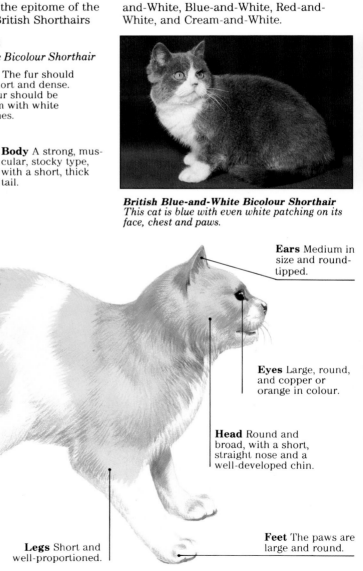

British Blue-and-White Bicolour Shorthair
This cat is blue with even white patching on its face, chest and paws.

Ears Medium in size and round-tipped.

Eyes Large, round, and copper or orange in colour.

Head Round and broad, with a short, straight nose and a well-developed chin.

Feet The paws are large and round.

Legs Short and well-proportioned.

British Smoke Shorthair

Like the longhaired Smoke (see p. 58), the shorthaired version has unusual fur, consisting of a one-coloured topcoat over a white undercoat. It is only when the cat moves that the effect of this is seen.

History Shorthaired British Smokes were developed in the late nineteenth century by crossing Silver Tabby and solid-coloured British Shorthairs.

Temperament The British Smoke is a good-natured, affectionate, intelligent cat.

Varieties There are two types of Smoke: the Black Smoke, with a black topcoat, and the Blue Smoke, with a blue topcoat.

KEY CHARACTERISTICS
British Blue Smoke Shorthair

Coat The fur should be short and dense. Undercoat colour should be white, with a blue topcoat of very long tipping.

Eyes Large, round, and copper, orange or deep gold in colour.

British Black Smoke Shorthair
This cat is often mistaken for a British Black because it looks solid-coloured until it moves, when the white undercoat shows through.

Ears Medium in size and round-tipped.

Head Round and broad, with a short, straight nose and a well-developed chin.

Body A strong, muscular type, with a short, thick tail.

Legs Short and well-proportioned.

Feet The paws are large and round.

British Tipped Shorthair

This breed is the shorthaired equivalent of the longhaired Chinchilla or Cameo (see pp. 56—7). It has a white undercoat tipped in a solid colour.

History The Tipped was developed from a complex breeding line involving cats with silver genes, Blues and Smokes.

Temperament The Tipped is a good-natured, affectionate, intelligent cat.

Varieties A British Tipped Shorthair can have tips in any British colour, plus chocolate and lilac. The eyes are copper or orange, unless the cat is tipped in black, when they are green.

British Silver Tipped Shorthair
A green-eyed variety, the Silver Tipped has short black tips on white, which sparkle when the cat moves.

KEY CHARACTERISTICS

British Red Tipped Shorthair

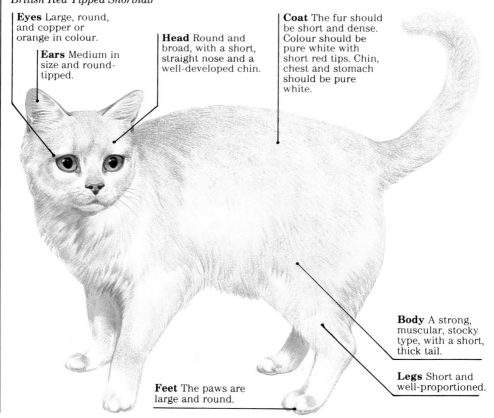

Eyes Large, round, and copper or orange in colour.

Ears Medium in size and round-tipped.

Head Round and broad, with a short, straight nose and a well-developed chin.

Coat The fur should be short and dense. Colour should be pure white with short red tips. Chin, chest and stomach should be pure white.

Body A strong, muscular, stocky type, with a short, thick tail.

Legs Short and well-proportioned.

Feet The paws are large and round.

Manx

An unusual, tail-less breed, the Manx has a similar build to the British Shorthair, except that its hind legs are longer than its forelegs, giving it a rabbit-like gait. The test of a true Manx or "Rumpy" is if you can put the end of your thumb in the hollow where its tail should be. A Manx with a rudimentary tail is a "Stumpy".

History This poor cat was late for the Ark and caught its tail as Noah was closing the door — or so the story goes. In fact, the real reason for its lack of tail is far less colourful. It is thought that the original Manx cats were mutants brought to the Isle of Man in the sixteenth century by galleons from the Far East. Due to the geographical isolation of the island, the tail-lessness was perpetuated. The Manx's unique appearance has made it very popular over the centuries. However, if it had appeared as a new breed today, it would be unlikely to be accepted, as it is based on a genetic abnormality.

Temperament The Manx is a good-natured, affectionate, intelligent cat.

Varieties This breed can occur in any recognized Shorthair pattern or colouring, and can be a "Rumpy" or "Stumpy" type.

KEY CHARACTERISTICS
Black-and-White Bicolour Rumpy Manx

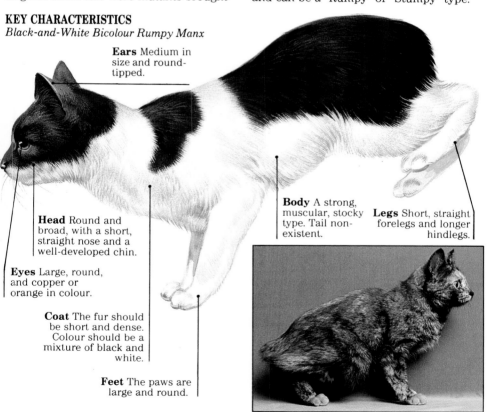

Ears Medium in size and round-tipped.

Head Round and broad, with a short, straight nose and a well-developed chin.

Eyes Large, round, and copper or orange in colour.

Coat The fur should be short and dense. Colour should be a mixture of black and white.

Feet The paws are large and round.

Body A strong, muscular, stocky type. Tail non-existent.

Legs Short, straight forelegs and longer hindlegs.

Tortoiseshell Stumpy Manx
Unlike the Rumpy Manx shown above, this cat has a rudimentary tail.

American Shorthair

A very athletic cat, the American Shorthair has a larger, leaner, and more powerfully built body than its relation, the British Shorthair (see pp. 78—88).
History When settlers sailed from Europe to North America they carried cats on board ship to protect the stores from mice. Most of these cats "settled" in the New World, interbred, and developed special characteristics to help them cope with their new life and climate. Early this century a selective breeding programme was established to develop the best qualities of these cats.
Temperament True to its ancestry, the American Shorthair is a real pioneer; its tough background has made it very hardy, healthy and bold.
Varieties The American Shorthair is bred in a wide range of colours and coat patterns, as shown in the chart opposite.

American Red Tabby Shorthair
This golden-eyed cat has dark red Classic-patterned markings on a rich red ground. It is larger and sturdier than its British cousin (see p. 83).

KEY CHARACTERISTICS *American Shaded Silver Shorthair*

Coat The fur should be thick, dense and hard. The undercoat should be white, with dark grey tipping over the spine that shades out to white.

Ears Medium in size and round-tipped.

Eyes Large, round, with a slight slant to the outer edge. Green in colour.

Head Oval, with a square muzzle, a medium-length nose and a well-developed chin.

Body An athletic, lean and strong type.

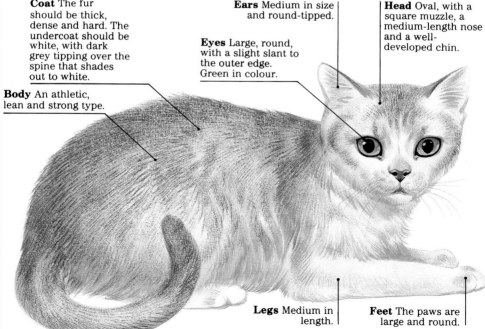

Legs Medium in length.

Feet The paws are large and round.

Varieties	Coat	Markings	Eyes
White	Pure white	None	Deep blue, brilliant gold, or odd-eyed
Black	Dense black	None	Brilliant gold
Blue	Pale blue-grey	None	Brilliant gold
Red	Deep rich red	None	Brilliant gold
Cream	Buff-cream	None	Brilliant gold
Bicolor	White	Black, red, blue or cream patches	Gold
Shaded Silver	White undercoat	Dark grey-tipped spine lightens towards white underside	Green or blue-green
Chinchilla	Pure white undercoat	Black tipping on back, flanks, head and tail	Rich emerald- or blue-green
Shell Cameo	White undercoat	Red tipping on back, flanks, head and tail	Brilliant gold
Shaded Cameo	White undercoat	Like Shell, longer tips	Brilliant gold
Cameo Smoke	White undercoat	Very deep red tipping	Brilliant gold
Black Smoke	White undercoat	Tipped with black	Brilliant gold
Blue Smoke	White undercoat	Very deep blue tipping	Brilliant gold
Blue-Cream	Blue	Clear patches of cream	Gold
Tortoiseshell	Black	Red and cream patches	Gold
Tortoiseshell Smoke	White undercoat	Black, red and cream tips in tortie pattern	Brilliant gold
Calico	White	Black and red patches	Gold
Brown Tabby	Rich brown	Black Classic or Mackerel pattern	Gold
Red Tabby	Rich red	Dark red Classic or Mackerel pattern	Gold
Silver Tabby	Clear grey	Black Classic or Mackerel pattern	Green or hazel
Blue Tabby	Bluish-ivory	Dark grey Classic or Mackerel pattern	Gold
Cream Tabby	Light cream	Buff-cream Classic or Mackerel pattern	Gold
Cameo Tabby	Off-white	Red Classic or Mackerel pattern tips	Gold
Patched Tabby	Silver, brown or blue	Black, dark grey or pale silver Classic/Mackerel; red/cream patches	Gold or hazel (Silver only)

American Wirehair

The "permed" version of the American Shorthair, the Wirehair has the same build, but with a crimped, woolly coat. This breed isn't recognized in Britain.

History This cat was developed from a spontaneous mutation that appeared in a litter of American Shorthairs in the 1970s.

Temperament The Wirehair is a good-tempered, active and intelligent cat.

Varieties The Wirehair is bred in the same colours as the American Shorthair (see p. 91).

KEY CHARACTERISTICS
American Blue Wirehair

Coat The fur should be thick, curly, woolly and coarse. Colour should be pale blue-grey.

American Brown Tabby Wirehair
This cat has curly, rich brown fur with black markings and gold eyes.

Eyes Large, round, with a slight slant to the outer edge, and brilliant gold in colour.

Ears Medium in size and round-tipped.

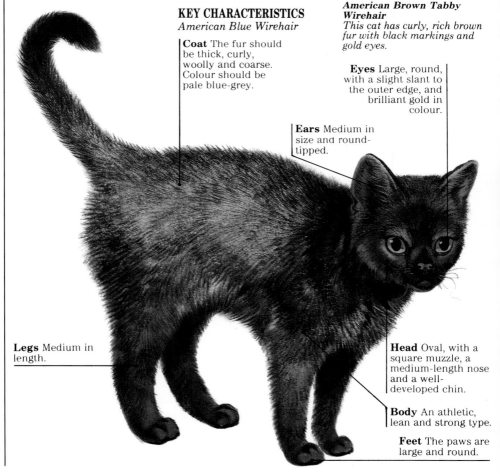

Legs Medium in length.

Head Oval, with a square muzzle, a medium-length nose and a well-developed chin.

Body An athletic, lean and strong type.

Feet The paws are large and round.

Exotic Shorthair

The Exotic has a similar coat to the American Shorthair (see pp. 90—1), but with the cobby body and the attractive round, snub-nosed face of the Longhair (see pp. 50—69).

History This new "man-made" cat was arrived at by selective breeding. In the early 1960s breeders in the U.S. worked out a programme for interbreeding Longhairs with American Shorthairs to produce a cat that combined the attractive, rounded looks of the Longhair breed, with the more manageable coat of the American Shorthair.

Temperament The Exotic Shorthair has the best features of both its "parents". It has a calm, affectionate nature like the Longhair, yet it is playful and alert like an American Shorthair cat.

Varieties The Exotic Shorthair is bred in all the coat colours and patterns found in the Longhair (see pp. 50—69) and the American Shorthair (see p. 91) — a total of about 40 varieties to choose from.

KEY CHARACTERISTICS *Exotic Black Smoke Shorthair*

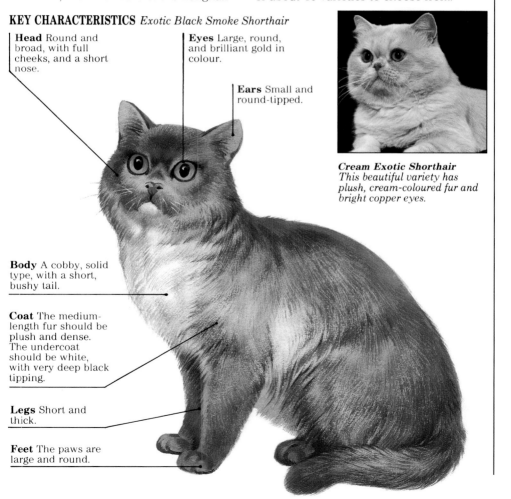

Head Round and broad, with full cheeks, and a short nose.

Eyes Large, round, and brilliant gold in colour.

Ears Small and round-tipped.

Body A cobby, solid type, with a short, bushy tail.

Coat The medium-length fur should be plush and dense. The undercoat should be white, with very deep black tipping.

Legs Short and thick.

Feet The paws are large and round.

Cream Exotic Shorthair
This beautiful variety has plush, cream-coloured fur and bright copper eyes.

Siamese

This spectacular-looking cat has a very characteristic colouring pattern of dark points against a pale coat, and sapphire-coloured, almond-shaped eyes.

History Definitely of Eastern origin, this breed was known to have been kept as a pet in the Royal court of Siam as early as the late sixteenth century, but it probably originated from even further east.

Temperament The Siamese is a real extrovert, and adores company. It is a very affectionate animal, and if you give it plenty of attention it will become a loyal friend. However, this breed has some disadvantages: a Siamese can be very

Seal-point Siamese queen and kittens
Like other Siamese kittens, Seal-points are born all-white, and their contrasting body and point colouring develops gradually.

KEY CHARACTERISTICS *Blue-point Siamese*

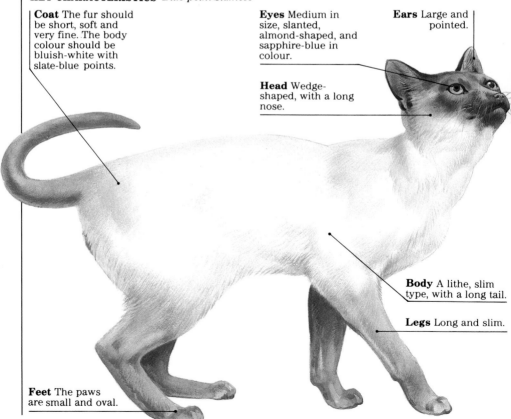

Coat The fur should be short, soft and very fine. The body colour should be bluish-white with slate-blue points.

Eyes Medium in size, slanted, almond-shaped, and sapphire-blue in colour.

Ears Large and pointed.

Head Wedge-shaped, with a long nose.

Body A lithe, slim type, with a long tail.

Legs Long and slim.

Feet The paws are small and oval.

SHORTHAIRED CATS | 95

Cream-point Siamese
*The Cream is a new variety
with very subtle colouring. It
has a white body shading to
pale cream, and warm cream-
coloured points.*

Red-point Siamese
*This new variety has a white
body that shades to apricot,
and reddish-gold points.*

demanding, it is often "jealous" of rivals, and it can be rather noisy as it has a loud, distinctive voice that is impossible to ignore. (When breeders euphemistically refer to Siamese as being "vocal" this is what they mean.)

Varieties There are four classic varieties of Siamese: Seal-point, Blue-point, Chocolate-point, and Lilac-point, as shown in the chart below. New varieties, called Colorpoint Shorthairs in the U.S., have been produced by mating Siamese with other breeds to introduce new colours and patterns on the points. Subsequent generations were mated to Siamese only, so the proportion of non-Siamese blood in these varieties is minimal.

Varieties	Coat	Markings
Seal-point	Warm cream	Seal-brown
Blue-point	Bluish-white	Slate-blue
Chocolate-point	Ivory	Milk choc. brown
Lilac-point	Magnolia	Pinkish-grey
Red-point	Clear white shading to apricot	Reddish-gold
Cream-point	White shading to pale cream	Warm cream
Tabby-point	White	Tabby

Varieties	Coat	Markings
Seal Tortie-point	Pale seal-brown	Seal-brown patched in cream
Blue Tortie-point	Pale blue	Blue patched in cream
Chocolate Tortie-point	Pale choc. brown	Choc. brown patched in cream
Lilac Tortie-point	Pale pinkish-grey	Pinkish-grey patched in cream

Russian Blue

Today's Russian Blue is a very distinguished-looking cat, with a lithe, slender body and short, plush, silvery blue fur that resembles sealskin.

History There has been some confusion about the origins of this breed, probably because it has had three different names. At first, it was known as the Archangel Blue, and only acquired its current name in the 1940s. And at one time it was known as the Maltese cat. The evidence suggests that the breed did originate from Russia because similar cats are found in the colder regions there today. It is thought that sailors first brought this blue-coloured cat to Britain in the 1860s from its home port of Archangel in Northern Russia.

Temperament This cat is very quiet, shy, and willing to please. In fact, Blues are so quiet that if you have a queen you may find it difficult to tell when she is calling. However, Russian Blues don't usually wander, preferring an indoor life, so the risk of an accidental mating is quite small.

Varieties An experimental white variety of Russian Blue was produced in Britain, but it didn't attract much interest, and is now quite rare.

KEY CHARACTERISTICS

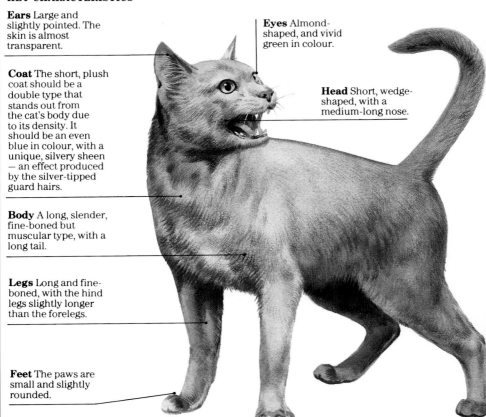

Ears Large and slightly pointed. The skin is almost transparent.

Coat The short, plush coat should be a double type that stands out from the cat's body due to its density. It should be an even blue in colour, with a unique, silvery sheen — an effect produced by the silver-tipped guard hairs.

Body A long, slender, fine-boned but muscular type, with a long tail.

Legs Long and fine-boned, with the hind legs slightly longer than the forelegs.

Feet The paws are small and slightly rounded.

Eyes Almond-shaped, and vivid green in colour.

Head Short, wedge-shaped, with a medium-long nose.

Abyssinian and Somali

Even that difficult breed of human, the cat-hater, falls for these cats' charms. When you look at an Abyssinian or the longhaired version, the Somali, it isn't difficult to see why. They both have a captivating, expressive face and an elegant Foreign build, though they aren't as fine-boned as the Siamese.

History Some of these cats were brought to England from Abyssinia in the 1860s. One common belief is that they are direct descendants of the Sacred Cat of Egypt.

Temperament In addition to irresistible good looks, Abyssinians and Somalis are blessed with a most appealing personality, they are very intelligent, and learn tricks quickly. They love freedom, and become restless when kept confined. They aren't therefore suited to apartment life.

Varieties There are three different coat patterns: the Usual Abyssinian or Somali has a ruddy brown coat ticked with bands of darker brown or black; the Sorrel or Red has a copper-red coat ticked with chocolate; and the Blue has a blue-grey coat ticked with steel blue. In all types of Abyssinian and Somali eye colour can be either amber, hazel or green.

The Somali
Basically a longhaired Abyssinian, the Somali has an identically patterned coat, but with medium-long, slightly shaggy fur.

KEY CHARACTERISTICS *Usual Abyssinian*

Coat The fur should be short and very thick. Colour should be pale brown, ticked with two or three bands of darker brown.

Body A medium-long, slender, lithe type, with a long tail.

Legs Long, slender and fine-boned.

Feet The paws are small and oval.

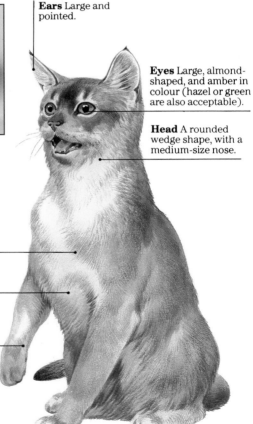

Ears Large and pointed.

Eyes Large, almond-shaped, and amber in colour (hazel or green are also acceptable).

Head A rounded wedge shape, with a medium-size nose.

Foreign Shorthairs

As you would expect from their name, these cats have the typical Foreign build (see p. 76). Basically, they are Siamese (see pp. 94–5) without point markings.

History Some Foreign Shorthairs, such as the Blue, occur naturally in Siamese litters. Others, like the Tortoiseshell, are "man-made" varieties, produced by crossing Siamese and domestic short-haired cats.

Temperament Energetic and inquisitive, Foreign Shorthairs are lively pets that need plenty of exercise and play.

Varieties There are 12 varieties of Foreign Shorthair, as shown in the chart on the right.

Varieties	Coat	Eyes
Black	Jet black	Green
White	Pure white	China-blue
Blue	Light bluish-grey	Green
Smoke	White under-coat; black, blue, lilac, cameo, chocolate or tortie tips	Green
Lilac	Pale pinkish-grey	Green
Red	Bright red	Green/amber
Cream	Buff-cream	Green/amber

KEY CHARACTERISTICS *Foreign Blue Shorthair*

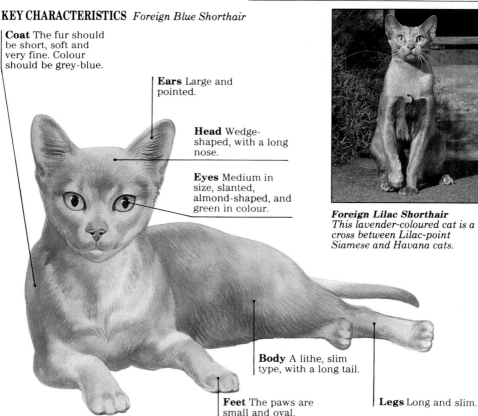

Coat The fur should be short, soft and very fine. Colour should be grey-blue.

Ears Large and pointed.

Head Wedge-shaped, with a long nose.

Eyes Medium in size, slanted, almond-shaped, and green in colour.

Foreign Lilac Shorthair
This lavender-coloured cat is a cross between Lilac-point Siamese and Havana cats.

Body A lithe, slim type, with a long tail.

Feet The paws are small and oval.

Legs Long and slim.

Varieties	Coat	Eyes
Shaded Silver	White; black tips	Green
Shaded Cameo	White; red tips	Green
Tabbies	Brown, Blue, Silver, Cream, Lilac or Red; Classic/ Mackerel pattern	Green
Torties	Black with red and cream patches	Green/ amber
Blue-Cream	Blue with cream patches	Green

Foreign White Shorthair
Unlike many blue-eyed white cats, the Foreign White isn't prone to deafness.

KEY CHARACTERISTICS *Foreign Black Shorthair*

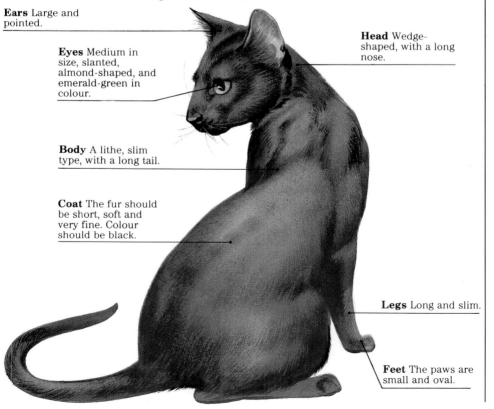

Ears Large and pointed.

Eyes Medium in size, slanted, almond-shaped, and emerald-green in colour.

Head Wedge-shaped, with a long nose.

Body A lithe, slim type, with a long tail.

Coat The fur should be short, soft and very fine. Colour should be black.

Legs Long and slim.

Feet The paws are small and oval.

Korat

A rare cat, even in its native Thailand, the silver-blue Korat has large, green eyes and an unusual, heart-shaped face. Its body isn't as long or skinny as that of the typical Foreign Shorthair, the Siamese.

History This breed was imported into America from Thailand in 1959, and was recognized by the U.S. cat fancy in 1965. In Britain recognition came 10 years later. Named after the Thai province where it originated, the Korat was known there as "Si-Sawat", meaning good fortune. A pair of these lucky cats were a traditional present to Thai brides.

Temperament The Korat has a sweet, quiet, loving nature.

Varieties There are no varieties of Korat.

Korat kittens
Young Korats have yellow or amber eyes which turn green by the time they are two.

KEY CHARACTERISTICS

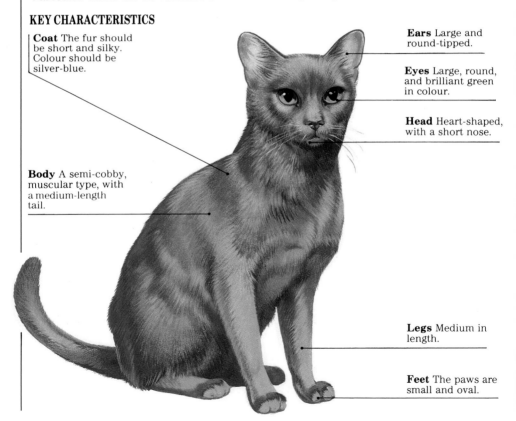

Coat The fur should be short and silky. Colour should be silver-blue.

Body A semi-cobby, muscular type, with a medium-length tail.

Ears Large and round-tipped.

Eyes Large, round, and brilliant green in colour.

Head Heart-shaped, with a short nose.

Legs Medium in length.

Feet The paws are small and oval.

Burmese

Prized for its glossy, smooth coat, the Burmese is more round-bodied than the typical Foreign cat, the Siamese.
History Virtually all Burmese cats are descended from a Foreign-type brown female imported into the U.S. from Burma in the 1930s. Because no male was available, she was mated to a Siamese.
Temperament Less vocal than the Siamese, but with the same love of people, the Burmese is an exceptionally affectionate, friendly and playful cat.
Varieties In addition to the Brown, there are nine varieties of Burmese, as shown right. All types of Burmese have yellow eyes. American breeders prefer a rounder body, head and eyes to the British.

Varieties	Coat	Markings
Blue	Silver-grey	Silver sheen
Chocolate	Warm milk-chocolate	None
Lilac	Pinkish-grey	None
Red	Light tangerine	Ears are darker than back
Cream	Rich cream	None
Brown Tortie	Brown	Red patches
Chocolate Tortie	Chocolate	Red patches
Lilac Tortie	Pinkish-grey	Cream patches
Blue Tortie	Grey-blue	Cream patches

KEY CHARACTERISTICS *British Brown Burmese*

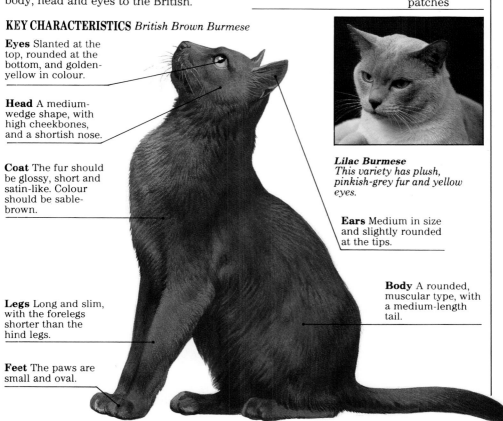

Eyes Slanted at the top, rounded at the bottom, and golden-yellow in colour.

Head A medium-wedge shape, with high cheekbones, and a shortish nose.

Coat The fur should be glossy, short and satin-like. Colour should be sable-brown.

Legs Long and slim, with the forelegs shorter than the hind legs.

Feet The paws are small and oval.

Lilac Burmese
This variety has plush, pinkish-grey fur and yellow eyes.

Ears Medium in size and slightly rounded at the tips.

Body A rounded, muscular type, with a medium-length tail.

Havana

The short coat of the Havana is a rich, chestnut-brown colour, rather like the cigar that the cat is named after. The Havana has a Siamese-type build, and almond-shaped, green eyes.

History This "man-made" breed was the result of a selective breeding programme carried out in Britain in the 1950s. A group of breeders produced a cat with the fine, graceful build of the Siamese, but without its point-patterned coat.

Temperament True to its Siamese blood, the Havana is intelligent and affectionate, but demands a great deal of attention.

Varieties There are no varieties of Havana. However, like the Burmese, this breed is judged by different criteria on opposite sides of the Atlantic. The British Havana is a Siamese-type cat that looks more like the American Oriental Self Brown. The American Havana Brown's physique is nearer to that of the Russian Blue than the Siamese: it has a shorter head and longer fur than the Havana, and its body is semi-cobby rather than a rounded, muscular type.

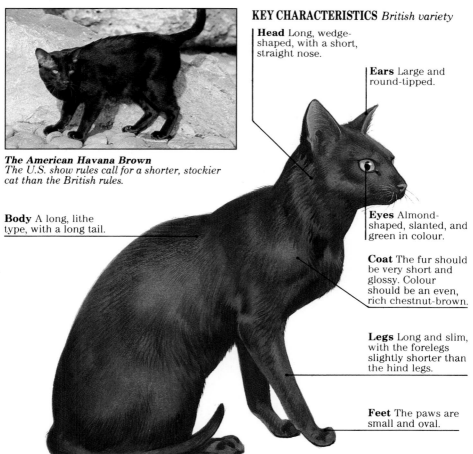

The American Havana Brown
The U.S. show rules call for a shorter, stockier cat than the British rules.

KEY CHARACTERISTICS *British variety*

Head Long, wedge-shaped, with a short, straight nose.

Ears Large and round-tipped.

Body A long, lithe type, with a long tail.

Eyes Almond-shaped, slanted, and green in colour.

Coat The fur should be very short and glossy. Colour should be an even, rich chestnut-brown.

Legs Long and slim, with the forelegs slightly shorter than the hind legs.

Feet The paws are small and oval.

Japanese Bobtail

A very unusual cat, the Japanese Bobtail's main feature is its unique tail. This is very short and curled, with hair growing outwards in all directions, producing a fluffy, bobbed effect rather like a rabbit's tail. The Bobtail doesn't have the full Foreign look; although slender, it is more muscular than other Foreign-type cats. This breed isn't recognized in Britain.

History The Bobtail occurs naturally in Japan, where it can be traced back over many centuries. When seated, it often raises one front paw, and this gesture is said to represent good luck. The tortoise-shell-and-white pattern (known as the Mi-Ke) is considered particularly lucky.

Temperament A friendly cat, the Bobtail has a lot of character.

Varieties The most popular varieties are the Mi-Ke (black, red and white or tortoiseshell with white), Black, White, Red, Black-and-White, Red-and-White, and Tortoiseshell (black, red and cream). However, any other pedigree colouring is allowed, except for the Siamese and Abyssinian patterns.

KEY CHARACTERISTICS *Mi-Ke Japanese Bobtail*

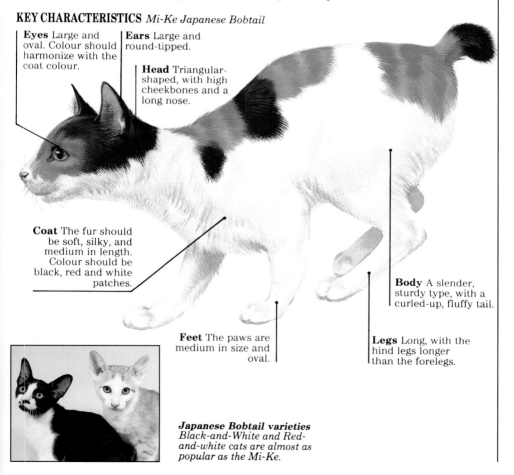

Eyes Large and oval. Colour should harmonize with the coat colour.

Ears Large and round-tipped.

Head Triangular-shaped, with high cheekbones and a long nose.

Coat The fur should be soft, silky, and medium in length. Colour should be black, red and white patches.

Body A slender, sturdy type, with a curled-up, fluffy tail.

Feet The paws are medium in size and oval.

Legs Long, with the hind legs longer than the forelegs.

Japanese Bobtail varieties
Black-and-White and Red-and-white cats are almost as popular as the Mi-Ke.

Singapura

The ivory-and-brown ticked coat of the Sing-apura looks rather like that of an Abyssinian. However, it is easy to tell the two cats apart, as the Singapura has a much smaller body than average. This is probably a result of its deprived lifestyle: in its native Singapore it roams wild and shelters in drains, and is therefore known as the "Drain Cat".

History Recently imported into the U.S. from Singapore, the Singapura is still rare in the West, and isn't recognized for showing in Britain at present.

Temperament Cats are unpopular in Singapore, so this breed is reserved and unaccustomed to human attention. It is a great pity that Singaporeans are so unfriendly towards cats, because, given the chance, the Singapura is very affectionate, though quiet, and loves human company.

Varieties At present, only ivory-coloured cats ticked with brown are available in the U.S., but several colour combinations are found in Singapore, and it is likely that other varieties will be exported in the future.

KEY CHARACTERISTICS

Eyes Large, slanted, almond-shaped, and hazel, green or gold in colour.

Ears Large and pointed.

Coat The fur should be short, soft and silky. Colour should be pale beige, with bands of dark bronze and warm cream ticking.

Body A small, stocky type, with a slightly arched back and a medium-long tail.

Head Rounded, with a short nose and a full chin.

Legs Medium in length.

Feet The paws are small and oval.

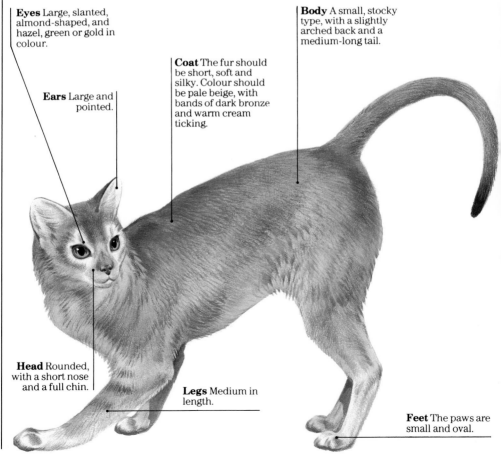

Tonkinese

A cross between the Siamese and the Burmese, the Tonkinese is bred in the U.S. and Britain, but it isn't recognized for showing in the U.K..

History This Siamese-Burmese cross was developed in North America in the 1970s.

Temperament The Tonkinese adores people. Unfortunately, its affectionate nature can put it in danger, as it associates cars with humans and has a habit of straying too close.

Varieties There are five varieties of Tonkinese, as shown in the chart on the right.

Varieties	Coat	Markings
Natural Mink	Warm brown	Dark chocolate
Blue Mink	Bluish-grey	Light or slate-blue
Honey Mink	Ruddy brown	Chocolate
Champagne Mink	Warm beige	Pale brown
Platinum Mink	Pale grey	Dark grey

KEY CHARACTERISTICS *Platinum Mink Tonkinese*

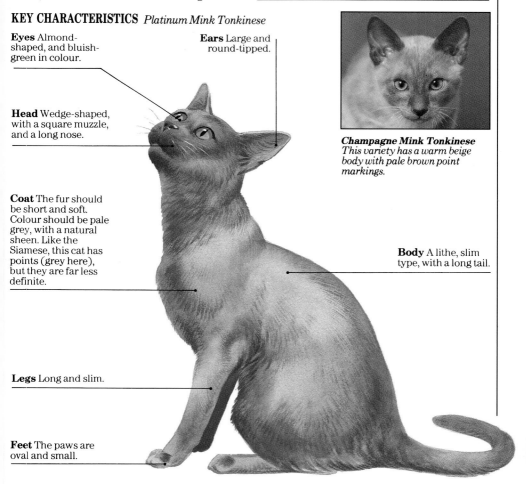

Eyes Almond-shaped, and bluish-green in colour.

Ears Large and round-tipped.

Head Wedge-shaped, with a square muzzle, and a long nose.

Coat The fur should be short and soft. Colour should be pale grey, with a natural sheen. Like the Siamese, this cat has points (grey here), but they are far less definite.

Body A lithe, slim type, with a long tail.

Legs Long and slim.

Feet The paws are oval and small.

Champagne Mink Tonkinese
This variety has a warm beige body with pale brown point markings.

Bombay

Named after the all-black Indian leopard, the Bombay's principal feature is its unique coat. This is jet black, with a distinctive sheen, and is very short and close-lying, giving the appearance of patent leather. The Bombay isn't recognized in Britain.

History Created in the U.S. in the 1970s, like the Tonkinese (see p. 105), the Bombay is a Burmese cross, this time with the black American Shorthair.

Temperament The Bombay has a marvellous nature, and it rarely stops purring. It craves companionship, and therefore shouldn't be left alone for long periods.

Varieties There are no varieties of the Bombay.

KEY CHARACTERISTICS

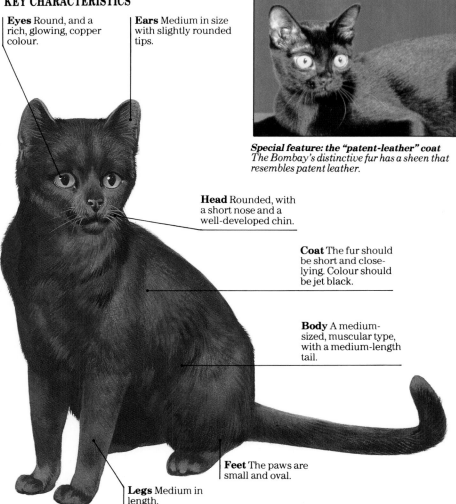

Eyes Round, and a rich, glowing, copper colour.

Ears Medium in size with slightly rounded tips.

Special feature: the "patent-leather" coat
The Bombay's distinctive fur has a sheen that resembles patent leather.

Head Rounded, with a short nose and a well-developed chin.

Coat The fur should be short and close-lying. Colour should be jet black.

Body A medium-sized, muscular type, with a medium-length tail.

Feet The paws are small and oval.

Legs Medium in length.

Snowshoe

The strikingly marked mask, ears, legs and tail of the Snowshoe are a much darker shade of its body colour, its chest and stomach are very pale, and its feet are white. The Snowshoe isn't recognized in Britain.

History This recently developed U.S. breed is a cross between a Siamese and a bi-coloured American Shorthair.

Temperament The Snowshoe is a lively, good-natured cat.

Varieties There are two varieties: the Seal-point, which has a warm fawn body, pale fawn chest and stomach, and seal-brown points; and the Blue-point, with a bluish-white body, a paler chest and stomach, and deep grey-blue points.

KEY CHARACTERISTICS *Blue-point Snowshoe*

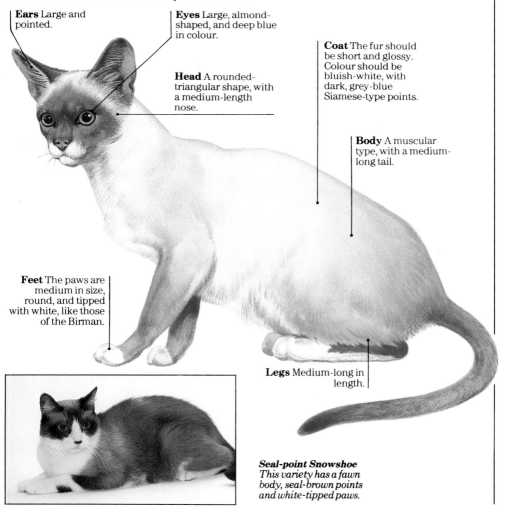

Ears Large and pointed.

Eyes Large, almond-shaped, and deep blue in colour.

Coat The fur should be short and glossy. Colour should be bluish-white, with dark, grey-blue Siamese-type points.

Head A rounded-triangular shape, with a medium-length nose.

Body A muscular type, with a medium-long tail.

Feet The paws are medium in size, round, and tipped with white, like those of the Birman.

Legs Medium-long in length.

Seal-point Snowshoe
This variety has a fawn body, seal-brown points and white-tipped paws.

Rex

Two breeds of curly-coated cat, the Cornish and the Devon, were named "Rex" after a similar mutation in the rabbit. The Cornish Rex is basically a Foreign-type cat with a curly coat. The Devon Rex's build is also of a Foreign type, but its face is a unique "pixie" shape. The Devon has a very short, wavy coat like the Cornish, but its fur feels coarser to the touch.

History In 1950, a litter of farm kittens in Cornwall included one wavy-coated red-and-white male kitten with curly whiskers. The puzzled owner consulted her vet, who suggested mating the kitten to his mother.

Several curly-coated kittens resulted, and an experimental breeding programme was started.

In 1960 another curly cat was found in Britain, this time in Devon. At first, it was assumed that the two cats were related. But interbreeding resulted in straight-coated cats, which proved that the Devon and Cornish coats are caused by different genes (see p. 202).

Rex cats were first recognized for showing in Britain in 1967.

Temperament The Cornish Rex is an affectionate, energetic cat that loves games.

KEY CHARACTERISTICS *Red Devon Rex*

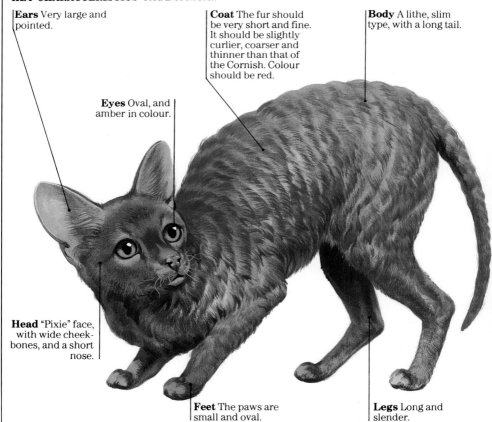

Ears Very large and pointed.

Coat The fur should be very short and fine. It should be slightly curlier, coarser and thinner than that of the Cornish. Colour should be red.

Body A lithe, slim type, with a long tail.

Eyes Oval, and amber in colour.

Head "Pixie" face, with wide cheek-bones, and a short nose.

Feet The paws are small and oval.

Legs Long and slender.

The Devon Rex is also a very playful, even mischievous animal. Apparently, when it is happy it wags its tail like a dog. This habit, in combination with the way that its coat looks has earned it the nickname "poodle cat".

Varieties Currently, two types of Rex are recognized: the Cornish and the Devon. For both breeds all coat colours and patterns except for the bi-colour pattern are acceptable. The eye colour should harmonize with the coat. Rex with the Siamese point pattern (see p. 94) are known as Si-Rex, and should have blue, green or yellow eyes.

Red-point Si-Rex
This blue-eyed variety has red Siamese-type point markings on a cream coat.

KEY CHARACTERISTICS *Blue-Cream Cornish Rex*

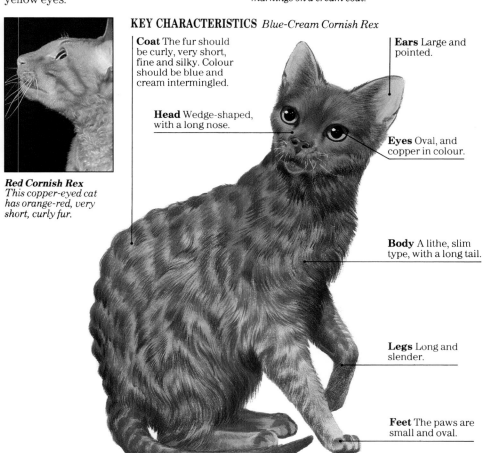

Red Cornish Rex
This copper-eyed cat has orange-red, very short, curly fur.

Coat The fur should be curly, very short, fine and silky. Colour should be blue and cream intermingled.

Head Wedge-shaped, with a long nose.

Ears Large and pointed.

Eyes Oval, and copper in colour.

Body A lithe, slim type, with a long tail.

Legs Long and slender.

Feet The paws are small and oval.

Egyptian Mau

The Egyptian Mau doesn't have the typical Foreign build (see p.76); instead it has a semi-cobby, muscular body. Its distinctively patterned coat is marked with elongated spots that are really broken stripes. This spotted coat attracts cat thieves, so it is best to keep a close guard on your Mau when it is outside. The Egyptian Mau isn't recognized for showing in Britain.

History The Mau is a natural breed which originates from Cairo, and was first brought to the U.S. in the late 1950s. It is reputed to be a descendant of the cat worshipped in ancient Egypt because it should have a pattern resembling a scarab beetle on its brow, and this pattern is often found on the foreheads of ancient cat figures. However, it is much more likely that the Mau was bred specifically to resemble that cat.

Temperament The Egyptian Mau is a friendly, playful, affectionate cat.

Varieties There are four varieties of Egyptian Mau: the Silver, which has a silver body with charcoal-grey markings; the Bronze, which has a honey-coloured body marked in dark brown; the Smoke, which has a charcoal-grey body with a white undercoat and jet black markings; and the Pewter, which has a pale fawn body with dark grey or brown markings.

KEY CHARACTERISTICS *Smoke Egyptian Mau*

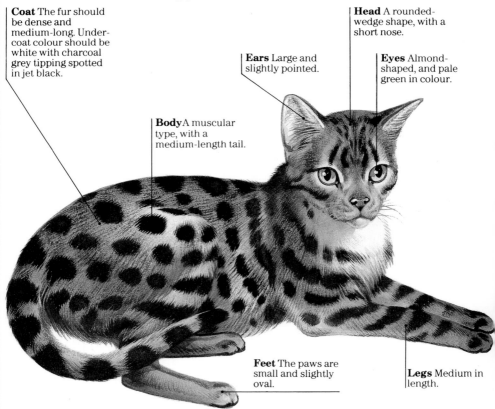

Coat The fur should be dense and medium-long. Undercoat colour should be white with charcoal grey tipping spotted in jet black.

Head A rounded-wedge shape, with a short nose.

Ears Large and slightly pointed.

Eyes Almond-shaped, and pale green in colour.

Body A muscular type, with a medium-length tail.

Feet The paws are small and slightly oval.

Legs Medium in length.

Sphynx

This has to be the most unusual breed in existence, as, unlike other cats, the Sphynx is hairless.

History First bred in Canada, this cat originated from a mutant hairless kitten that was born in a litter of shorthaired cats in 1966. The Sphynx is unknown in Britain, and rare in North America, where only a few small associations accept it.

Temperament The Sphynx is a quiet, affectionate cat. However, it doesn't like being cuddled.

Varieties The skin and down can be any recognized colour and pattern, and the eye colour should harmonize with the coat.

Blue Sphynx
A Sphynx's body feels warm to the touch, and should be taut and wrinkle-free.

KEY CHARACTERISTICS *Black Sphynx*

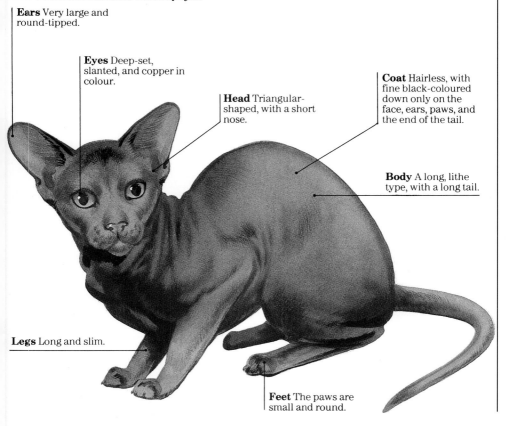

Ears Very large and round-tipped.

Eyes Deep-set, slanted, and copper in colour.

Head Triangular-shaped, with a short nose.

Coat Hairless, with fine black-coloured down only on the face, ears, paws, and the end of the tail.

Body A long, lithe type, with a long tail.

Legs Long and slim.

Feet The paws are small and round.

CHOOSING A CAT

A cat is an ideal pet, whatever your personal circumstances.
Whether you are a busy would-be owner who doesn't
have time to exercise a dog or an elderly or infirm person
who would appreciate some companionship,
you will find that a cat is affectionate and easy to care for.
Another advantage is that a cat requires very little space — if
necessary, it can be kept permanently indoors (see pp. 145—7)
— and is therefore suitable for the city apartment-owner.
When looking for a cat, follow the guidance
in this chapter to make sure that you
choose a healthy specimen.

Making the right choice

Once you are committed to the idea of owning a cat, there are a number of decisions to be made, the most important being: pedigree or non-pedigree.

Why choose a pedigree cat?

If you are interested in showing or breeding, you should buy a pedigree cat. Selecting a breed is largely a question of personal taste, but bear in mind that longhairs require daily grooming (see p. 170), and that Siamese and Burmese can be demanding and vociferous and may mature more quickly than other cats.

Choosing a pedigree cat demands more than just a fitness check. The points, quality and prize-winning potential of any feline can only be gauged by an expert eye. You should therefore take along someone who is very familiar with the breed in question and who understands exactly what you hope for from the cat.

Unfortunately pedigree cats are expensive, but if you can't afford the full price there are two ways of getting a "bargain": buying a "pet-quality" cat or making a breeding agreement. The features of "pet-quality" animals may not match the standards required for showing, but such cats will nevertheless make good pets. Under a breeding agreement, you buy a show-quality cat, and return it to the vendor at prearranged times for breeding. You should discuss who will own the kittens, and put whatever is agreed in writing.

Why choose a non-pedigree cat?

In general, the main object of owning a cat is as a companion and if this is your motive, I think that there is little point in going for a pedigree type, especially if you live in a town as thieves tend to target breeds like Persians and Siamese.

There are always plenty of inexpensive cross-bred felines in need of homes.

Which sex should it be?

In my view, there is nothing to choose between the castrated tom and the spayed queen: both sexes make equally good, affectionate pets. I would advise against an un-neutered tom as it will spray pungent urine, frequently go wandering and get into far more fights, with consequent wounds and infections. And an un-neutered queen should be avoided for similar reasons: she will have frequent heat periods (oestrus) at certain times of the year, and if you don't confine her indoors she may have unwanted pregnancies. Neutering eliminates these disadvantages, and may make the cat more affectionate.

Should you choose a kitten or an adult?

When choosing a pet, the attraction of a tiny, defenceless kitten is obvious, but it will demand lots of attention, and will need to be house-trained. On the plus side, a kitten will usually adapt quite quickly to its new environment.

For many people a fully grown cat is a wise choice, particularly if you are out at work all day, or would find a kitten too boisterous or too difficult to train. If you decide on a mature cat, keep it indoors for the first few days or it may try to return to its previous home.

Should you obtain one cat or a pair?

More than one cat may well be out of the question if you have a limited budget or live in a small flat. Nevertheless, in a household where everyone is out during the day, a solitary cat can become lonely, and you may therefore choose two cats to provide companionship for each other.

Obtaining a healthy cat

It is possible to buy a cat from a number of sources. Personal recommendation is a good guide, but your choice will depend on the type of cat you have decided to purchase and the amount of money you wish to spend. Never be rushed into buying any animal before you have checked out the source.

Buying a cat from a breeder
If you have decided on a pedigree cat, your best source is a specialist breeder although this will probably be the most expensive. Your local cat club will be able to supply a list of names and addresses, or you may prefer to visit a cat show and meet a number of breeders. Although some of the cats at a show may be for sale, it is better to see the whole litter at home. There you will be able to observe the conditions under which they have been brought up, and see how each kitten behaves away from the bustle and excitement of a show.

Buying a cat from a pet shop
If you have a choice, I would advise against obtaining a cat from a pet shop as young cats are particularly susceptible to disease and infection, and these can spread easily in pet shops. If you do buy a cat from such a source, be especially thorough when inspecting the animal. Cats purchased in pet shops will usually be moderately priced.

Obtaining a cat from a clinic
Humane clinics are another ready source of non-pedigree animals, and will usually let you have a cat for little or no money.

Health certificates and vaccinations
A veterinary examination before purchase is the ideal, and if you are buying an expensive pedigree cat, it is essential.

Ask your own vet to perform it, and provide a written certificate of health. Where a kitten or cat is obtained from a humane society, a veterinary inspection is usually carried out before the animal is handed over. Nevertheless, wherever you obtain your cat, it is most important to arrange a check by a vet as soon as possible after acquisition.

With a kitten, make sure that it has been vaccinated against Feline Enteritis and Feline Influenza (see pp. 238 and 229) at least one week before purchase, and with an adult animal check that it has been vaccinated as a youngster and given regular "boosters" thereafter. Proof of vaccination and "boosting" must come in the form of a written veterinary certificate. In addition, if you have other cats and are anxious to keep them free from Feline Leukaemia (see p. 259), ask a vet to carry out a blood test on the new cat and provide evidence that the result was negative. Healthy cats which test negative can be vaccinated against Feline Leukaemia from 9 weeks of age.

Pedigree registration
All pedigree animals should be registered under an individual name, along with details of their colour and parents, when they are about five weeks old. Unless this is done, they won't be permitted to enter a cat show in a pedigree class.

Has the cat a good temperament?
When selecting a cat, you should make a point of looking for one that is alert, friendly, playful and willing to be handled. With kittens, it is best to go for the bigger, bolder, first-to-come-forward individual, rather than the smallest, most retiring member of the litter as it is more likely to be sickly and you may suffer the trauma of its early death.

Inspecting your prospective cat

Whatever kind of cat you are after, and no matter where you obtain it, there is one golden rule: always make a careful study of the cat's condition and state of health. *Never* take on a cat that is sick or not up to the mark, no matter how convincing the vendor's excuse may be. If your request to examine the cat is rejected, don't buy — any responsible vendor will realize it is reasonable to check a new pet thoroughly.

Before inspecting the animal, wash your hands thoroughly and play with the cat a little in order to put it at ease. Then grasp the body firmly but gently throughout the examination to prevent the cat from escaping. Take it slowly — any sudden movements may alarm the cat.

HOW TO EXAMINE A KITTEN

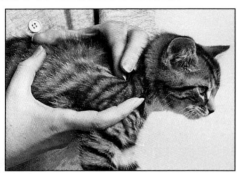

Coat
Feel the texture of the kitten's coat, which should be smooth and unmatted. And look for fleas or other pests.

Ears
The kitten's ears should be clean and dry. Make sure they aren't filled with wax (see p. 250).

Eyes and nose
Check that the "haws" (third eyelids, see p. 248) don't protrude, the eyes are clean and bright, and the nose is damp.

Mouth and teeth
A healthy kitten should have a pink mouth and white teeth. Check that the gums aren't inflamed.

WHAT SEX IS THE KITTEN?

Although sexing adult cats is fairly easy, differentiating between male and female kittens may not be. To do so, lift the tail and look at the opening beneath the anus. A female kitten can be distinguished by the closeness of her vulva to the anus, and the two openings may appear to be joined together. In the case of a male kitten, there is a raised dark area beneath the anus, which will develop into testicles, and below this, the penis.

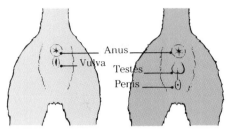

Female organs   **Male organs**

Anal area
Lift the kitten's tail and look for any signs of diarrhoea. The anal area should be clean.

Abdomen
Gently feel under the abdomen with one hand. It should be slightly rounded, but not hard. Make sure there are no lumps (a sign of a hernia). Then let the kitten move around freely so that you can see if it is lame.

Preparing for your cat's arrival

Before you collect your new kitten or cat, it is wise to have a number of pieces of equipment ready and waiting at home.

Essential items

The most important items to have ready for your new pet are the litter tray and the cat bed. Although your cat is quite likely to adopt the most comfortable place it can find as a sleeping area, it should be given its own bed (see pp. 140–1). The need for a litter tray speaks for itself (see p. 133).

Other necessities are feeding and water bowls (see p. 164). Each cat requires its own dishes, which must always be kept scrupulously clean and washed separately from household crockery. Your cat will also need some grooming tools (see pp. 171 and 173), a carrying container of some sort (see p. 149), and a collar with a name tag. You must choose a collar that is partially elasticized so that the cat won't choke if the collar gets caught (for example, on a branch when tree-climbing).

Useful items

Aside from these essentials, you might like to provide your cat with certain other items. A playpen may be useful, particularly for kittens, as it will provide a safe environment until they have become used to their new home. A scratching post or pad (see p. 146) may stop the cat from using the furniture to sharpen its claws, particularly if it is confined to the house. Where a cat is to be allowed outdoors, you might consider installing a cat flap (see p. 143) so that you don't need to be on hand to let the animal in and out.

All cats love to play, and there are now many cat toys on the market. Simple household items like cotton reels make equally good playthings, but avoid giving soft rubber objects as toys — they can cause choking or internal disorders if cats swallow them.

INTRODUCING YOUR CAT TO OTHER PETS

When you bring your new cat or kitten home, keep other pets away until it has had time to explore. Only then should you introduce the new cat to other animals. Let them into the room where you are holding the newcomer, supervising the initial encounters carefully. There will be antipathy in most cases; this may last hours or weeks, but it will gradually fade. Eventually, there will be a reasonable accommodation on all sides, and generally good friendship. Make sure you give both animals affection and don't neglect your old pet in favour of the new one. Remember that cats are territorial animals and the new cat is an interloper. Social adjustments have to be made and only the animals can work these out.

Forming friendships
If you already have other pets, it is a good idea to choose a kitten rather than a mature cat as it is more likely to be accepted.

EQUIPMENT FOR A NEW CAT

Although pet shops sell a wide range of equipment for cats, few items are vital. Of the selection shown here, only the following are essential: a cat basket, litter tray and scoop, carrying basket, food and water dishes, grooming tools and a collar. Other items can be purchased as the kitten grows if you feel they are necessary.

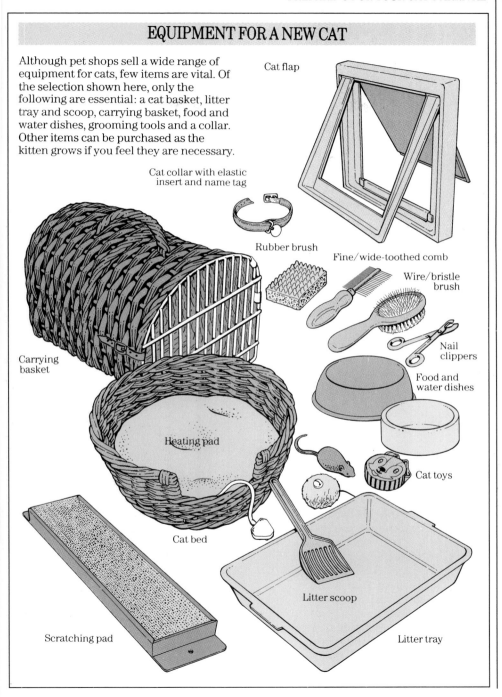

Cat flap

Cat collar with elastic insert and name tag

Rubber brush

Fine/wide-toothed comb

Wire/bristle brush

Nail clippers

Food and water dishes

Carrying basket

Heating pad

Cat toys

Cat bed

Litter scoop

Scratching pad

Litter tray

First steps with your new cat

Having prepared all the equipment you will need for your new cat (see p. 119), you should have a good look at your home to make sure that it is safe for an inquisitive cat. Then you can fetch the newcomer.

Bringing your cat home

It is important to transport the cat in a proper container: a custom-built carrier (see p. 149) rather than a cardboard grocery box. If you are acquiring a "second-hand" adult from a friend, you should ask if you can bring back an object with which the animal is familiar. If the cat has its usual litter tray or bed for example, it will feel more secure, and hopefully settle in more quickly.

Settling in

Once at your home, allow the arrival to explore its surroundings thoroughly on its own, introducing it to one room at a time, and without interference from other pets (see p. 118). It is also a good idea not to let young children worry the cat or kitten, particularly if they haven't had a pet before.

Allowing the cat out of doors

In the first week, handle and fuss over the cat as much as possible prior to any planned release into the garden or backyard. Find out from the previous owner what the animal's favourite titbits are and spoil it with them. When the cat is eventually allowed outdoors, make sure you accompany it on its first few "sallies", and fit it with a suitable cat collar bearing your name and address in case it gets lost. In particular, young cats shouldn't be allowed outdoors in inclement weather, and no newly arrived cat, whatever its age, should be allowed to roam at night.

SAFETY IN THE HOME

The inquisitive nature of cats can lead them into danger, even in a seemingly harmless environment. Before your cat arrives, think carefully about potential hazards and move any dangerous objects out of the cat's range.

Cooking Keep your cat away from the hob or fit a guard.

Open doors Keep washing machine, fridge, freezer and oven doors shut at all times.

Plants Make sure that the plants you keep, indoors and in the garden, are non-toxic. Several plants are poisonous to cats (see p. 147).

Rubbish bins Make sure all refuse is inaccessible to your cat.

SAFETY TIPS

- Don't leave sharp utensils out
- Don't leave toxic household products in accessible places
- Don't permit your cat to walk on kitchen surfaces, especially the hob
- Don't let your cat near when you are cooking with boiling liquids
- Don't leave polythene bags out — if a cat climbs inside it may suffocate
- Don't put a hot electric iron where your cat could knock into it
- Don't leave small objects where your cat may swallow or step on them
- Don't allow cats onto a high balcony

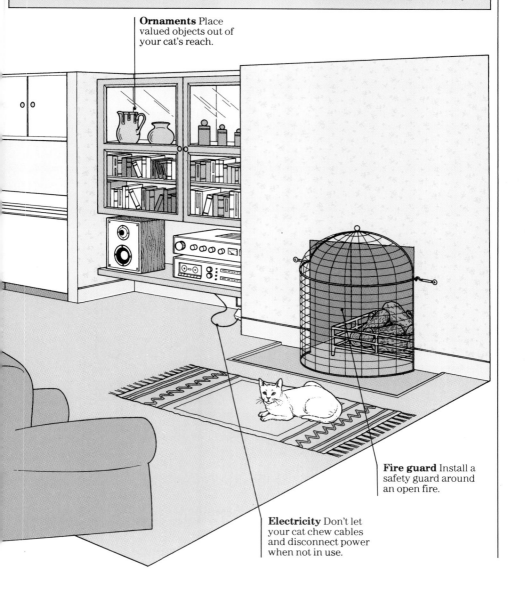

Ornaments Place valued objects out of your cat's reach.

Fire guard Install a safety guard around an open fire.

Electricity Don't let your cat chew cables and disconnect power when not in use.

Responsible ownership

Deciding to become a cat owner isn't something that should be undertaken lightly: you will need to spend some time training the animal to behave in an acceptable fashion, and you will also have certain legal responsibilities.

Training

The best way to train your cat is to establish a routine right from the beginning of its life. Toilet training in particular must begin then (see p. 133). Wherever possible, feeding and grooming should be carried out at regular times of the day.

All cats should be taught to respond to their own name — many have been rescued because they have called out in response to their owner's voice when trapped or in danger. If you use its name regularly, your cat will learn to respond without too much difficulty, particularly at feeding time.

Another useful skill is the ability to use a cat flap. Your cat will probably hesitate to do so at first, because of the fear of being trapped, but it isn't difficult to train it (see p. 143).

Your cat may also need some "negative" training, for example to dissuade it from biting or jumping on people. The most effective way to do this is to say a firm "No" from kittenhood. It is not a good idea to chase the cat away as this may encourage it to think you are playing a game. It will be less likely to scratch the furniture if you allow it outdoors and introduce a scratching post (see p. 146).

Some owners like to teach their cats tricks such as begging for food. This can be done by rewarding with titbits or stroking. However, a cat will only "perform" if it wants to, and no amount of training will make it do something that it doesn't want to do.

Your legal rights and responsibilities

Looking after a cat is a considerable commitment: you can be prosecuted for neglect or for causing suffering. This not only includes intentional physical harm, but failing to give the cat medical attention when it is ill or injured, not making provisions to look after it when you go away on holiday, or keeping it in unsuitable conditions.

Buying and selling cats

In the U.K., it isn't necessary to hold a licence in order to own cats or to breed them, but there are some restrictions on the sale of cats. If you buy a pedigree cat it must be as described on its registration papers, and you can sue for compensation if these prove to be incorrect. Also, if the cat was seriously ill at the time of purchase and you were unaware of this, you may be able to reclaim all or part of your money.

Damage caused by cats

Unlike dogs, cats aren't easy to control or confine to a particular area, but fortunately you won't be liable if your cat should trespass on someone else's property. Nevertheless, you may be held responsible if it causes any damage, provided it isn't a result of normal feline behaviour (such as digging in the garden to bury faeces) and provided the cat wasn't provoked.

Travelling with a cat

If you transport your cat in your car and you don't have a human passenger present to restrain the cat, it is an offence not to confine it to a carrying basket. When travelling further afield, there are strict rabies control laws that forbid you to import or export your cat without subjecting it to quarantine (see p. 151).

BASIC RULES FOR EVERY CAT OWNER

Feed your cat at regular times from its own bowl. Keep this dish separate from the family's crockery.

Give your cat its own bed — don't let it use yours.

Clean the litter tray out daily.

If you don't want your new kitten to be a mother or father, consult the vet about neutering it.

Register your cat with your chosen vet as a matter of routine (don't wait for an emergency).

Make sure that your pet's "booster" vaccinations are kept up-to-date.

Groom your cat regularly — daily if it is a longhair — and check for the presence of fleas.

Establish behaviour rules early on — it is no good trying to stop a cat scratching the furniture after several years.

When you go on holiday, make arrangements for someone to look after your pet beforehand.

Keep your cat indoors during celebrations involving fireworks.

If you obtain a new cat or move home, never let your pet out until it has had time to adjust to its new environment.

If your queen is breeding, don't take the kittens from her until they are at least 6 weeks old.

Other people and your cat

If someone is involved in a motor accident with your cat they aren't legally obliged to report it. However, if the animal is injured in the accident, they could be prosecuted for failure to relieve its suffering.

Cat thieves

Cat theft is a criminal offence — as is receiving a stolen feline. However, adopting a cat can also be termed as stealing, so be wary of looking after an apparent stray and always try to find out who it belongs to. If someone has "adopted" your cat, you are entitled to reclaim it anytime up to six years after its disappearance.

American laws

The laws governing cat ownership and treatment vary from state to state. For example, in some cities in the U.S., cats are only allowed out on a lead. Some states will prosecute for neglect of a cat much as under English law, but in other areas there are no restrictions on abandoning pet cats and only "wilful" cruelty is outlawed.

KITTEN CARE

The first few months of a kitten's life are fascinating to watch.
Moreover, this is an extremely important time because
both the physical and mental health of the adult cat are shaped
by its early experiences. When newly born,
the young kitten is a blind, helpless, furry sausage-shaped
object, but over a period of a few weeks it changes
into a sleek, hunting carnivore. The intelligent owner,
in the role of good foster-parent or "nanny", must therefore
monitor the kitten carefully, learning to anticipate its needs and
to recognize any signs of distress. Your care will be amply
rewarded as you will gain the affection and
friendship of the new cat.

The newly born kitten

At birth, each kitten is between 11 and 15 cms long, and weighs between 70 and 135 grams. Kittens are born with their eyelids closed and their ears folded back, so they can't see or hear. They are unable to walk, and are totally dependent on their mother for survival. Over a period of eight weeks, the kittens gain their independence: their first advance is when their eyes begin to open at 5—10 days old. Fully open once the cats are 8—20 days old, the eyes are usually grey-blue, but this early colour begins to change at around 12 weeks of age. At 16—20 days old, the kittens start to crawl, they begin to eat solids at 3—4 weeks, and are fully weaned at about eight weeks old.

Maternal bonding

At first, feline mothers will accept kittens other than their own, but as they familiarize themselves with their litter, a bond between the queen and her own offspring builds up. Once this is established, the cat will no longer accept a strange kitten easily. Later on, when the partly weaned kittens start living independently, the bond weakens, and the queen tends not to differentiate between her own and other cat's kittens.

Getting to know each other
By rubbing heads, this queen and her 2-week-old kitten are able to sniff each other's sweat glands, and thereby reinforce their newly established bond.

MILESTONES IN A KITTEN'S DEVELOPMENT

Even within a litter, the individual development of kittens may vary — some become independent relatively quickly, whilst others rely heavily on their mother. Similarly, their physical growth rates may vary, although the runt will always be the smallest and weakest. The figures given in this chart are for an average kitten.

Vision
- Eyes open: 8—20 days
- Eyes change to permanent shade: 12 weeks

Mobility
- Crawls: 16—20 days
- Walks: 21—5 days
- Runs: 4—5 weeks

Weaning
- Eats first solids: 3—4 weeks
- Fully weaned: 8 weeks

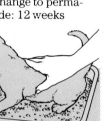

Training
- Start toilet training: 3—4 weeks

Teeth
- All milk teeth: 8 weeks
- Permanent teeth appear: 12—18 weeks

Learning
- Washing: 4—5 weeks
- Play begins: 4—5 weeks
- Starts practising hunting: 6—8 weeks

Registration
- Register pedigree kittens: 5 weeks

Veterinary attention
- 1st vaccination: 9 weeks
- 2nd vaccination: 12 weeks
- Spaying (f): 16 weeks
- Neutering (m): 36 weeks

Independence
- Earliest age can leave mother: 6—8 weeks
- Totally independent of mother: 6 months

The first weeks of life

Female cats know how to care for their new kittens by instinct — even a first-time mother knows what to do without any instruction. Although human substitutes can perform some tasks such as feeding and nest-building, the feline behaviour from which the kittens learn (hunting and fighting, for example) can't be copied.

Nest-building

During the first few days after the birth, the mother may move the kittens, sometimes frequently, to a new "nest". This often occurs in the wild, and is an instinctual act, the purpose of which is to protect the kittens from predators. If your queen does this, move the original kittening box into her newly selected site.

Feeding

After the birth, the queen's appetite usually increases to cope with the milk supply, and sufficient food must be provided.

If the kittens are restless, cry constantly, and fail to settle at the teats in a row, there may be a problem with the queen's milk supply. As the kittens suckle, they push their forepaws against the mother's body, thereby stimulating her to let down milk. The queen may not be "letting down" milk due to stress, inexperience or lack of hormones. Consult your vet, as treatment with hormones will remedy this. In rare cases the queen may be unable to produce sufficient milk, and the kittens will need fostering or artificial rearing (see p. 130). If only one kitten is having difficulty, ask your vet to examine it for a congenital defect such as a cleft palate.

At around three weeks old, kittens are ready to take solid food, so make sure that suitable food is provided (see p. 132).

Keeping warm in the litter
Young kittens often huddle together in a group, possibly because the warmth and the sound of their heartbeats remind them of being in their mother's womb and therefore comforts them.

Communication

Vocal communication between mother and offspring is important, and maternal noises may be used for scolding, greeting, calling together or warning the litter. For example, the kittens know that their mother's growl is a signal for them to scatter. And if in distress kittens will call out, to which their mother will respond with a feline "there, there!"

Once the family is old enough to go on "walkabout", visual signals like the tail are used, as shown opposite.

Instinctive behaviour

Although kittens learn some behaviour by watching older cats, other reactions are obviously instinctive as they will respond to certain stimuli even before their eyes are open. For example, if disturbed, they may hiss or spit.

Another natural habit is for kittens to rest only when in close contact with siblings. This serves two purposes: it keeps the kittens warm and prevents separation of the litter. However, the temperature of their environment may influence this behaviour.

THE MOTHER'S CARE

The care and attention a queen lavishes on her litter is usually second-to-none. Not only is she responsible for their food and grooming, but she also protects them when they are tiny, and then teaches them to defend and care for themselves in preparation for their independence.

Feeding
Each kitten adopts its own individual teat, and there is rarely any moving about the "milk-bar".

Licking
Queens lick their kittens frequently, particularly their rear ends. This is important as it stimulates urination and defecation.

Carrying
When moving her nest, the mother may use her mouth to pick up her kittens by the scruff. However, don't assume you can safely pick them up by the scruff.

Leading
In long grass, kittens keep together by watching the queen's tail held high with the top bent backwards.

Fostering

If a queen turns out to be a neglectful mother, is deficient in milk, or dies, unless you decide to take unwanted kittens to the vet for painless euthanasia (see p. 271), you have two choices: fostering or bottle rearing. If you want to keep the kittens, your local vet, breeder, cat club or pet shop may be able to put you in touch with somebody who has a newly kittened queen with spare teat capacity. Ideally, the fostering should begin as soon as possible after the foster mother has given birth and before she has bonded strongly to her own kittens. The best way to transfer kittens to a new mother is to smear them with a little butter — in general, once the foster mother has licked the butter off, she will regard the foundlings as her own.

During fostering, regular weighing of the kittens is important to check that they are getting enough milk.

Bottle feeding

If no foster mother is available, you can rear kittens artificially using a bottle. To provide kittens with important antibodies that will protect them from disease, it is very valuable to give them one meal of their mother's colostrum (milk secreted in the first few days after the birth) if at all possible. Milk a few drops from the teats for each kitten and give it to them by dropper.

Preparing substitute milks

Cat's milk is richer in protein and fat than that of cows or humans, and it contains slightly less sugar than cow's milk and considerably less than the human product. Pure cow or goat milk is therefore too weak for cats. However, there are several alternatives:
● Special cat milk substitute powder with water added as instructed
● Human milk powder made up to double the strength for babies with lime water or water
● Evaporated tinned milk made up to double the strength for human babies with lime water or water

Care of bottle-fed kittens

After feeding, a kitten needs to be stimulated in order to encourage urination and defecation. Gently wipe its anal area with cotton wool moistened in warm water and stroke its belly with your fingers. Keep the area beneath the tail clean and dry by sponging, drying with towelling and anointing with nappy cream.

Between feeds keep the kittens warm in a clean, snug box with disposable bedding, a heating pad or infra-red lamp, and some sort of mother substitute such as a hot water bottle wrapped in a woolly cover. The box temperature should be 25–30°C for the first two weeks, gradually reduced to 20°C by the sixth week.

QUANTITY AND FREQUENCY OF FEEDS

Age	Amount	Frequency
Up to 7 days	3–6 ml	Every 2 hours
7–14 days	6–8 ml	Every 2 hours during the day, every 4 hours during the night
14–21 days	8–10 ml	Every 2 hours during the day and once between 11 p.m. and 8 a.m.

FEEDING PROCEDURE

There are three common pieces of equipment you can use to administer milk feeds: a simple eye dropper, a 2 ml hypodermic syringe with a 5 cm length of plastic tube attached in place of the needle or, ideally, a specially designed, curved kitten-feeding bottle. If these are unavailable, a premature baby bottle can be used.

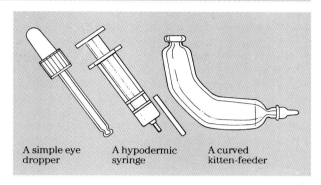

A simple eye dropper

A hypodermic syringe

A curved kitten-feeder

Feeding method

The bottle method is suitable for most kittens. But where a kitten is a weak sucker or a poor swallower, the hypodermic syringe and plastic tube method is best as the tube can be gently slid over the back of the tongue, down the gullet and into the kitten's stomach. However, this should only be attempted on a vet's advice, as if the tube is passed into the trachea instead of the gullet, the kitten may choke.

Whatever method you use, the milk must first be heated to approximately blood temperature (38°C). To do this, make the milk up with hot water (it won't mix properly if you use cold water), and leave to cool. Then fill the bottle and place it in a bowl of hot water for a few minutes. Before feeding the kittens, test the milk on the back of your wrist to ensure it is neither too hot nor too cold.

1 As with human babies, hygiene is extremely important to prevent your kitten catching an infection. All equipment must be thoroughly washed and sterilized (use the products sold for sterilizing babies' bottles) between feeds.

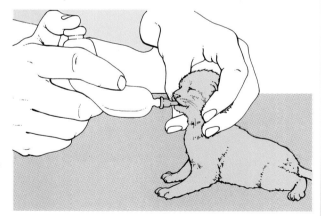

2 Grasp the kitten gently around the neck and push the teat of the bottle into the kitten's mouth. Try not to rush this, thereby frightening the kitten. Light pressure on the bottle will deliver the meal without fuss.

Raising kittens

Cats are at their most vulnerable in the early weeks of their lives, and whether reared by their mothers or bottle-fed, they also demand a great deal of attention from their owners at this time. Your involvement is particularly important at the weaning stage.

Weaning

The process of acclimatizing the kitten's digestive system to take food other than milk is known as weaning, and can usually begin when the kitten is three weeks old. Starting with milky liquids, cereal and then meat are gradually introduced to the diet until the kitten is fully weaned at eight weeks of age, as shown in the chart below. As the food the kitten learns to accept will establish feeding patterns for its adult life, it is worth encouraging good eating habits from the start by providing a varied, balanced diet.

WEANING AFTER NATURAL REARING

Age	Food	Feeding method
3 weeks old	Give powdered cat milk substitute or tinned milk diluted with water as for human babies, but at double strength.	Offer the liquid on a teaspoon, 4 times a day.
4 weeks old	Provide milk, as above, with a little baby cereal, puréed, tinned or bottled baby food (fish, meat or cheese varieties) added to the milk mixture.	Place in a shallow tray or saucer, 4 times a day. Give the kittens as much as they will take.
5 weeks old	Substitute finely minced best meat, finely chopped tinned cat food, or chopped, boiled or milk-poached fish for one of the 4 milk feeds.	Place in a shallow tray or saucer. Give the kittens as much as they will eat once a day, but don't put too much down at once.
6–8 weeks old	Increase the amount of solid minced food, preferably concentrating on balanced tinned cat food.	Provide as above. Gradually replace 2 more of the milk feeds with these solid meals.
8 weeks and older	Kittens are normally fully weaned. Give them 2 or 3 solid meals a day, and a saucer of cow's milk. If preferred, the milk can be substituted with fresh water once the kittens are 6 months old.	Provide solid food on a saucer. Milk or water should be available all the time, but change it 2–3 times a day.

Vitamins

It is a good idea to give each kitten once a day one drop of a proprietary multi-vitamin syrup of the type used for human babies. Mix it with a feed from the beginning of weaning right through to at least six months of age.

Taking kittens from their mother

Except under special circumstances (i.e., for medical reasons), don't take kittens from their mother before they are at least six weeks old. Ideally, you should wait until they are fully weaned at about eight weeks of age.

After bottle rearing

The weaning of artificially reared kittens should also begin at three weeks. Add about half-a-teaspoonful of the finest human baby cereal, smoothly blended baby food purée (meat, fish or cheese) or calf's-foot jelly to the bottle feed for a few days. Thereafter the kittens can be weaned in exactly the same way as naturally reared kittens, as shown in the chart on the opposite page.

Toilet training

When the kittens first begin to eat solids at three to four weeks of age the time has come to introduce them to toilet training. Place the cat litter tray in a convenient, easily reached but quiet spot and put the kittens in it frequently, particularly when they look ready to urinate or defecate, or indeed have begun to do so. You can tell if your kitten is about to urinate or defecate as it will crouch with its tail raised. *Never* rub the kittens' noses in their urine or droppings when they relieve themselves in the wrong place or, attracted by the scent, they will regard that area as their permanent "toilet". Always clean these areas scrupulously to avoid repetition of the soiling.

LEARNING TO USE A LITTER TRAY

As cats are very clean animals by nature, toilet training is relatively simple (see above), especially where a kitten has been brought up by its natural mother. With fostered kittens, their natural instinct to cover their faeces means that most will readily adopt the litter tray. However, if your kitten won't use it, check that the tray is in a quiet place where the kitten isn't being disturbed, and that the litter is fresh. Alternatively, it may be that your pet doesn't like the odour of the litter you are providing.

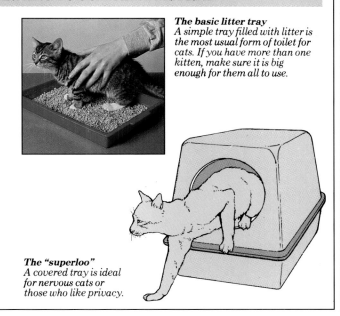

The basic litter tray
A simple tray filled with litter is the most usual form of toilet for cats. If you have more than one kitten, make sure it is big enough for them all to use.

The "superloo"
A covered tray is ideal for nervous cats or those who like privacy.

Growing up

Kittens develop quickly from weak, defenceless animals when newly born to fully independent cats at around six months (see p.127). As they grow, they have increasing control over their bodies, and begin to develop new skills such as hunting and playing. Some of their behaviour is instinctual whilst the rest is only learnt through experience.

Learning to hunt

Queens who are allowed to range outdoors begin to bring back prey to the litter when the kittens are around three weeks old. The purpose of this is to teach the youngsters how to kill through observation, practice and competition. At first, the mother will bring back dead prey and eat it in the kittens' presence. Later, she will leave dead prey for her offspring to eat. Finally, she will bring live prey and allow the kittens to kill it. She doesn't instruct them by actually killing her "catch", but she does remain with them to prevent the luckless victim from escaping. If the kittens are to fend for themselves, they must learn to hunt as well as deal with prey.

Kittens learn hunting techniques by watching their mothers at work (see p. 190). Interestingly, they learn more quickly from their own mother's example than by watching an unrelated adult, however competent and friendly.

Fighting in play
Don't be alarmed if your kittens appear to be engaged in a battle — it is usually only a game. In fact, such mock fights are extremely important, as the kittens learn how to attack and defend themselves.

Toys for kittens
Although pet shops do sell special toys designed for cats, an inquisitive kitten will quickly discover household items, such as a ball of wool, that will keep it equally amused.

AVERAGE WEIGHT OF KITTENS	
Age in days	Weight in grams
1	70—135
5	90—220
10	130—280
15	175—335
20	210—415
25	230—480
30	260—520
35	290—620
40	305—670
45	380—765
50	390—880

Providing a safe environment
Kittens love to explore baskets, boxes and other openings, so make sure that anything they might climb into is safe (see pp. 120—1).

Play

Like the young of other carnivores, kittens love to play. For them games serve as practice for independent adult life. Offensive and defensive roles, attack, pursuit, ambush and killing techniques are rehearsed, but without carrying things too far or inflicting damage on playmates.

There is an air of exaggeration, excitement and bravura in the way that kittens play games, clearly showing they enjoy having fun for its own sake. Play also serves to develop a social sense among cats. Kittens that aren't able to play with others during their development period can become rather anti-social, sometimes neurotic, adults.

Caring for the new "family"

When the kittens are three weeks old, you should discuss worming them with your vet. It is also the ideal time to begin to accustom them to being handled, petted, groomed and inspected for general health.

Keep all kittens (and their mothers if at all possible) indoors until they have been vaccinated at nine weeks of age and for at least one week after vaccination.

The queen should be kept away from tom cats until well after the kittens have been weaned. This is because she may come into oestrus within a few days of giving birth and conceive again, and an unremitting sequence of pregnancies is likely to damage her health.

Occasionally, fully weaned, three-month-old kittens continue to pester their mother for milk. They should be discouraged: the queen frequently looks thinner than normal, and is in need of a good rest. Build her up with several more weeks of extra feeding, and dissuade the kittens from raiding the "milk bar" by smearing her teats with a bitter mixture of petroleum jelly and quinine or by spraying them with a non-toxic repellent.

KITTEN CARE DON'TS

- Don't pick up young kittens by the scruff of the neck
- Don't drown unwanted kittens — ask the vet to put them down
- Don't give cow's milk to very young kittens
- Don't take kittens from their mother until they are at least six weeks old
- Don't allow a kitten outdoors before its first vaccination

6

HOUSING
AND HANDLING

Adding a cat to your household isn't just
a matter of bringing one home. You will have to learn how
to treat and care for your cat on a day-to-day basis — from
picking it up correctly to transporting it safely. This may
sound like a lot of work, but don't be alarmed. Cat
care is basically a matter of commonsense, and won't
take up too much of your time. Like you, the new member
of the household will need its own "possessions" and
equipment. This chapter covers the cat's "furniture": its bed,
travelling container, door flap and pen. Equipment for
feeding and grooming is dealt with in the relevant chapters
(see pp. 154—65, and 166—75), and toilet training
equipment is dealt with in *Kitten Care*
(see p. 133).

Handling techniques

It is almost impossible to resist handling a cat. And if they are handled correctly, most cats adore being picked up and cuddled. For a cat to enjoy being picked up it must feel comfortable and secure, and trust you completely. A cat's body must always be supported; if you pick it up incorrectly, with your hands under its arms and the rest of its body dangling in mid-air, a tolerant cat will wag its tail to show its displeasure, but a less placid animal will probably struggle, or even bite, to get free.

Correct handling is particularly important with new kittens, as their small rib cages are very fragile and can be bruised easily. And a sick cat will also need special handling; this method is covered in the chapter on *Health Care* (see pp. 270–1).

How often can I pick my cat up?

The number of times you handle your cat will depend on its temperament and on the treatment you want it to get used to. If you intend to show your pet you should get it used to being held up high at arm's length as a judge would when examining it. It is also a good idea to ask any visitors to make a point of handling it as this will help it to grow accustomed to the attentions of strangers.

Children and cats
It is very important that children are taught how to handle cats correctly, so that they always support the body firmly. If a child picks up a cat incorrectly it will scratch or bite in order to be freed.

Cradling a cat
Although humans like to hold a cat like a baby, tummy facing upwards and face looking into theirs, not all cats enjoy this. If your cat objects, don't insist on carrying it in this manner.

HOW TO PICK UP AND HOLD A CAT

Grown cats can be picked up with one hand around the stomach, just behind the front paws, and the other under the hind quarters. Once picked up, a cat will probably be happiest sitting in the crook of your arm, with its forepaws either leaning against your shoulder or held in your other hand. Your arms should be taking most of the cat's weight, and it should be sitting upright.

Don't pick up a kitten by the scruff of the neck as a mother cat would. Instead place one hand around its stomach and the other hand under its hind legs. A kitten should be small enough to sit on your palm as long as you have your other hand around its neck to support the head.

1 To pick up a cat without hurting it, place one hand under its front legs, and scoop it up by pushing your other hand under its hind quarters.

2 Bring the cat up level with your chest, all the time keeping one hand firmly under its hind quarters in order to support its full weight.

3 Lean the cat against you, using both arms and hands to support it.

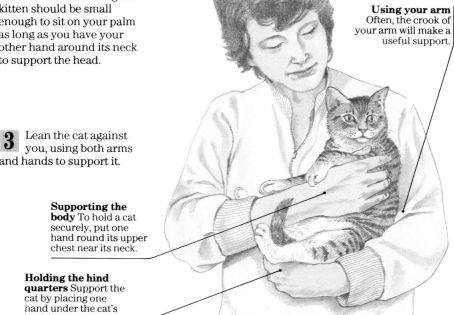

Using your arm
Often, the crook of your arm will make a useful support.

Supporting the body To hold a cat securely, put one hand round its upper chest near its neck.

Holding the hind quarters Support the cat by placing one hand under the cat's back legs.

Cat beds

Even if your cat spends most nights snuggled up with you, it will also need a sleeping place of its own. Your cat may not use its bed, preferring to nap on yours or on a particular cushion or chair. But in times of illness or insecurity its own bed will be an important retreat, satisfying a deep psychological need.

Buying a bed

Nowadays, most pet shops sell cat beds, and you may wish to treat your feline friend to one of these. They range from the bean-bag type (large, round cushions filled with polystyrene granules) to cat "igloos" (as the name suggests, these are igloo-shaped beds — but made out of plastic, not ice!). The traditional wicker basket looks very attractive, and kittens are said to find its creaking very soothing, but it isn't very easy to clean thoroughly. As a less expensive alternative, a wooden or cardboard box lined with plenty of newspaper will provide equally suitable living quarters. Moreover, since cardboard is disposable, you can simply replace the bed when it gets dirty.

You should always make your cat's bed comfortable and inviting by providing soft, warm bedding. You can do this by lining the bed, first with newspaper, then some soft fabric. An old woolly jumper can easily be transformed into a luxurious cat blanket. If you have a new kitten who may be missing its mother and siblings you could also add a soft toy as a bed pal.

Cleaning the bed

Cats are, by nature, clean creatures, and they will turn their noses up at a dirty bed. You should therefore clean the bed and bedding regularly. Plastic types are by far the easiest to wash, and they have

Wicker basket
These look attractive, but they are draughty and difficult to clean.

Plastic bed
Your cat won't suffer from draughts with this type of bed, and you will avoid cleaning problems since plastic is easy to wash down.

the added advantage of being unpopular with fleas. Wash the bed by scrubbing it thoroughly with a non-toxic disinfectant diluted in some hot water. Once the bed is dry, add a fresh layer of newspaper, then launder or replace the fabric bedding.

Where should the cat's bedroom be?

Cats have an uncanny knack of finding the warmest place in the house in which to curl up for a nap. If you have central heating, your cat will probably choose a sleeping place near the boiler. As long as this spot is draught-free and reasonably secluded, it is the best place to put your pet's bed.

In colder weather, you could add a heating pad (an electrically heated pad that acts like an electric blanket) to your cat's basket for extra warmth. However, you should make sure that the bed has a warm and a cold area by placing the pad to one side, not centrally, so that your cat can choose the temperature it prefers.

Feline bedtime

You can lead a cat to bed, but you can't make it stay there and go to sleep. A great many cats have trouble coming to terms with their family status. Even if you were to equip your cat with its own four-poster bed, chances are that it would be found curled up in your own when bedtime arrives. If you don't object to sharing your bed with a furry hot-water bottle this isn't a problem. But if you like a quiet night's sleep, you must lay down the rules of the house firmly while the animal is still a small kitten.

Start a night time routine by putting your cat in its own bed just before you plan to retire. Switch off the light, and shut the door to its "bedroom". Don't forget to leave its litter tray and water bowl accessible. To start with, your kitten probably won't like this enforced segregation, and may even protest loudly, but in a week or two, once the routine is established, it will settle down quietly each night.

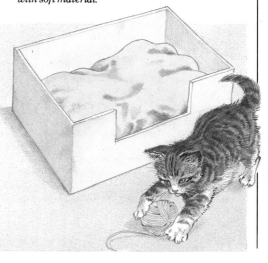

Cardboard box
For a cat's bed that costs nothing, take a cardboard box and cut out a large piece at the front to give easy access. Then line the box with soft material.

Bean-bag
Cats enjoy trampling these polystyrene-bead-filled "sacks" to form a warm nest. Choose one with a washable cover.

Cat pens and cages

Although your cat will have the run of the house most of the time, there may be occasions when you should restrict it to a pen. You can buy metal or fibreglass cages in varying sizes, and your choice will depend on the length of time the cat will spend in the pen. A small wire pen is sufficient for an hour or two, but if the period of confinement is to be longer you will need a larger pen with space for bedding, water and feed dishes, a litter tray, and a toy. A large pen is also useful to contain kittens when you are out .

Metal pens are usually made from plastic-coated wire so, like the fibreglass type, they are very easy to clean. After use, wipe the bars of the pen with cotton wool soaked in diluted, non-toxic disinfectant. This procedure is particularly important if you have used the pen to contain a cat with an infection.

USES FOR A PEN

- Recovery from an operation or illness
- For an overnight stay in a cattery
- To isolate your cat from other pets
- To contain young kittens safely
- To keep a bathed cat near a heater

BUILDING AN OUTDOOR RUN

If you own an un-neutered tom cat it is unlikely that he will be able to live in the house. A tom will invariably spray indoors, and the strong, unpleasant odour of his urine will mean that he can't live with you as a neuter or a female cat can. If you take on the responsibility of a male cat, it is essential that you provide him with separate living quarters. Provided you have a garden, the solution is to build an outdoor run. The ideal run will be as large as possible, with a "house" for shelter, a place to sunbathe, a cat tree, and various "perches".

Most runs consist of a basic wooden frame covered with chicken wire. It is important to cover the top of the run to prevent the cat simply climbing out. The house area should be draught-free, with a heating device for use in colder weather; and should contain the tom's bed and feeding dishes. When you take the cat his meals, play with him for a while so that he doesn't feel neglected.

A simple, smaller garden run can be useful for any cat if you live in a hazardous traffic area.

Shelter The run should have a shelter that is large enough for the tom to sleep in.

Tree A climbing tree, whether natural or man-made, provides excellent exercise.

Cat doors

A cat door is only useful if you want to give your cat the freedom to come and go as it pleases. The door is basically a flap-covered opening in an outside door that is large enough to allow a cat to pass comfortably through. Plastic or rubber flaps (from pet shops) can be fitted to a hole of the correct size cut in your door. Once fitted, your cat will be able to enter via the flap whenever it wants.

There are several different types of cat door, but whichever you choose it should be set no higher than six cms from the base of the door so that your cat can step rather than jump through it. Flaps either

The cat door
Once a cat has learnt to use a flap, it will enjoy the freedom it provides.

open both ways, or they allow the cat to enter the house, but not to leave. A flap must have a locking device as a pre-caution against unwanted visitors. If your pet is female and calling, the local toms will regard a cat door as an invitation! Fix a small bolt on the inside so that you can lock the flap whenever necessary.

One disadvantage of a cat door is the draught it can cause. However, flaps with magnetic strips along the sides are available. These keep the flap firmly closed except when pushed open by the cat.

Teaching your cat to use a cat flap

Some cats are veritable Houdinis, and need no instruction in the art of using cat doors, whilst others may need some encouragement. Begin by fastening the flap open and allowing your cat to investigate it. If you place some food on the other side this may tempt the cat through, but make sure that the flap is firmly fastened and won't drop down and alarm the cat. Once your pet has stepped through, release the flap and use a titbit to encourage it to step back, but this time help it to push the flap open.

A tom's run
This outdoor run incorporates a shelter, perches, areas of grass and concrete, and a tree. It is made of wire mesh on a wooden frame.

Roof The top of the run must be escape-proof.

Shelves The cat should have a choice of perches, so that he can sit in the sun or shade.

Flooring Part grass, part concrete is the best choice for a pen base. The tom will select part of the grassed area to serve as a lavatory.

Exercise

Fortunately for those of us who aren't fitness fanatics, cats don't need a daily five-mile hike. They get their exercise from regular jaunts around the garden, climbing trees, hunting birds and small rodents, chasing trespassing cats, dodging the local dog and exploring their immediate terrain.

ACTION GAMES

Playing is important to a cat's well-being — as well as providing beneficial exercise, it has other useful purposes. For example, chasing a toy helps a kitten to practice its hunting techniques, and tree-climbing is your pet's equivalent of a visit to the manicurist.

Climbing tree or frame
If your cat has access to the outdoors, a tree will provide plenty of opportunity for exercise. For a housebound cat, a frame will act as a substitute for climbing and scratching.

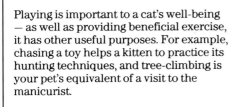

Cardboard boxes
Your cat will love to jump in and out of these, often ambushing passers-by!

Rolled-up tin foil
Your cat will enjoy chasing this around obstacles like chairs or table legs.

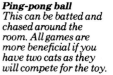

Ping-pong ball
This can be batted and chased around the room. All games are more beneficial if you have two cats as they will compete for the toy.

Fitness for the indoor cat

You may be forced to confine your cat indoors if you live in a high-rise apartment or near heavy traffic (see p.146). In such circumstances, many cats can live perfectly contented lives providing alternative exercise is created. If you supply devices such as scratching posts and climbing frames this will give your housebound cat similar sorts of exercise to a cat that has access to a garden. You should select a breed that is suited to these living conditions, rather than one that is renowned for its wanderlust. Breeds that don't take to a permanent indoor life include the Somali, Abyssinian and Rex.

You must encourage your housebound cat in an alternative form of exercise to replace the hours it would have spent in the garden. Don't panic — this doesn't mean that you have to enroll your pet in the local aerobics class! An hour or so of play each day is sufficient to keep a cat fit and healthy. If you encourage your cat to play with a toy from an early age it will keep itself fit and happy without any further effort on your part.

Cats and leads

In general, unlike dogs, cats don't enjoy walking on a lead. Only cats with a suitable "dog-like" temperament will accept this practice. Certain breeds of cat (see below right) seem to take more readily to it than others. Personally, I think that, with the exception of the odd, stylish Siamese, a cat on a lead doesn't look quite right. If your cat doesn't object, you can take it on short walks using a safe lead, but you should never drag it out against its will, and only walk as far as it chooses.

Teaching a cat to walk on a lead
Unlike dogs, cats aren't easy to train to walk on a lead. Begin with a weaned kitten, getting it accustomed to wearing a

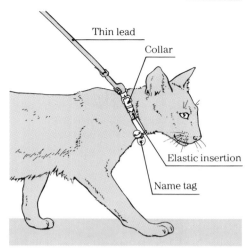

Thin lead
Collar
Elastic insertion
Name tag

Walking the cat
Some shorthaired cats (see below) will tolerate standing in for a dog during your daily constitutional, but don't force your cat to walk on a lead against its will.

collar first. Choose one with an elastic insertion that acts as a safety device. If your pet gets caught — for example, in a branch when climbing a tree — the elastic allows it to escape. Once your kitten is used to the collar, attach a long, thin lead or cord and start to walk with it, first in the house, then in the garden, and, later perhaps, on the pavement. Patience and regular practice may bring results. However, cats are supreme individualists, and so will never submit as easily as a dog to being led anywhere. Ultimately, you can never force a cat to walk on a lead if it doesn't want to.

BREEDS FOR LEADS

- Siamese
- Burmese
- Russian Blue
- Foreign White
- Foreign Black
- Foreign Blue
- Foreign Smoke

The housebound cat

Keeping a cat indoors is much less of a problem than restricting a dog to the house. If outside access simply isn't possible — because you live in a high-rise apartment or next to a major road, for example — it is quite feasible to keep a cat indoors permanently. If you plan to do this, try to start with a kitten, not an adult cat that is already used to an outdoor life. And choose a breed that is suited to sitting at home, rather than one renowned for hunting and exploring.

Territorial requirements

Any size of dwelling — from an apartment or cottage to a mansion or palace — is acceptable to a cat as a sufficient area of territory. Cats have several advantages over dogs: they are proportionately smaller in most cases, they are neater in build, and they can utilize the third dimension by going up. Thus, they will fit in contentedly, even in a home where there is "barely room to swing a cat".

COPING WITH AN INDOOR CAT

Scratching

The main problem you will have with a cat confined indoors is damage to furniture by scratching. Certain covering materials like velvet or leather seem to be, to your cat's way of thinking, ideal for keeping its claws neatly manicured.

The only solution to this is training. As soon as you acquire your cat you should discourage it from lacerating your furniture. At the first sign of an attack, grab it by the scruff and thrust it firmly at an alternative, and even more claw-grabbingly attractive, object — one specially contrived for the purpose. Pet shops sell special pillars on wooden bases covered with a tough material like sacking. But, as an alternative, you can make one of these "scratching posts" yourself. Make sure it is stable enough to take the weight of a clawing cat.

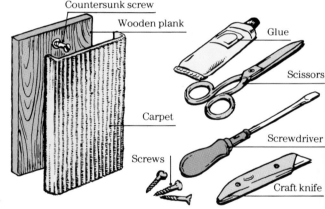

Countersunk screw
Wooden plank
Glue
Scissors
Carpet
Screwdriver
Screws
Craft knife

Making a scratching post
Screw a 30—60 cms long piece of wood planking to the wall in an unobtrusive corner of the room. Then glue your chosen material — hessian, carpet or bark — to the wood upright.

Natural scratching posts
Your furniture is less likely to be assaulted if your cat has the opportunity to go outdoors and file its nails on rough wooden fencing or the bark of tree trunks.

Leaving cats unattended

A cat can be left alone in a house or apartment for 24 hours as long as adequate food, water and a tray of cat litter are provided. But it is unwise to leave your cat for more than 24 hours without arranging for someone to visit and change the supplies. Litter trays must be cleaned and replenished, and fresh water provided. If you are going away for more than a day, it is better to get a neighbour to call each morning to feed your cat and empty its tray than to send it to a cattery. The cat will be much happier and there is less risk of disease.

Declawing

A cat's claws can be removed once and for all in a mutilating operation carried out under a general anaesthetic. Except for medical reasons, it is illegal in the U.K. In the U.S., however, this unpleasant practice is still allowed. I am totally opposed to declawing — it removes the cat's main defensive weapons purely for the protection of inanimate objects.

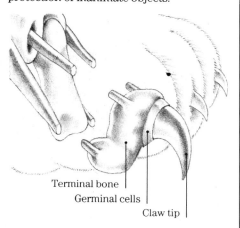

Terminal bone
Germinal cells
Claw tip

How declawing is done
Surgical declawing includes removal of the germinal cells and some or all of the terminal bone in the toe.

BEFORE GOING OUT CHECK:

- A litter tray is available
- Adequate food is available
- Fresh water is available
- Any doors you want shut are shut
- There are no safety hazards

Cats and indoor plants

Some cats have a tendency to vandalize certain species of indoor plant. They may stomp about on, root out, chew or scratch your choicest blooms. In fact, a cat usually acts in this manner out of love for the particular plant — the aroma, texture, and an instinctive requirement for tasty vegetable extracts turn your cat on.

If you have a determined feline gardener of this kind, spray your plants with an odour-free (to humans), cat-repellent aerosol. And if your cat hasn't access to a garden, provide it with a small seedbox planted with herbs and weeds.

Plants to grow for a cat
Catmint, Thyme, Sage, Parsley, Chickweed, Lawn grass, Colt's foot grass, Cereal grass such as wheat or oats.

PLANTS TO AVOID:

Certain houseplants are poisonous and you shouldn't allow your pet access to them, particularly if it is prone to nibble plants.

Philodendrons Tree lovers
Dieffenbachia Dumb cane
Hedera True ivy
Caladiums Elephant's ears
Euphorbia pulcherrima Poinsettia
Solanum capiscastrum False Jerusalem cherry
Oleander
Rhododendron Azalea
Prunus laurocerasus Common or cherry laurel
Mistletoe

Moving house with a cat

Most cats are taken along when a family moves house. In general, they raise no objection to this, and quickly set about staking out their new territory. Some cats, however, decide that they prefer the old home, with its familiar hideaways, rodents and promiscuous members of the opposite sex. They turn their noses up at the new residence, and set out for their original haunt.

Lost cats frequently track down their old homes, often travelling very long distances. The longest recorded journey by a cat is 950 miles — from Boston to Chicago! This ability to make for home doesn't work if the family moves house and leaves its cat behind — it is the place not the people that the cat tracks down.

Where is the cat's homing device?

Modern research suggests that the key to the homing ability of cats lies in a form of inbuilt celestial navigation, similar to that employed by birds. It is thought to work because, during the months or years that the cat lived in its original home, its brain automatically registered the angle of the sun at certain times of day.

But how does the cat tell what time it is? After all, it doesn't wear a watch. Like man and other higher mammals, cats are thought to possess internal biological clocks. Therefore, if a cat is uprooted to a new home where the sun's angle at a certain time is slightly different, and it wants to put it right, it works by trial and error. Moving in one direction, it finds the angle gets worse. It tries another and the angle improves, so it concludes that that must be the direction to travel in. Of course, this is a subconscious activity, but as the cat gradually gets the sun in the right spot in the sky it finds itself in a neighbourhood where the smells, sights and sounds are familiar. And pretty soon, it arrives at its old home. The cat doesn't need a clear day to navigate, like birds, in overcast weather it uses polarized light.

HOUSE-MOVING PROCEDURE

Moving a cat
When transporting a cat by car, don't carry it loose: use a suitable container (see opposite).

1 Don't send the cat in the furniture van — put it in its carrier and take it in the car with you.

2 When you arrive at the new house you must shut all the doors before releasing your cat.

3 Feed your cat as soon as possible to endear it to the new home.

4 Make sure that your cat is fitted with a collar and tag giving your new address and telephone number before you allow it outdoors.

Travelling

There will be many occasions when your cat needs to travel — for example, to a show, a new home, or just down the road to the vet's surgery. Cats don't enjoy enforced journeys, but as long as you follow the advice given here, transporting your pet without causing it distress won't be a problem.

Choosing a carrier

No cat owner can be without that essential piece of travelling equipment — the cat carrier. At most pet shops you will find a variety of travelling baskets to choose from. Look for one that is large enough for your cat, well-ventilated, completely "cat-proof", and easy to clean and carry.

If your pet isn't a regular traveller, then a disposable cardboard carrier will probably suffice. These very cheap boxes are suitable for an occasional trip to the vet, but they aren't strong enough for long-distance travelling. Moreover, once these carriers are soiled, they have to be thrown away.

For more frequent trips, and where public transport is involved, you should choose a vinyl "hold-all" carrier. These are more escape-proof than the cardboard type. If you show your cat regularly, you will need a fibreglass or polyethylene carrier. These are the most expensive option, but they are long-lasting and very secure.

You can still buy the traditional wicker carriers, but although they are most attractive, they have two major drawbacks — they are draughty, and they are difficult to clean. If you have one, it is a good idea to wrap newspaper or polythene around the sides in cold weather in order to keep your cat warm, but take care to leave the top and bottom clear for ventilation.

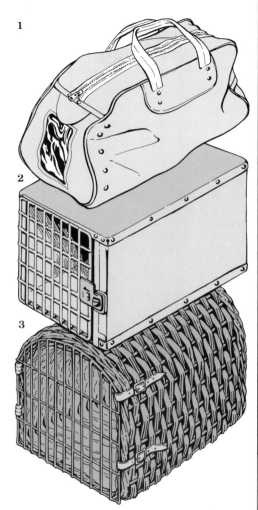

Types of carrier

1 Vinyl carrier
This has two large handles, a zip running along the top, a clear vinyl window at one end, and ventilation holes.

2 Fibreglass carrier
A secure carrier for show cats, this has a lockable door and a metal ventilation grille.

3 Wicker carrying basket
This traditional cat carrier is fairly secure. The cat gains access via the ventilation grille.

Preparing for a journey

For a short winter journey simply put the cat's blanket inside the carrier. For a longer journey in cold weather it is a good idea to buy a special insulator — many pet shops sell a type of polyester fur fabric designed for putting inside a travel carrier.

On hot-weather journeys it is enough to use a thin, lightweight blanket. For a long journey in exceptionally hot weather, you should dampen a cloth in cold water and place it over the basket to keep the temperature down inside.

Introducing your cat to its carrier

Your cat's first encounter with its carrier should be in a closed room. This is because cats are very quick to realize that a carrier means an unwelcome journey, and you don't want to arrive late because you have spent several hours chasing a frightened cat around the house. You can try to encourage it into the basket with some dried food, but you will probably have to pick the cat up, supporting the hind legs and holding the scruff, and lift it into the carrier. Before you start to put your cat in its carrier, remember to let it use its litter tray.

Travelling by car

Some cats, if started early as kittens, travel well in cars. Older cats, though, get distinctly alarmed when first brought face-to-face with an auto interior. Many cats aren't keen on travelling, and complain vocally, but as long as they are in safe, comfortable accomodation it won't do them any harm.

If the journey lasts for more than half-an-hour, you should stop the car at reasonable intervals to allow your cat to use the litter tray and to eat and drink. You should keep all the doors and windows closed when you make this "comfort" stop, as the cat may try to escape if given the chance.

Sedatives
Opinion is divided on the use of sedatives for cats that don't travel well. I would never advise their use without a vet's recommendation, as they may do more harm than good. Your vet may also be able to prescribe drugs to prevent motion sickness.

Restraining a cat in a car
Cats can behave in a most distressed manner when left loose in a car. Some owners allow their cat to travel loose, but this isn't advisable, and if your cat isn't used to travelling, you must restrict it to a carrier. There are two practical reasons for this. First, a nervous, loose cat may well get in the driver's way, and secondly, if it is car sick, you will find a carrier easier to clean than the car upholstery. In fact, in Britain it is an offence to have a loose cat in a car if the driver is the only occupant. If your cat is a well-seasoned traveller and doesn't need to be kept in a carrier, it is a good idea to put a collar and lead on it and ask a back-seat passenger to hold the lead.

Leaving a cat in a car
As with dogs, there is a grave risk of illness or even death if you leave a cat inside a car on a warm day. Overheating and death from hyperthermia can and do occur very easily as the sun heats up the car, rather like a greenhouse. You should always leave a window partly open if you must leave your cat unattended for any length of time.

ITEMS YOU SHOULD PACK:

- Litter tray
- Food
- Water
- Feeding dishes
- Blanket
- Toy
- Carrier (see p. 149)

Travelling abroad

Transporting a cat to other countries calls for a great deal of organization. Your first priority will be to investigate the quarantine regulations both in the country you are travelling to, and the country you are travelling from.

Britain is one of the world's few rabies-free countries, and remains so by imposing very strict quarantine laws.

When you bring a cat into the U.K. from abroad, it will be quarantined for a period of six months, and during this time it will be given two anti-rabies inoculations. Even though Britain is rabies-free, a short quarantine period and/or an inoculation will often be required if you take a cat (or any other susceptible animal) from Britain to another controlled country.

RABIES

Rabies is a potentially fatal virus transmitted in the saliva of infected animals. The disease is endemic in many countries, and rabies-free countries impose strict quarantine regulations to stop its spread. Anyone who tries to evade quarantine regulations when taking a cat (or any other controlled species) into a country with disease-control regulations breaks the law and endangers lives.

Rabies-free countries

These countries have very strict quarantine laws:
● Britain
● Australia
● New Zealand
● Hawaii

Precautions

In all countries without anti-rabies legislation take the following precautions:
● Avoid close contact with free-roaming animals
● Don't allow your household pets any contact with wild or feral animals
● Get your cat vaccinated regularly

Emergency action

If bitten by a suspect cat:
● Clean the wound with soap or disinfectant immediately. If this isn't possible, wash it with clean water or alcohol
● Seek medical attention immediately — prompt treatment with vaccine will save your life
● If possible, restrain the animal for investigation, but take care to avoid further injury
● If you can't catch the cat, inform the local police

Incubation period

The rabies virus has a long incubation period (usually 10−120 days, but sometimes up to six months). The quarantine system is therefore an essential part of the safe-guards designed to keep the human and animal populations of rabies-free countries safe.

United Kingdom quarantine regulations

If you buy a cat abroad or take your cat overseas and then return to Britain with it, even if it has been vaccinated abroad, it will still be subject to quarantine here. This six-month confinement is essential in order to keep Britain rabies-free.

Registered quarantine catteries are comfortable, well-run establishments. Of course, they have all the disadvantages of commercial catteries, including cost, but in this case they are unavoidable.

If you plan to bring a cat into Britain, you must obtain the necessary documents before you make your journey.

Anti-rabies vaccinations

British policy is *not* to use vaccines, for various sound scientific reasons applicable to an island that has been free of infection for many years. However, if you are going to live or work abroad and you intend to take a cat to a country where rabies vaccination is advisable or compulsory, vaccine can be given in the U.K. by your vet under licence.

Travelling by air

Air travel isn't very costly for small, light animals like cats, and its speed makes it an ideal way of shipping animals from country to country — the period of distress is minimized and the animal is never more than a few hours away from veterinary attention. If you ship your cat by air, you must contain it securely in a basket or box which complies with the regulations laid down by the airlines through the International Air Transport Association (I.A.T.A). A reputable airline won't accept animals for transport unless the minimum standards of packing are met. As well as the I.A.T.A. rules, some airlines add their own. You must find these out from the airline you are using well before you travel. For example, on long-haul intercontinental routes, British Caledonian won't accept cats under 16 weeks old, whilst Pan-Am insists on special containers.

It is recommended that the animal should be given a light meal and a short drink two hours before dispatch. If the animal is nervous, you can give it a tranquilizer (prescribed by the vet) shortly before you deliver it to the airline's office. It is a good idea to put a familiar article in the container with the cat, as this may help to keep it in good spirits. Always make sure that your documents are in order before going to the airport.

Air travel regulations

For fibreglass, metal, rigid plastic, and wooden containers:

1 The containers must be stoutly constructed, and the joints must be made so that there is no chance of the animal escaping as a result of clawing or biting at the structure.

2 The whole of one end of the container must be open and covered with bars, weldmesh or smooth expanded metal. (This is the main ventilation source).

3 The container must have a sliding or hinged door designed to prevent accidental opening. This door can also be the main ventilation source (see point 2).

4 In addition to the main ventilation opening, there must be additional slots or holes distributed regularly over the opposite end of the container from top to bottom, as well as over the top third of the sides, covering not less than 14 percent of the surface of all the walls. This can be achieved by drilling 0.7 cm holes at 10 cm horizontal and vertical intervals.

For wickerwork containers:

1 The height of the container must be at least the length of the cat plus half its height from ground to elbow joint.

2 The width of the container must be at least twice the width of the cat across its shoulders.

Other regulations:

● Females suckling young and unweaned animals aren't acceptable for transport.
● The animal's name should be marked on the outside of the container.
● On board the aircraft, containers with cats and containers with dogs must be kept apart unless they come from the same home.
● Some countries insist that each cat is crated separately. The only exception to this rule is a consignment of a mother with a weaned litter.
● The airline must fix a "This Way Up" label and a green "Live Animal" label to the container.

Additional regulations for the U.K.:

● The carriage of live animals in the passenger cabin is prohibited.
● Animals destined for Britain must have a red "Rabies Control" label on their container.

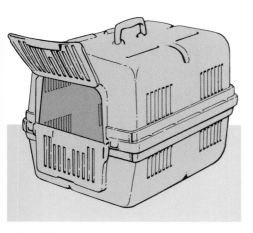

Air freight container
This rigid plastic container is specially designed for transporting a cat by air. The cat gains access via the "door" at one end.

● Containers made principally of wire mesh must be sufficiently rigid to prevent damage or distortion during normal handling. They must also possess external lifting handles, have a solid floor or tray, and they must be padlocked or bolted when in use.
● Where mesh is used for cat containers, it must not be larger than 2.5 cm square, and not thinner than 0.4 cm.
● Cats can only be imported into the U.K. through the following airports: London Gatwick, London Heathrow, Birmingham, Edinburgh, Glasgow, Leeds, Manchester and Prestwick.

Additional regulations for the U.S.:

● The cat must not be presented to the carrying airline more than four hours before the scheduled departure time.
● Animal shipments to, from or via the U.S. must have written instructions concerning food and water requirements fixed on the outside of the container.
● The container must have ventilation openings on two opposite walls (at least 16 percent of the area of each wall) or on all four walls (at least eight percent of the area of each wall).

● At least ⅓ of the minimum ventilation area must be in the lower half of the container, and ⅓ in the upper half.
● If there are any ventilation openings on three walls, they must be at least eight percent of the area of two opposite walls and 50 percent of the area of the third wall. The total combined ventilation and opening area must be at least 14 percent of the total area of all four walls.
● The outside of the ventilated wall must have a rim or other separation device 2 cm deep to prevent obstructions of the openings.
● The container must be marked on the top and at least one side with the words "Live Animals" in letters not less than 2.5 cm high.
● A maximum of one cat over six months old may be transported in a single container. Two 8—24-week-old kittens less than 9 kg each and of comparable size may be carried in one container.

Travelling by rail and sea

Broadly speaking, the recommendations for containers for air travel should be observed. Some rail companies will allow you to keep the cat with you as long as you restrict it to its carrier; others will insist on it travelling in its carrier in the luggage compartment.

Cats can be sent by sea, but this isn't such a desirable method as air travel, and will probably be costlier. Unless the owner is also on board, daily attendance will have to be provided by a crew member. Cats usually travel well by sea, and I have never heard of a seasick cat, but sea travel has the disadvantage that no specialized veterinary care is available on board in case of illness.

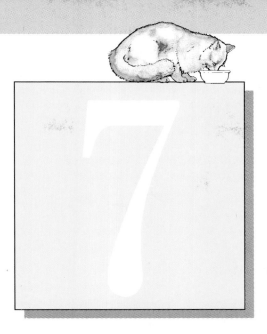

FEEDING

A correctly brought-up cat isn't very faddy, although it is often
fussier than many humans are about freshness and hygiene in
the kitchen. Don't make the mistake of turning your cat into a
spoilt and unhealthy pet by feeding it continuously on its
"favourite" brand of pet food; to keep it fit and well,
you should give it a varied, well-balanced diet as described
in this chapter. For special information on feeding kittens and
pregnant queens consult the *Kitten Care* (see p. 132) and
Breeding chapters (see p. 209).
Advice on preparing meals for sick or elderly cats is given in
the *Health Care* chapter (see pp. 272 and 274).

The dietary needs of a cat

There is no such thing as a vegetarian cat: all cats are carnivores and must have meat to survive. But this doesn't mean that cats don't like or need to eat some fruit or vegetable matter. Several wild cat species like to supplement their meat with the occasional fruit or vegetable titbit. Lions and tigers, for example, often go straight for their victim's stomach after making a kill, devouring the soup or digesting vegetation as a starter, before progressing to the main course of prime fillet and porterhouse.

Nutritional requirements
Variety is the key principle to observe when feeding a cat. You should accustom a kitten to a wide variety of food from the day that it is weaned. Although pet cats should have a diet that is at least 25 percent protein, they ought to follow the lead of their wild cousins and eat a varied menu that contains a little vegetable matter in addition to the staple meat and fish diet.

Providing fats and carbohydrates in your cat's diet as sources of energy makes good sense as, to an extent, an all-protein diet of meat or fish is wasted. This is because some of the expensive foodstuff is simply burnt by the cat's body to provide calories instead of being used to repair cells (see p. 158). Another reason for not feeding an all-protein menu is that it can be unhealthy. Over-doing the raw meat content of your pet's diet can have harmful effects: a cat that is fed on nothing but fish can develop vitamin B1 deficiency, a liver-only menu can upset its bowels, and a diet of nothing but prime lean meat produces calcium and vitamin deficiencies.

If you provide a varied selection of food that supplies adequate quantities of the essential nutrients shown in the chart opposite, the animal should balance its diet instinctively. If you inherit an old animal that is set in its ways, a little culinary effort may winkle it out of its determination to fast to death unless given a monotonous diet of crayfish or caviar. When acting as a chef to a recently arrived "faddy" cat, the best way to introduce a new, healthier diet is gradually, adding the new foods one by one over several weeks.

Giving supplements
If your cat is in good health, and you feed it a broad, varied diet, if shouldn't need extra vitamin or mineral supplements. If you give it extra vitamins or minerals, these will simply be excreted. However, supplements are sometimes beneficial to sick animals; for example, iron tablets help an anaemic cat to recover. Such treatment should only be given on a vet's advice. Supplements are also useful for pregnant and nursing queens (see p. 209).

How long can a cat go without food?
A cat can survive without food for much longer than humans, as it can lose as much as 40 percent of its body weight without dying (though 10–14 percent loss of the total water in a cat's body is normally fatal). Cats have been known to survive for weeks without food or water in exceptional circumstances. For example, Chips, a marmalade tom from Liverpool, was inadvertently packed into a crate of machine parts and shipped by sea to Mombasa. Four weeks later, when the crate was opened in Africa, Chips was still alive, although he was somewhat thinner. He was thought to have survived by eating some of the grease coating the machinery and lapping up what little moisture developed from condensation.

THE NUTRITIONAL REQUIREMENTS OF A CAT

Constituent	Daily requirement	Source	Comment
Protein	**Kitten**: 35—40 percent by weight of total diet **Adult**: 25 percent by weight of total diet	Meat, fish, eggs, cheese and milk	Needs much more than a dog (13 percent)
Fat	25—30 percent by weight of total diet	Animal and vegetable oils and fats	Needs much more than a dog (5—10 percent)
Carbohydrate	Up to 33 percent by weight of total diet	Potatoes, cereals and bread	Not essential, but fibre beneficial to bowel function
Vitamin A	2000 i.u.	Milk, egg, liver, cod liver oil, carrots	An overdose can be dangerous — don't give supplements
Vitamin B2 Vitamin B6	0.5 mg 0.5 mg 0.3 mg	Meat, liver, yeast, green vegetables	Some is synthesized in the intestine
Vitamin B12	Not required	Unnecessary to cat	
Vitamin C	Not required	Synthesized by cat	
Vitamin D	150 i.u.	Effect of sunlight on coat, cod liver oil, milk, eggs, oily fish	An overdose can be dangerous — don't give supplements
Vitamin E	5 mg	Cereals, some meat	
Vitamin K	Not required	Synthesized by cat	
Biotin Folic acid	0.002 mg 0.1 mg	Meat, liver, yeast, green vegetables	Some is synthesized in the intestine
Minerals: Sodium Potassium Calcium Phosphorus Magnesium Iron Copper Iodine Manganese Zinc Cobalt	1500 mg 200 mg 400 mg 400 mg 10 mg 5 mg 0.2 mg 0.2 mg 0.2 mg 0.3 mg 0.2 mg	From a balanced diet	An overdose can be dangerous — don't give supplements. Nursing queens have higher requirements
Water	30 cc per 0.5 kg of body weight	The tap!	

Providing a healthy diet

Most of the dietary constituents that are essential to human life are just as important for a cat's well-being. However, they are needed and used in different proportions. Unlike us, the cat is a true carnivore, equipped to survive on a diet of other animals. When a cat eats its prey it consumes not just the muscle meat, but also the skin, bones and internal organs. This total diet contains almost everything that a cat needs to survive.

Proteins
Found in meat, fish, eggs and cheese, proteins provide the amino acids that are the essential building blocks of body tissue, and are vital for growth and repair. In the cat, proteins are also a source of energy calories. After being processed by the cat's body during digestion, proteins produce a high level of waste products. As a result, the kidneys have to be able to work hard to remove them from the body (see p. 163). A growing cat needs a minimum of about ten percent protein in its diet, and an adult cat requires six percent. However, a good feline diet should contain between 25 and 30 percent. While metabolizing protein in its body, a cat synthesizes an important amino-acid called taurine. This chemical is vital for health of the eyes, nervous system, skeleton and heart. Cats don't produce enough, and must get the rest of their taurine in foodstuffs where it is found almost solely in raw fish and meat. Balanced cat foods and most special cat milks contain added taurine.

Fats
A key source of calories for a cat, fats should form 15–40 percent of your pet's ration. The advantage of fats is that they don't load the kidneys with waste products, and therefore the fat content of your cat's diet should be increased as it gets older. Don't feed fats that are old or rancid, it can make it ill.

Carbohydrates
Another source of energy calories, carbohydrates are found in starchy food such as bread or potatoes. Although they aren't essential to a cat, if you want to include them in your pet's menu you can give up to 50 percent of its diet in this form. This type of food is also a useful source of the bulk (fibre) needed for a healthy bowel.

Minerals
As in humans, minerals of all kinds are essential for a cat's growth, and the maintenance of its body structures and vital functions. If you feed your cat a well-composed, varied diet, mineral deficiencies are most unlikely to occur.

Vitamins
Eating the complete prey animal, together with exposure to sunlight, provides wild cats with all the vitamins that they need. The domestic cat gets all its requirements either from a balanced diet, or from the supplements which are added to manufactured cat food. The cat doesn't need the vitamins B12, C and K. B12 is unnecessary to it, and C and K are synthesized within its body.

Choosing the right foods
Cats' meals should vary, so it is impossible to lay down a fixed diet sheet. Many different foods can be fed to a cat; the chart on the opposite page gives the pros and cons of the major types. When feeding your cat, you should vary its diet, using all the foods mentioned in the chart. A useful guide is to give two parts by weight of a selection from the protein foods to one part of a selection of the fillers.

THE MAJOR FOODS

Type	Preparation	Value	Comments
PROTEIN **Manufactured** — dried, soft-moist and canned	● Ready-to-serve, no cooking involved	Formulated to provide a balanced diet	Convenient to use
Meat — beef, lamb or pork	● Bake or grill, then cut into small cubes	High in protein	Don't buy from knacker's yard. If you must boil it, use water as gravy on dried food
Offal	● Must always be cooked	High in protein	Don't buy from knacker's yard
Poultry and **rabbit**	● Feed cooked scraps	High in protein	Don't feed bones
Egg	● Serve whole, cooked and chopped ● Raw, separated yolks can be fed	Good source of protein	Don't feed raw egg whites. Don't give more than two whole eggs a week
Milk	● Pour it from the bottle!	Good source of protein and calcium	Gives some cats upset stomachs
Cheese	● Serve raw and grated ● Can be cooked with other foods	Excellent source of protein	
Fish	● Serve fresh and raw, steamed or grilled. If larger than a herring, chop and bone it ● Tinned fish in tomato or oil can be given	High in protein. Oily fish helps to dispel fur balls from the stomach	A diet of nothing but fish is unbalanced
FILLERS **Vegetables**	● Add cooked to meat or fish	Provides bulk and vitamins	No more than one- third of meal
Starchy foods	● Mix crumbled toast, pasta or potato with gravy or fish stock ● Cereal can be used with milk	Provides bulk	No more than one- third of meal
Fruit	● Occasional slices or segments	Source of vitamins	An occasional "treat" food

Pre-packed foods

There are three main kinds of pre-packed food marketed for cats: canned meat, soft-moist products and dried foods. All three types, convenient as they may be, should be used as a component of the full diet, not as a complete diet. Ideally, you should feed a meal of fresh food (see p.162) at least twice a week. This is because proprietary foods don't provide the nutritional completeness that a cat demands if it is to live a long and healthy life. They claim to be complete, and many types match the recommended protein content of a cat's diet (25—30 percent). However, like us, cats should have some fresh food to obtain sufficient vitamins and minerals. Also, such food is very dull as the sole item on the menu, even though some animals can put up with a great deal of monotony. And in terms of the nutritional value, pre-packed food is fairly expensive.

However, at certain times you may find it necessary to use pre-packed food as the sole element in the diet. As long as this is for weeks rather than months, and plenty of water is provided with dried types, your cat won't suffer.

You will find that food technologists add the same chemicals to processed cat foods as those with which they lace packaged food for humans. I suspect that most of these substances are included to make the product more acceptable to the store buyer and the cat's owner than to the cat. Of course, the last word on which of these products is best lies with the consumers — the cats. They won't be influenced by advertisements; they will either like the taste or not.

Canned food

These products usually contain meat, fish salts, jellying agents, vitamins, colouring chemicals, water and, sometimes, cereals. Most recipes are based on fish, chicken, beef, rabbit or offal. They contain 25—30 percent protein, and can therefore be used as a large component of a cat's rations.

Cans are useful because they are sterile and easy to store. But they can work out to be relatively expensive as you are buying a fair quantity of water, particularly in a type that has a lot of jelly. Also, the canning process and storage time can reduce the level of vitamins.

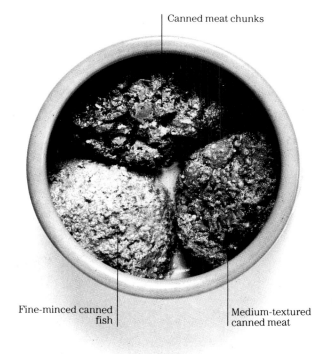

Canned meat chunks

Fine-minced canned fish

Medium-textured canned meat

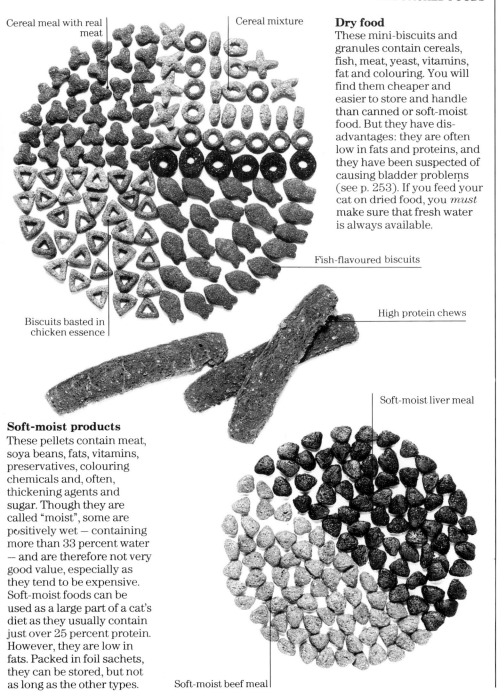

Cereal meal with real meat

Cereal mixture

Fish-flavoured biscuits

Biscuits basted in chicken essence

High protein chews

Soft-moist liver meal

Soft-moist beef meal

Dry food

These mini-biscuits and granules contain cereals, fish, meat, yeast, vitamins, fat and colouring. You will find them cheaper and easier to store and handle than canned or soft-moist food. But they have dis-advantages: they are often low in fats and proteins, and they have been suspected of causing bladder problems (see p. 253). If you feed your cat on dried food, you *must* make sure that fresh water is always available.

Soft-moist products

These pellets contain meat, soya beans, fats, vitamins, preservatives, colouring chemicals and, often, thickening agents and sugar. Though they are called "moist", some are positively wet — containing more than 33 percent water — and are therefore not very good value, especially as they tend to be expensive. Soft-moist foods can be used as a large part of a cat's diet as they usually contain just over 25 percent protein. However, they are low in fats. Packed in foil sachets, they can be stored, but not as long as the other types.

Fresh foods

If you feed mostly tinned food, you may like to give your cat a once- or twice-weekly meal of any of the fresh foods in the chart on p.159, as this will help to keep it healthy. If you do cook specially for your cat, season the food with iodized salt. This trace element is particularly important for pregnant queens, as it prevents re-absorption of the foetuses within the womb.

Meat

To avoid Toxoplasmosis (see p. 241), all meats should be cooked.

Because of the construction of their teeth, cats can't chew (see p.25), so you should either mince or chop the food finely, or serve it in large lumps so that your cat can tear it up. If you give your cat chicken make sure that you have removed all the bones, as it can easily choke on them.

Eating grass

Don't be alarmed if your pet insists on chewing grass or weeds. Grass is good for cats: it contains certain vitamins, and acts as an efficient emetic, helping the animal to regurgitate unwanted matter such as furballs. However, if your cat often grazes on your lawn, make sure that any fertilizer you use is non-toxic.

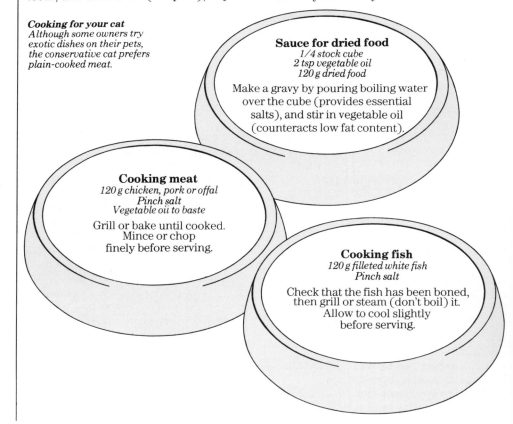

Cooking for your cat
Although some owners try exotic dishes on their pets, the conservative cat prefers plain-cooked meat.

Sauce for dried food
1/4 stock cube
2 tsp vegetable oil
120 g dried food
Make a gravy by pouring boiling water over the cube (provides essential salts), and stir in vegetable oil (counteracts low fat content).

Cooking meat
120 g chicken, pork or offal
Pinch salt
Vegetable oil to baste
Grill or bake until cooked. Mince or chop finely before serving.

Cooking fish
120 g filleted white fish
Pinch salt
Check that the fish has been boned, then grill or steam (don't boil) it. Allow to cool slightly before serving.

Liquids

Liquids are essential to feline health, although a cat can survive with a lower fluid intake than us in proportion to body size.

Water

Although this isn't strictly a food, it is a necessary part of a cat's diet. Meat diets should contain high levels of water as well as of protein. An animal on a rich protein diet will produce plenty of urea, and therefore will need a good volume of water to flush this waste product away via the kidneys. So do cats need a larger quantity of water for their size than we do? In fact, they need less, because they are able to produce a far higher concentration of urea in their urine than we can (almost three times as strong), and this helps them to conserve water. And cats lose very little water through panting or sweating, and an insignificant quantity evaporates during breathing. Even big cats like lions have been recorded as going without a drink for up to 10 days.

Diets that contain cooked fish, tripe and some tinned foods should give a creature the size of a cat much of the water that it needs. In addition, cats get a large proportion of their daily water requirements by chemical action. The fats and carbohydrates in their food are "burnt" within their bodies and produce water molecules.

As long as fresh, clean water is always available, don't worry about how little of the stuff your pet seems to be drinking, unless you have settled for the lazy owner's diet of nothing but dried food pellets – in which case, an adequate intake of water is important to prevent urinary problems (see p. 253). Some cats don't drink at all in their owner's presence, but probably tipple at a puddle, or, like mine, imbibe bath water.

Lapping
A cat transfers liquid into its mouth by collecting it in its long tongue, which it curls into a spoon shape for the purpose.

Milk

Milk is a source of liquid and food, but while water must always be available for a cat, milk is not essential for an adult cat. Its prime value is as a source of calcium and phosphorus – a 200 ml serving will provide an adult cat's daily needs. However, cow's milk gives some cats diarrhoea (see p. 238).

Alcohol

Unfortunately, some cats do fall victim to this human vice. Jack, a black tom from Brooklyn, was said to have given up drinking water at the tender age of three, preferring milk laced with Pernod. As he grew older, he demanded stiffer and stiffer saucers of "milk", until it was a question of lacing the Pernod lightly with milk. Jack died when he was eight years old, and a post-mortem found his liver in a sorry state. Do not give a cat alcohol, however small the quantity. Except when administered under veterinary advice as an antidote to anti-freeze poisoning, alcohol should never be given to cats.

Feeding methods

Cats are "fussy" eaters: they like to eat fresh food little and often, out of clean bowls, and in a place that is free from noise, strong light or bustle.

Where to feed your cat
You should serve your pet's meals somewhere out of the general flow of traffic in the house, for example in a corner of the kitchen. Ideally, the cat should have a regular feeding area where it can eat in peace, and where the floor is impervious and easy to clean. Put a tray, mat or newspaper underneath the bowls to catch spills. If possible, avoid feeding your cat outdoors as meals spoil more readily in the open air, and there is also a risk of attracting rodents.

Bad feeding habits
Cats should be discouraged from foraging for food in dustbins or other unhealthy sites.

FEEDING EQUIPMENT

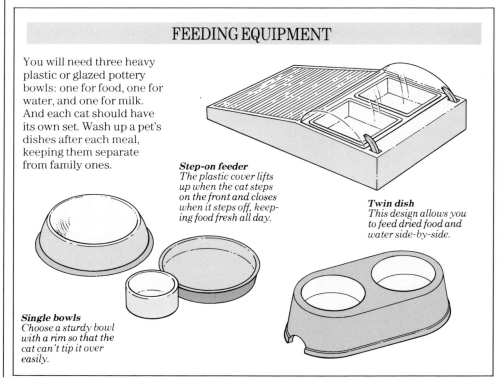

You will need three heavy plastic or glazed pottery bowls: one for food, one for water, and one for milk. And each cat should have its own set. Wash up a pet's dishes after each meal, keeping them separate from family ones.

Step-on feeder
The plastic cover lifts up when the cat steps on the front and closes when it steps off, keeping food fresh all day.

Twin dish
This design allows you to feed dried food and water side-by-side.

Single bowls
Choose a sturdy bowl with a rim so that the cat can't tip it over easily.

How much food should you provide?

Scientists have calculated that the daily requirement of a cat on a diet that contains 25 percent protein is 14 g of food per 450 g of body weight. The table below gives the total daily serving of food that a cat requires at different stages in its life. However, in practice, cats' appetites vary widely – so use it as a guideline only.

Obese cats don't generally have health problems. It may be necessary to watch the outlines of show cats, but the ordinary fireside pet doesn't need to slim.

How often should you feed a cat?

Use the table below to assess how many meals a day your cat should have. Because fresh food and water is a "must" for cats, the main rule for feeding a cat is to give small amounts frequently. This will avoid waste, as a cat will stalk away from any dish that seems stale.

Coping with loss of appetite

A cat that has lost its appetite isn't necessarily ill. It may have been upset by travelling, or be feeling the effects of hot, humid weather. And queens on heat sometimes forget about their food until they "cool down". Another reason for a cat rejecting food may be that it has spoilt, as meat or fish that is slightly "off" produces chemicals that a highly sensitive feline

DIET DON'TS

- Don't feed knacker's meat – it may be teeming with bacteria
- Don't feed poultry bones as these are small and splintery, and could choke a cat
- Don't give raw egg white – this contains avidin, which neutralizes biotin (an essential vitamin), making it unavailable to the cat
- Don't give a cat more than two eggs a week
- Don't boil fish – you will destroy the nutriments
- Don't feed dried food to a cat with bladder problems
- Don't give a cat proprietary dog food – the protein balance is not suitable for them

nose can detect immediately. If none of these explanations fits, consider whether your pet may be obtaining food elsewhere. Duplicitous gourmandizing is not uncommon, and can lead to a disinterest in the food you provide, particularly if all you have to offer is the same old food.

However, if your pet rejects fresh food for more than half a day, and you are certain that none of the explanations given apply, it may well be unwell (see p. 233). If your cat has refused food for more than 24 hours, take it to the vet.

Prescription diets

Cats with special needs or suffering from a wide range of ailments can, with veterinary advice, be fed on special proprietary liquid or canned diet foods. There are low protein diets for animals with weak kidneys, low calorie diets for the obese, pH control diets for urinary problems and many more.

PLANNING YOUR CAT'S MEALS

Age	Meals per day	Amount in grams
KITTENS		
Weaning – 3 months	4 – 6	80 – 190
4 – 5 months	4 – 5	275
6 – 7 months	3 – 4	370
7 – 8 months	3	370
ADULTS		
Over 9 months	2 – 3	400
Pregnant queens	3 – 5	420 – 60
Senior citizens	3 – 6	300 – 70

GROOMING

Cats have a reputation for cleanliness. In fact,
they often devote a good part of their day to grooming
themselves. If you watch your cat cleaning itself, you will
notice how it reaches almost every part of its fur with its
tongue, giving its coat a thorough washing.
But what is the importance of this fastidious grooming
routine? The most obvious reason for the cat's behaviour is
to keep its coat soft, glossy and clean. However, grooming has
other functions too — it removes dead hair and skin, and tones
up the muscles, as well as stimulating the blood circulation
(this is one of the reasons why a mother cat cleans her newly
born kittens so frequently). Although cats groom
themselves regularly, they require some additional
help from their owners, particularly
if they are longhaired.

The first steps in grooming

The best place to groom your cat, if the weather allows, is out of doors. An outdoor grooming session will keep dirt, hair and fleas out of the house and will also help people who are allergic to cats' fur and skin dust. If an outdoor session isn't possible, the next best location is a porch, bathroom or utility area. Indoors, it is a good idea to stand your pet on a sheet of paper or plastic whilst the session takes place.

Inspecting ears, eyes and claws

Before you begin brushing and combing your cat you should take the opportunity to check its ears, eyes and claws for cleanliness and any signs of potential health problems.

Care of the ears

If your cat is healthy, its ears won't need much attention. Examine the inside of the inner flap for dirt, and clean it out with a piece of cotton wool dipped in olive oil. If your cat scratches its ears persistently it may have an infection — look for dark, waxy marks inside the ears (see p. 250). If the ears seem to be clean, however, an infection is unlikely. An alternative explanation for persistent scratching may be that the ears are blocked by ear wax — try massaging

Self-grooming
At first, the queen cleans her kittens herself. This maternal licking also has the effect of stimulating the bodily functions of the newborn. However, after a few weeks, with mother's help, a kitten soon learns how to keep itself clean.

externally to loosen the blockage. If the cat continues to scratch, consult a vet.

Cleaning the face
Longhaired cats are prone to blockages in the tear ducts. When this occurs, tears run down the cat's cheeks, leaving unsightly dark marks on its face. To remove this discoloration, you should wipe the fur with cotton wool dipped in a mild salt solution. If the problem is recurrent, you will need to consult a vet.

Inspecting the mouth
Examine your cat's teeth for tartar. Ideally, you should clean its teeth once a week (see p. 234) to prevent a build-up. However, your pet may refuse this undignified treatment, in which case an annual trip to the vet for a "scale-and-polish" will be necessary.

CARE OF THE EYES

Dirt around a cat's eyes can be simply wiped away. Your cat's eyes should be bright and clear — if there is any inflammation or discharge the animal may have a serious health problem (see p. 244).

Cleaning the eyes
To clean a cat's eyes moisten a cotton wad in warm water and gently wipe the dirt away.

CARE OF THE CLAWS

A healthy, active cat's claws are trimmed automatically because they are worn down as it exercises. However, if your cat is old, or confined indoors, you should check its claws regularly as they may need trimming. Untrimmed claws may grow into the pad of the paw, and the cat will then need veterinary attention.

Trimming claws
If you need to cut a cat's claws, hold the animal firmly in your lap and press the pad of its paw with your fingers to make the claws come forward. Examine the claw carefully — the main part includes the pinkish-coloured quick which contains nerves. You must *not* cut this. The white tips are dead tissue, and cutting them won't hurt the cat.

Cleaning claws
Cat's claws don't often become caked with dirt, but if they do, you can clean them quite easily using damp cotton wool.

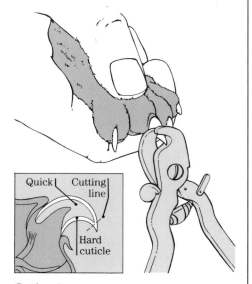

Quick | Cutting line

Hard cuticle

Cutting claws
Using very sharp scissors or special clippers, cut off the white tip. Make sure that you don't cut the quick.

Grooming a longhaired cat

In the wild, a longhaired cat would moult in the winter only, but because domestic cats are kept in artificially lit and heated conditions, they moult all year round. As a result, longhaired cats need daily grooming — two 15—30 minute sessions — otherwise their coats will mat. If the matted balls of fur aren't dealt with at an early stage they will become painful, and

you will have to get a vet to shave them off while the cat is anaesthetized. This isn't just painful for the cat — your pocket will be hurt too!

Before you start a grooming session take the opportunity to check your cat's ears, eyes, mouth and claws for cleanliness and signs of health problems (see p.169).

GROOMING METHOD

1 With a wide-toothed comb, remove debris and tease out mats. Once this comb runs through the hair easily, change to a fine-toothed type.

3 Brush some talcum powder or fuller's earth into the coat. This adds body and helps to separate the hairs. Brush out the powder immediately.

2 Using a wire brush, remove all dead hair. Pay particular attention to the rump, where you will probably be able to brush it out by the handful.

4 Run the fine-toothed comb through the hair in an upwards movement, brushing the fur out around the neck so that it forms a ruff.

GROOMING EQUIPMENT

You will need a wide and fine-toothed comb, a bristle and wire brush for the coat, and a toothbrush. You should also have blunt-ended scissors to cut mats, and bay rum conditioner (dark cats) or talc (light cats) to rub into the fur. And for a show cat use a slicker brush on the tail.

Slicker brush

Wire and bristle brush

Fine/wide-toothed comb

Toothbrush for cleaning face

5 With a toothbrush, gently brush the shorter hairs on the cat's face. Be careful not to get too close to its eyes.

6 Finally, repeat Step 4 with the wide-toothed comb, to separate the hair and help it to stand up. For show cats, use a slicker brush to fluff out the tail (see p. 182).

Grooming a shorthaired cat

A shorthaired cat doesn't need daily grooming as its coat is much easier to manage than that of a longhaired type. Moreover, shorthaired cats have longer tongues than their longhaired cousins, and so are efficient self-groomers. Two half-hour grooming sessions a week are therefore ample.

In fact, some people believe that if you groom a shorthaired cat more than twice a week it may stop grooming itself altogether. If you are an eager cat beautician and this news disappoints you, don't despair. There is a way in which you can indulge your love of grooming — you can spend some time every day conditioning the coat by stroking it along the lie of the hair.

GROOMING METHOD

1 With a fine-toothed metal comb, work down the cat from its head to its tail. As you comb, look for black, shiny specks — a sign of fleas (see p. 267).

3 With some shorthairs you may prefer to use a soft natural bristle brush, rather than the rubber type. Again, work along the lie of the hair.

2 Use a rubber brush to brush along the lie of the hair. If your cat is Rex-coated, this brush is essential as it won't scratch the skin.

4 After brushing and combing, rub in some bay rum conditioner. This removes grease from the coat and brings out the brilliance of its colour.

GROOMING EQUIPMENT

You will need a fine-toothed metal comb, and a soft natural bristle or rubber brush. You should also have some bay rum conditioner to rub into the fur (suits all coat colours), and a velvet, silk or chamois leather cloth to polish the coat.

Fine-toothed comb

Soft natural bristle brush

Rubber brush

Chamois cloth

5 Finally, to bring up the glossy quality of a shorthaired cat's coat, especially just before a show, "polish" it with a piece of silk or velvet or a chamois leather cloth. Between grooming sessions you can keep up the shine by gently stroking the cat with a clean hand along the lie of the hair.

Problems with a cat's coat

As well as posing a cleaning problem, ungroomed or soiled fur can lead to matting. Longhaired cats are particularly susceptible to mats, and therefore they need more regular attention.

Cleaning dirty fur

Cats don't usually need washing, as generally they clean themselves, but if your cat's coat is very dirty or greasy, you will need to clean it. And light-coloured show cats may need a bath a few days before being exhibited.

Wet method

Unless your cat is of the Turkish swimming variety, its first encounter with bath water will undoubtedly turn it into a sourpuss. You should give it plenty of love and attention, so that the bathing session doesn't turn into a wrestling match. The usual method is shown opposite.

Dry method

If your cat objects violently to water, you can give it a bran bath as an alternative. This "dry shampoo" should only be used on shorthaired cats, and is effective as long as the cat isn't too dirty. Start by heating $\frac{1}{2}$–1 kg of bran in an oven set to 150° C for 20 minutes. Then stand your cat on a newspaper and massage the warm bran into its coat. When you have covered all the fur with the bran, then comb it out.

Coping with matted fur

Ungroomed hair or hair that is contaminated with faeces will become matted, and form dense balls of unkempt, dirty fur. These masses form the perfect environment for parasites, and encourage the development of inflammatory skin diseases (see p. 266). A matted fur mass isn't easy to remove; pulling at the mat with a comb only hurts the animal, and may damage the skin. You should never try to cut matted fur off as you may cut through adjacent skin. Cats in this condition require a vet's care — he or she will sedate the cat, then shave off the matted lumps.

The effects of swallowed fur

The other major problem connected with grooming is ingested accumulations of loose hair, known as "furballs", within a cat's stomach or intestines. There are two causes for this — lack of grooming by the owner, or over-enthusiastic self-grooming by the cat. The natural mucus of the alimentary canal "glues" the hairs together, and they build up into sausage-like masses which upset the cat's digestive functions by obstructing its bowel (see p. 238).

Many cats will regurgitate these dark masses of fur automatically, but others aren't so fortunate. Episodes of furball trouble occur regularly in some long-haired cats, and while daily grooming may control the problem, a fastidious cat may still ingest enough hair to make furballs. If your cat is such an animal, you can help by giving it liquid paraffin oil, either directly or mixed in with its food or drink. This will soften the furball mass, so that it can be passed through the bowel and out with the stools. I would suggest a dose of one tsp of the oil once a day for three days every three to four weeks. Don't give your cat liquid paraffin every day as continual dosing will cut down its absorption of the essential vitamins.

BATHING A CAT

The kitchen sink will probably make the best "bath". Before you start, make sure that all the doors and windows are closed, and that the room is free from cold draughts. Place a rubber mat in the sink to stop the cat slipping.

If you think that your cat is going to struggle, put it in a cotton sack, leaving only its head visible. Pour the shampoo into the sack and lower the cat and sack into the water. You can then massage the cat through the sack and form a lather.

A shower attachment is the best way to wet a cat

A sponge will help to work the water into the fur

A warm, dry towel should be to hand

A rubber mat will prevent the cat slipping

Hold the cat firmly but gently

1 Fill the sink with about 5—10 cms of warm water. The water temperature should be as close to your cat's blood heat of 38.6°C as possible. To lift the cat in put one hand under its hind quarters, and hold the scruff of its neck with the other. If your cat prefers, allow it to rest its front paws out of the water.

2 Using a sponge, wet the cat's fur all over, except for its face. Next, rub a non-toxic cat or baby shampoo into the coat to produce a lather. Once the fur is full of soapy lather, rinse it thoroughly with warm water until there is no trace of soap in the rinse water. You will find that a spray attachment is the most efficient tool for this.

3 Lift the cat out of the sink and wrap it in a large, warm towel. Now you can wash its face with cotton wool dipped in warm water. Until the cat is totally dry you must keep it in a warm place. If it isn't afraid of hairdryers, you can use one on a low setting, taking care not to singe the coat. Once the fur is dry, comb it gently.

9

SHOWING

Introducing your cat to "show business" requires a
great deal of time and effort, so you must decide whether
the pleasure you will gain is worth the investment.
If you think it might be, start by going along to a local
cat show for the day as a spectator. Like most exhibitors,
you will probably end up simply showing your pet as a
hobby. However, for some people breeding and showing
pedigree cats is a full-time business, and there is
always the chance that your interest will flower
to such an extent that you become one
of these "professional" stage parents.

What is a cat show?

The cat show has only been established for just over a century, although there are records of one held as long ago as 1598 — at a fair in England. However, the practice of exhibiting cats really began in 1871, with a large show held at the Crystal Palace in London for British Shorthair and Persian types. At around the same time, the first American cat show was held in New England for the Maine Coon breed.

In Britain the way shows are run is still similar to the early days, with judges going to the pens. Later, one or two shows had a ring class where cats were led around a ring by their owners for judging. This often resulted in chaos, with fights breaking out and potential champions receiving battle scars which ruined their show career! At the very early shows, cats ran a very high risk of catching fatal infections. Fortunately today, vaccinations (see pp. 238 and 229) will guard against this danger.

Judging at an early show
At this show held at the turn of the century, the judges are seen visiting the cats in their pens.

Judging in the ring
Some early shows, such as this one held in London, featured multiple judging in the ring.

Pedigree organizations

Each country has a controlling authority for all the cat clubs and societies. In Britain, this is the Governing Council of the Cat Fancy (G.C.C.F.). In the U.S., the largest body is the Cat Fanciers' Association (C.F.A.). Their most important duties are laying down formally approved standards for all breeds, providing for the registration of pedigrees and transfers of ownership, and approving show dates.

When you apply for a show, you will be sent a schedule giving details of the show rules and classes, together with an entry form. Show rules are laid down to ensure fairness and to protect the interest of the cats. For example, no cat or kitten may be shown in Britain unless it has been inoculated against the killer disease, Feline Infectious Enteritis (see p. 238). Also, after showing a cat you must wait at least a fortnight before exhibiting it again. Another rule prohibits the use of any colouring matter which could alter a cat's appearance — punk Persians and bottle-blonde Burmese are taboo!

Types of show

In Britain there are three types of show: Championship, Sanction and Exemption.

Championship

This is a major showing event and attracts the *crème de la crème*. Probably the largest championship in the world is the National Cat Club Show, held in London, which has over 2,000 entries.

Challenge certificates are awarded to Open-Class winners if of a high quality. A cat with three certificates is eligible for the Champion of Champions Class. A three-time winner of this class becomes a Grand Champion. (Neutered cats become Premiers and Grand Premiers.)

Sanction

These shows follow the same rules as Championship shows, but Challenge Certificates aren't awarded.

Exemption

At Exemption shows regulations aren't applied so stringently. Such shows are the ideal starting point for beginners.

HOW IS A SHOW ORGANIZED?

There are usually four entry categories: the Open, Side and Club classes, plus Household Pet classes.

Open class

This is the most important class, and is open to all pedigree-registered cats, neuters and kittens. If your cat is eligible it must be entered in an open class.

Side class

Exhibits usually have to be entered in at least four classes, and these can include the various side classes. For example, if your cat has never won at a show before, one of its entries could be for the "Maiden" class.

Club class

Sponsored by particular cat clubs, these classes are open to members only.

Household Pet class

This class is solely for neuters of unknown or unregistered parentage.

Making an entry

Write to the show's organizers, preferably at least 16 weeks before the show. You will receive a schedule containing all the information you need.

When deciding which classes to enter, it is a good idea to get advice from a more experienced cat-club member. Read the entry form carefully, because if it is incorrectly filled-in, your cat can be disqualified, and send it off as soon as possible.

What makes a good show cat?

If you want to take part in a show, you must decide whether your cat is a suitable competitor. Don't be discouraged if it isn't a pedigree (see p. 45) — cats of unknown or unregistered parentage qualify for the "Household Pet class" held at most shows. If it is pretty or full of character, it may win a prize.

Obtaining a show quality cat
If your cat isn't suitable for showing, then consider purchasing a pedigree cat (see p. 114). A good-quality adult cat will be prohibitively expensive — if available at all — and therefore you will probably

A prize-winning non-pedigree cat
Your pet may lack the right forebears, but if it is as attractive as this cat, it can win rosettes.

HOW A SHOW CAT IS JUDGED

Pedigree cats are judged against a scale of points for their particular breed. The maximum number of points is 100, with marks deducted for features that don't match the breed standard. These two cats are "perfect" show animals.

Points awarded to a champion Blue Longhair

Head — type and shape: 25 points
The shape of this specimen's broad head shows all the requisite features including full cheeks and a short nose.

For a full description of the breed standards, see p. 54.

Eyes — colour and shape: 20 points
Cats with green-rimmed eyes are heavily penalized. This cat, however, has ideal ones: large, round and copper-coloured.

Condition: 10 points An ideal specimen, this sturdy cat is neither too thin nor too fat, and has bright eyes and an alert look. Its fur stands well away from the body, and isn't lank and clinging.

Coat: 20 points This conforms to the standard texture, and the frill is particularly fine. It has gained full marks because it is pale blue in colour and without markings.

Body: 15 points
Maximum points are awarded for a sturdy looking body of the cobby type.

Tail: 10 points Blue Longhairs mustn't have a kink in the tail. This one is quite straight, and beautifully groomed into a bushy brush.

choose a kitten. Once you have obtained a pedigree kitten for showing you *must* check that it is registered with the governing body, and be sure to complete and post the transfer form showing change of ownership.

Breeding for a cat show

The best way to start breeding cats for shows is with one or two female kittens. Don't buy an entire male (stud). If the breed you choose is rare, bear in mind the impracticalities and expense of finding a suitable stud. If at all possible, discuss your plans with an experienced cat breeder.

You should wait until your chosen kitten is a year old before you start the breeding programme (see p. 203), but you can start looking for a suitable stud straight away. Your local cat club will probably be able to recommend some professional cat breeders with studs.

Choosing a stud
To produce a litter of kittens with excellent showing potential, you should try to improve on the queen. Compare the pedigrees of various studs and select the one that is most suited to that of your queen. A good tip is to study his kittens at shows. Choose a champion with features that compensate for any weaknesses in your queen. For example, if her ears are too large for her type, choose a stud which has ears of the correct size.

Points awarded to a champion Siamese

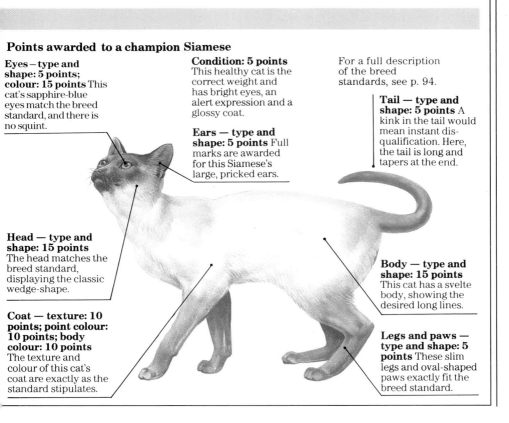

Eyes – type and shape: 5 points; colour: 15 points This cat's sapphire-blue eyes match the breed standard, and there is no squint.

Condition: 5 points This healthy cat is the correct weight and has bright eyes, an alert expression and a glossy coat.

Ears — type and shape: 5 points Full marks are awarded for this Siamese's large, pricked ears.

For a full description of the breed standards, see p. 94.

Tail — type and shape: 5 points A kink in the tail would mean instant disqualification. Here, the tail is long and tapers at the end.

Head — type and shape: 15 points The head matches the breed standard, displaying the classic wedge-shape.

Coat — texture: 10 points; point colour: 10 points; body colour: 10 points The texture and colour of this cat's coat are exactly as the standard stipulates.

Body — type and shape: 15 points This cat has a svelte body, showing the desired long lines.

Legs and paws — type and shape: 5 points These slim legs and oval-shaped paws exactly fit the breed standard.

Preparing for a cat show

The following guidelines will help you prepare your cat for the show:

● Inoculate your cat well in advance of the show, and check for any signs of illness.

● Accustom your cat to being penned. Begin by putting it in a pen for a few minutes a day, and gradually extend the time. Cats unused to being restrained may turn aggressive, and an animal that bites an official on three occasions will probably be disqualified from showing.

● Make sure your cat is used to car travel. If it suffers from car sickness, the symptoms may be such that it fails the vetting-in.

● Groom your cat daily, and pay special attention to its diet. But be realistic — crash dieting won't turn an overweight cat into a perfectly conditioned one.

Grooming a longhair for showing

The coat of a longhaired show cat should appear massive, with the fur standing well away from its body, particularly around its head. For the correct brushing method see pp. 170—1.

Don't use grooming powder if the show is less than two days away as traces of powder in the coat will be penalized. If your cat's coat is white or has a lot of white patches in it, you can brush in a chalk-based powder or even babies' talcum powder to enhance the whiteness. Again, make sure you brush it all out. However, if your cat's coat is black, tortie or any other dark colour combination, don't use white powder as it is difficult to remove and deadens the colours. If you feel it necessary, use fullers' earth then bay rum conditioner.

Grooming a shorthair for showing

Shorthaired coats should be groomed in the usual way (see pp. 172—3). As grooming powder will tone down dark and contrasting colours, use bay rum conditioner instead. To achieve the final "gloss", polish the cat with velvet or chamois leather.

General inspection

Eyes Remove any staining (see p. 169).
Ears Clean them carefully and thoroughly (see p. 168).
Mouth The teeth must be clean and white. To prevent a build up of tartar, give your cat a chunk of solid meat once a fortnight and clean its teeth regularly (see p. 234).
Claws If necessary, trim them (see p. 169), but *never* consider declawing your cat — declawed exhibits are disqualified.

Grooming a longhair's tail
Brush the tail with a slicker brush (see p. 171) so that it is full and bushy.

Show day

Before you set off in the morning, check that you have everything you need:
- White litter tray
- Newspaper and litter for tray
- White show blanket
- White feeding dish
- White water bowl
- Bottle for carrying water
- Tally (the small white disc showing your cat's show entry number)
- White ribbon or elastic for attaching the tally to cat's neck
- Travelling container
- Old blanket for travelling
- Cat food
- Disinfectant and cloth
- Brushes and combs
- Schedule of classes entered
- Entrance ticket and pass-out card
- Vetting-in card
- Current F.I.E. certificate

Feeding

If you are showing a kitten, you will need to feed it before you leave. Otherwise, it is best to wait until after the show. If you do decide to feed your cat beforehand, give it lean, raw meat and not milky foods.

Vetting-in

The first thing that happens at the show is vetting-in. You may have to show your F.I.E. certificate (see p. 238), so have it ready. The vet will give each cat a thorough health check, and if for some reason, such as fleas, runny eyes or sore gums, the cat fails the examination, you will have to take it home and forfeit your entry fee.

Penning

After vetting-in, you can take your cat to its pen — a metal cage displaying the

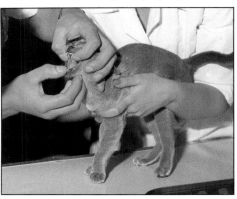

Mouth inspection
As part of the vetting-in procedure, the vet will check each cat's mouth for any signs of sickness, such as bleeding or red gums.

Vetting-in
To prevent the spread of disease and infection, all the cats at a show are inspected by a fully qualified vet. Although your cat may not enjoy the vetting-in, it will soon become accustomed to it, and the vet's assistant will stop it from struggling too much.

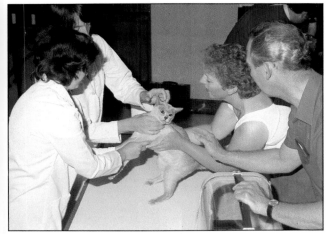

same number as that on the cat's tally. Although the show organizers will have checked that the cages are clean, it is safest to wipe down the bars with some non-toxic disinfectant.

Arrange the clean white blanket, litter tray and filled water bowl in the pen. In the United Kingdom, these are the only items allowed in with the cat. The reason for this is to make sure that the judges aren't influenced by the surroundings and that the cats are judged on their merit alone. In America, however, judging takes place away from the pens so you can decorate your cat's cage.

Final touches

1 Check that the tally is securely tied around your cat's neck.

2 Give your cat a final grooming — if it is shorthaired, rub it over with a velvet cloth to make its coat shine; if longhaired, give the hair a final upward brushing, concentrating on the ruff. Powder isn't allowed at this stage.

3 Check the corners of its eyes for dirt, and gently wipe them clean with a fine linen cloth.

4 If you have fed the cat in the pen, remove the bowl, and change the litter in the tray.

5 Place the cat basket under the bench with the name tag hidden.

6 You may be asked to leave the hall whilst the judging takes place.

Judging

Well in advance of the judging, the steward will arrange the judge's mobile table, checking that it has a filled disinfectant spray bottle and paper towels. He or she will also check that all the cats are in the right pens.

When judging commences, the steward will take the first cat out of its pen, place it on the table and allow the judge to make his or her assessment. Between cats, the table is disinfected.

For each pedigree breed there is a standard of points against which the cat will be assessed (see pp. 180−1). In the case of a household pet, where there is no scale of points, the cat will be judged on condition, grooming, colouring, attractive features, and temperament when handled.

After examining each cat, the judge will write his or her comments in a judging book. A judging slip is then placed on the award board. If a slip is marked with "CC", the cat has been awarded a challenge certificate. When all the entries have been assessed, each judge will nominate a best cat, neuter and kitten from the exhibits he or she has judged. Then awards like "Best Cat", "Best Neuter", "Best Kitten", "Best Exhibit" and "Best in Show" are decided.

A winning cat will have an award card placed on its cage. Prizes may be small amounts of money or rosettes.

Judging
A steward is holding this cat as the judge assesses it. She will then record the marks awarded in the judging book.

The judging hall
At the National Cat Club Show in London (left), owners can watch the judging from the balconies, and wander along the rows of pens.

Public judging
In America, each cat is taken from its pen in turn, and brought to the judging table. It is then examined and assessed in full view .

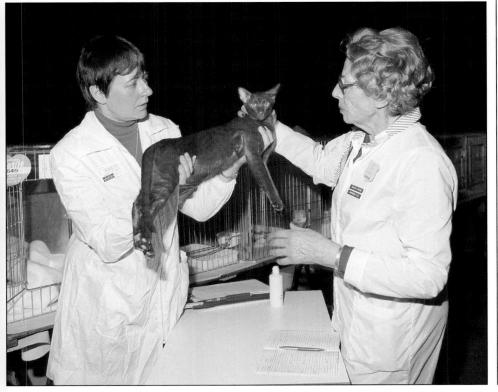

10

UNDERSTANDING YOUR CAT

Comprehending the attitudes and motivations of members of one's own species, even when you share a common language, isn't always easy. How much more difficult, then, is it to understand another species. Without a shared language and with no possibility of experiencing the world at first hand from a cat's point of view, there is a risk that you will interpret your pet's behaviour anthropomorphically — regarding it as a little human with whiskers and claws. But this would be a great mistake. Your cat is a fundamentally different animal to you, with its own set of motivations, attitudes and social behaviour.

Intelligence and awareness

The cat is a highly intelligent animal, with an acute awareness of the world about it. It can work out answers to problems, apply them, and then adapt solutions to different situations.

How clever is my cat?

The yardstick most commonly used to measure intelligence in animals is to compare brain weight with the length of the spinal cord. This shows how much grey matter controls how much body. The cat has a ratio of 4:1, compared to a monkey's 18:1 and our 50:1.

Can a cat learn?

Feline hunting actions aren't instinctive; they are learned from other cats. So kittens that are born to non-hunting mothers, or lack litter-mates, don't learn to hunt. Other habits, such as using a litter tray, may also be learned from the mother's example.

Cats can be trained to perform tricks, but unlike dogs, they don't take kindly to coercion by punishment or reward, only co-operating if they want to.

The cat's memory

A cat uses its learning ability and memory for useful "operations", generally for its own gain, such as:
● opening a door by jumping for the latch
● summoning humans by imperiously rattling objects, tapping on doors or launching itself at a door knocker or bell
● drinking water from a running tap
● scooping milk from a jug or dry food from a packet with its paw
● finding its way home (see p. 148)
● responding to its name by returning home when called (even if it forgets its name for most of the day, recall is usually 100 percent at mealtimes!).

What goals do cats have?

Cats don't subscribe to the work ethic. They will toil to attain an end (for example, to acquire food), but they won't work for work's sake in the manner of a hamster on a treadmill.

Do cats have a sixth sense?

As cats are, above all, creatures of the senses, they sometimes appear to be endowed with supernatural powers, sensing things that we are unconscious of. Their faculties of sight, hearing and detection of vibrations are far more developed than our own. I believe that all the cat's ultra-tuned reactions can be explained by its known senses — when a cat raises its hackles in alarm in an apparently quiet house it is reacting to sounds or vibrations we can't detect, and when a cat clears out of a dwelling just before a volcanic eruption it has picked up minute pre-tremors or changes in air pressure. As hunters, cats need and live by five super-efficient senses.

Curiosity and determination
A combination of curiosity and hunger has aroused

Feline dexterity
Through careful study of human behaviour, a clever cat can learn to open doors. If the handle is too high or requires a two-handed turn, it may pounce on it and make a dramatic flying entry.

Feline ingenuity
This cat has discovered that climbing onto the table and making a sly scoop into a container with its paw will get it forbidden fruits — or, in this case, cream.

this cat's adventurous spirit. Following its nose, it tests out the opening. Then in order to overcome the

limitations of its four-legged stature, the cat uses its body weight as a lever to swing open the door.

Hunting prey

Like its wild relatives, the domestic cat is built as a natural predator. However, this doesn't mean that it will hunt instinctively; its hunting urge is induced by competition and demonstration, and hunting skills are learned by observation, trial and error. For example, cats are particularly inefficient at catching birds unless they acquire the knack through practice, and offspring of a non-hunting mother are unlikely to hunt well.

Why do domestic cats hunt?

Unlike their wild "cousins", domestic cats don't often hunt to satisfy hunger, although they may on occasion eat part or all of their prey. Basically, they are in it for the fun of the game, rather like those humans in pink coats who hunt fox, but rarely tuck into fox pie after making a kill.

CATCHING METHOD

What sort of prey do cats hunt?

Cats will swipe at anything that moves, but the chase proper is generally confined to rodents such as mice and small birds. Pets like hamsters also come into this category, so if one of these forms part of your menagerie along with a cat, make sure that its cage is secure.

Returning with the spoils

When your cat carries the dead mouse, rabbit or bird proudly back home and presents it to you, it is doing what any hunter would do — bringing a token of success in the field to someone it regards as family. Wild cats will do this as a social gesture, and when your domestic cat brings you such a prized gift you should take it in the same vein.

What makes a good mouser?

Some cats excel at catching mice, others aren't interested in the sport. Mousing is an atavistic ritual, and some cats have a better developed "race memory" than

Stalking
As soon as the cat has located a suitable victim, it begins to approach it slowly and cautiously, using all available cover. Next, the cat travels forward rapidly in a movement known as a "slink run", with its belly pressed close to the ground.

Pausing
The slink run is interrupted by pauses, during which the cat intently observes its prey. The sequence of slink run and pause will be repeated several times until the cat reaches the nearest piece of cover to the target.

The "ambush"
When close enough, and crouched behind cover, the cat prepares for the final phase of its offensive. Its hind feet begin to make treading motions, its eyes follow the prey's movements, and its tail tip twitches in anticipation.

What should you do with proffered prey?
If your cat arrives at the door with a present of a dead mouse, accept it gratefully, but try to dispose of the gift promptly and discreetly as wild prey will often harbour disease and parasites.

the enemy's arrival. This is a good idea, but don't be disappointed if it doesn't work — I know of cats who manage to return home with catches despite being fitted with a bell. If you have a bird-feeding device in your garden make sure that it is sited in the open so that your cat can't slink up on the birds unnoticed.

Dealing with an injured bird
If you rescue a captured bird from your cat and find that it is still alive place it in a closed, ventilated box lined with soft material and seek guidance from a vet or an animal welfare organization. Unfortunately, many birds escape the cat's clutches only to succumb to death from shock or internal injuries.

others. You won't be able to change a non-mouser into an efficient rodent operative by starving it, as the mousing instinct isn't tied to hunger. Castrated toms make just as good mousers as uncastrated ones.

Catching birds
Many owners disapprove of their pet's attacks on wild birds, and fit a bell to its collar to warn visitors to the bird table of

Catching and eating flies
It is often said that cats that catch and eat flies become ill and thin. It is certainly true that if your cat eats a bluebottle there is a small risk of it ingesting disease bacteria, and there is a chance that worm eggs might be carried from one cat to another by a fly. But the risk is so low that it isn't worth worrying about.

The attack
The cat leaves its cover and shoots forward quickly, its body pressed to the ground. When within striking distance, it raises its foreparts and leaps on the prey.

Pinning down the prey
With its hind feet firmly planted on the ground, the cat uses its forepaws to pin down the prey, forcing it into a position where the death bite can be made.

The kill
If the victim struggles, the cat may release it and then repeat the final attack to get a better grip. Or it will maintain its grip, and throw itself onto its side, so that it can use its hind feet to rake the victim. Then it adminsters the death bite with its powerful jaws.

The cat's social behaviour

Cats communicate in a variety of ways:
● Vocalization — from contented purrs to angry screeches to plaintive mews
● Body signals — facial expressions, body postures and tail positions additionally emphasized by coat markings
● Touch — rubbing noses, grooming others
● Scent — tagging territory (see p. 196) or identifying individuals (see p. 193).

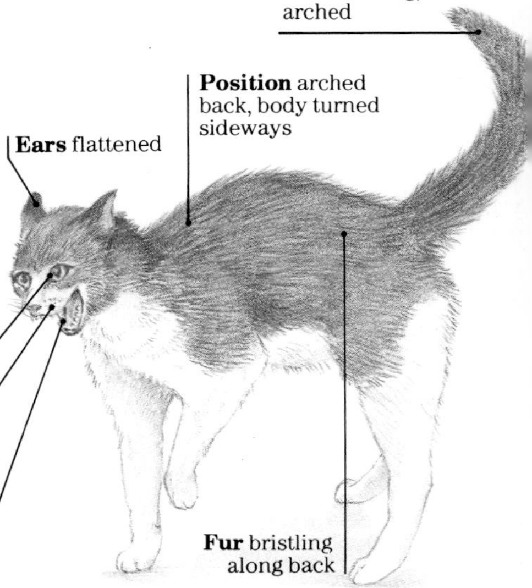

Tail bristling, arched

Position arched back, body turned sideways

Ears flattened

A defensive cat
When faced with a display of aggressive behaviour from another animal, a cat's first reaction is to stand its ground.

Pupils enlarged

Whiskers bristling

Mouth open, teeth on show. Makes hissing, spitting sounds

Fur bristling along back

An aggressive cat
A dominant cat will use body language to encourage its opponent to turn tail.

Position poised to strike

Ears pricked, furled back

Pupils closed to a slit

Whiskers bristle forwards

Mouth wide open, with lips curled back to emphasize snarl. Makes growling, hissing and spitting sounds

Fur smooth

Tail low and close, bristling, swishing to and fro

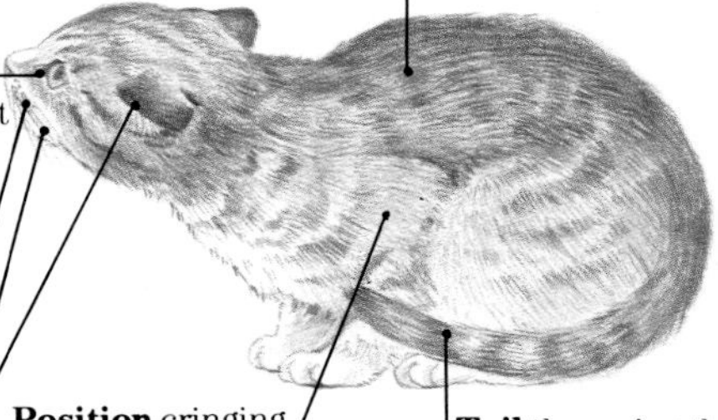

Fur flattened

Pupils enlarged

Mouth may open but not emit sound or half open for distress call

Whiskers flattened

Ears flattened

A submissive cat
When a cat is faced with an aggressor it is no match for, it will communicate its submission by its posture.

Position cringing

Tail thumping the ground

How are other cats identified?

The cat's equivalent of exchanging names and handshakes involves sniffing the other cat's head or beneath its tail. These areas are where scent glands are concentrated, and therefore they convey a wealth of personal information.

Social order

Cats are very social animals, and even if your pet is the only feline in your house, if it isn't confined it will be part of a community of cats in the neighbourhood, street, or apartment block. This cat community organizes itself into an "association" with a built-in hierarchy, rituals and rules that are laid down in a very precise way. All cats in the association know one another, and are allotted positions in the hierarchy. Imported strangers who aren't in the club have to fight to be accepted and allotted a place in the community.

The position of female cats

In a cat community, females are organized along matriarchal lines — the unneutered queen with the most kittens is at the top of the pecking order. When a queen is neutered, her social descent is very rapid.

The position of male cats

The hierarchical arrangement for male members of a cat community is along the usual lines for social male animals — by trial of strength. The roughest, toughest tom becomes the "top cat" in the area, with subordinates of varying ranks and levels of authority. It is rather like the Mafia: the "Godfather" at the top, with consiglieres, chiefs and button-men below, in a pyramid of power based on "respect". The organization is rigid, with occasional changes in position occurring when one member weakens and is overthrown in combat by an ambitious junior. Once in a while, a very tough outsider will arrive and break into the existing local hierarchy by sheer muscle power.

Unlike the set-up in the macho-hierarchical systems of animals such as monkeys or deer, dominant toms don't possess large harems of queens. In fact, they aren't necessarily granted priority in the courtship stakes as of right. Curiously, queens will sometimes select males well down the power pyramid as mates. However, top tom cats do rule the biggest area of territory. It seems therefore that land rather than sex is the marker of social status in feline society.

Unneutered toms have no place in this mafia "family". An entire tom with a social position gradually loses it after being castrated. After the operation the masculine odour of his urine will become weaker, paralleling the fall in testosterone circulating in his blood, and as this happens he will gradually descend the social ladder rung by rung until he reaches the bottom.

What does a single cat's territory consist of?

All cats are territorial by nature, including those confined indoors. With the latter, their territorial zone may be part of a room or a favourite armchair. Where several cats live in a household, indoor territorial claims gradually blur, until all the cats jointly "possess" the house and mutually defend it against feline outsiders.

Outdoors each cat, whatever its position in the local hierarchy, possesses some territory. Females and neuters hold onto fairly small patches, and fight harder than a big tom with a large area to retain what little they have. A large "landowner" may just have too much property to protect, and won't be able to fight 24 hours a day to drive off each and every intruder. But when he does decide to fight, he generally wins.

TERRITORIAL AREAS

Territory is very important to cats, and they
stake their claim by marking (see p. 196),
and defend their area vigorously. Toms
control more land than neuter or female cats
(queens) do.

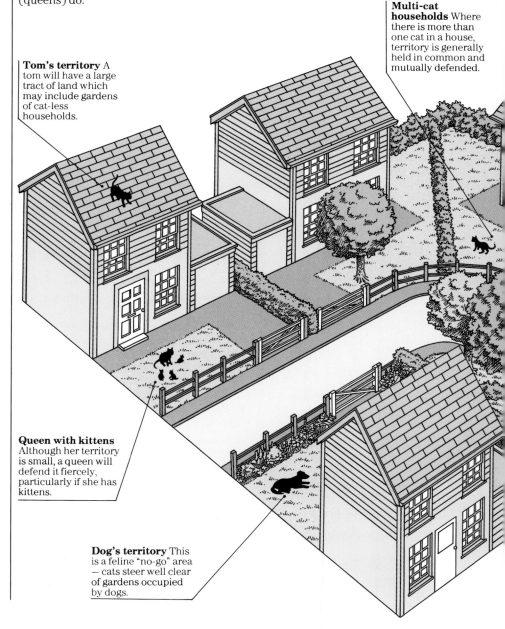

**Multi-cat
households** Where
there is more than
one cat in a house,
territory is generally
held in common and
mutually defended.

Tom's territory A
tom will have a large
tract of land which
may include gardens
of cat-less
households.

Queen with kittens
Although her territory
is small, a queen will
defend it fiercely,
particularly if she has
kittens.

Dog's territory This
is a feline "no-go" area
— cats steer well clear
of gardens occupied
by dogs.

How big is a cat's territory?

A cat's private outdoor territory may be as small as a city backyard, but it can also be very large — a dominant tom in an area with a low cat population may control 50 or so acres. Within its property a cat has favourite places for sleeping, observing, and catching the sun. The

Surveying territory
Cats often use areas like fences, gateposts and shed rooves as vantage points from which to keep an eye on their property.

extent of territory that a cat possesses can, to some degree, be influenced by humans. A newly arrived cat's owner can assist it in staking its claim by discouraging other cats or breaking up fights.

How are communal areas separated from the private territories?

Beyond the private territories lie commonly held hunting and meeting grounds. To reach these places cats have a well-worked out network of pathways which skirt other cat's private territories and non-cat areas (a garden occupied by a dog, for example). Some pathways are private to a particular cat, but the majority — the "main roads" — are communal. And like all main roads a "highway code" operates to avoid accidents and conflict. For example, any cat moving along a main pathway has an automatic and undisputed right-of-way over any other cat, whatever its social standing, approaching on an intersecting side path.

Common walkways
Where cat territories meet, the cats usually decide to use common walkways at different times to avoid conflict.

Meeting grounds In a street or block there is usually a communal area where all the local cats meet.

What happens at the meeting grounds?

In cat society, meeting grounds are important centres of feline social intercourse. Males and females congregrate from time to time in these communal places, sitting peacefully in groups 1—6 m from each other. Although the gatherings may sometimes be associated with the mating of a queen in season, most meetings aren't sexual in nature. What goes on we simply don't know, but these assemblies certainly aren't aimless. I like to think that there is some sort of communication between the club members, and that the meetings are an important part of feline social life.

Anti-social behaviour

A cat that is left alone indoors all day, deprived of feline or human companion-ship, may become lonely or bored and react by behaving badly — chewing the carpets, urinating in forbidden spots or biting at its fur. In such a case, consult the vet for advice on remedying the problem.

IDENTIFYING CAT TERRITORIES

Identification of territory is carried out in two main ways: spraying with urine to make "boundary posts" and scratching visual signals on trees or fences with the claws.

Scratching
As well as leaving a visible mark, this practice marks the tree with scent from sweat glands on the paw pads.

Spraying
A boundary marked by feline urine will be very noticeable, particularly if the cat is a tom.

Rubbing
Scent from the sebaceous glands is deposited by rubbing the head and face against an object.

Sleep

Whether wild or domestic, cats spend a surprisingly high proportion of their time asleep. Their specialized anatomical and physiological design indicates that their "machinery" is expected to be used in short bursts. In a hunter, high performance over short periods of time and distance are called for, not stamina and endurance. Consequently, cats take great delight in rest and relaxation. Their love of comfort — the warm spot on the windowsill or the favourite cushion — are important features of the feline lifestyle. After all, a cat sleeps on average 16 hours a day, albeit taken in short chunks of several minutes at a time (the ubiquitous "cat nap"). Why cats are the greatest sleepers amongst mammals isn't understood.

Cat nap sites
Your pet may choose a sleeping spot that seems strange to you, but the cat's main considerations when choosing a nap area are warmth and safety from attack. This dustbin lid fulfills both criteria admirably.

What happens when a cat sleeps?

Awake or asleep, cats are constantly receiving and programming information from environmental stimuli. In scientific experiments, cats have been placed in a totally stimulus-free environment and electro-encephalogram readings of their brain activity recorded. The effect of this deprivation of stimuli is that the feline brain gradually shuts down to a basic body-maintenance level. There is no evidence of spontaneous thought or the generation of ideas — a cat won't while away the hours composing poetry or recalling favourite incidents from its past, unlike a human placed under similar conditions.

Sleeping cats' brains have also been studied with electro-encephalographs, and phases of deep and light sleep distinguished: 30 percent is deep, 70 percent light. The phases alternate, and during deep sleep there is evidence that the cat dreams. You may see external signs of this: □ movement of the paws and claws □ twitching of the whiskers □ flicking of the ears □ in some cases, vocalization.

Curiously, in the deep-sleep levels a cat's brain is as active as when it is awake, and it is still constantly on the alert for incoming danger signals via its sensory apparatus. So don't try pulling a sleeping cat's tail in the mistaken belief that you can get away with it — the "rousing time" is instantaneous.

Sleeping places

Cats like warm spots to sleep — by the fire, on a sunny windowsill or on a central-heating boiler. Attracted by body heat, they may curl up alongside a baby, but this habit *must* be discouraged as there is a danger that the cat might unwittingly suffocate the child.

11

BREEDING

Whether you are about to make your debut into the pedigree
cat-breeding fraternity or are simply interested in
how to prevent your promiscuous queen from producing
unwanted kittens, you will need to understand
the basic principles and practice of feline reproduction
outlined in this chapter.
There are two diametrically opposed
attitudes to the merits of breeding cats, whether
wild or domestic. On the one hand, people are striving
to produce more pedigree domestic and rare wild felines
such as the Clouded Leopard; on the other,
neutering or contraception is urged for non-pedigree pet cats
and safari park lions. When it comes to your own animal the
decision to breed or not to breed is up to you,
but you should make sure that you can find good homes
for all the kittens before you proceed.

Heredity

The way in which animals inherit particular features from their parents has only been understood this century, when the work of Gregor Mendel (carried out in the nineteeth century) came to light. His research into the inheritance of characteristics began the study of genetics, which is the basis of the scientific breeding programmes for pedigree animals.

What are the "ingredients" of a cat?

All living things, including cats, are constructed of cells. Each cell is a minute package of a complex material called cytoplasm, in the middle of which lies a control centre known as the nucleus. The nucleus contains a certain number of chromosomes, depending on the animal. For example, the domestic cat has 38, arranged in pairs of 19, whereas humans have 46 in 23 pairs. Chromosomes can be regarded as blueprints for the design of the particular individual to which they belong. Imagine that each chromosome is a very long string of beads of a wide variety of colours, shapes, sizes and design arranged in a particular order. This order makes up a "code" which represents and controls, as if it were coded software in a computer, every detail of every structure within the body of the particular individual animal. Thus within each cell, whether it be at the tip of a cat's tail or deep in its tongue, is all the information on the design of the *total* cat's body.

What are the genes?

The many "beads" carried by the chromosomes are called genes. Each gene "describes" one (or occasionally more) particular characteristic of the whole body: some genes deal with the colour of the cat's coat, whilst others are concerned with its length. Other genes deal with the size of various parts of the body, or cope with the functioning of the internal organs or with behaviour.

How is the genetic information passed on to new cells?

When cells multiply by splitting into two, the 38 chromosomes produce 38 identical "copies" of themselves before cell division takes place. This is how the blueprint passes from one generation of cells to the next.

Sex chromosomes

Although for most purposes the 19 pairs of chromosomes in the nucleus of any cat cell are identical, one pair of chromosomes differ slightly. These are the chromosomes that determine the sex of the individual. A female carries a pair of "X" chromosomes, and is given the symbol "XX", whereas a male carries an "X" and a "Y" and is therefore referred to as "XY".

When reproduction occurs, two cells — egg and sperm — from different individuals come together. Eggs and sperms, commonly known as "germ cells", differ from all other body cells in possessing only *one* set of chromosomes within their nucleii, instead of a double set. This means that when they fuse together at the moment of conception they form standard chromosome pairs again. The single sex chromosome in the male's sperm can be either X or Y, whereas the chromosome of all the female's eggs are X. Thus, a kitten's sex depends on whether an X or Y sperm is first to reach the egg. If it is a Y sperm, it will combine with the egg's X chromosome to make a male XY pair. When eggs and sperm meet, the two single sets of chromosomes combine together in the nucleus of the now-fertilized egg. Each germ cell contributes its share of genes, and the resultant chromosome pairs contain the genes of both the sperm and the egg, but arranged in a slightly different order along the length of the chromosome "bead" chain. It is this new arrangement of the genes that gives the fertilized egg, and eventually the cat that it develops into, its unique individuality.

Other factors that influence development

Occasionally, X-rays, atomic radiation and certain chemicals can induce changes in the fundamental character of genes. These changes are called mutations, and the effect of them is that altered characteristics appear in the body that develops from the germ cells. Sometimes gene mutation occurs apparently spontaneously during the multiplication of cells. This *very* rare event is at the core of the evolutionary process, and results in the development of new breeds, colours, and types of cat.

Apart from rare mutations, many other factors influence the way genes "express" themselves in every individual case. Sometimes non-genetic, non-hereditary processes are involved — these are quirks that develop in the embryo *after* conception. Cells arrange themselves in the growing tissues in a slightly imprecise fashion, and this type of congenital, non-hereditary occurrence results in such modifications as the

---

HOW ARE CHARACTERISTICS PASSED ON?

The new cat receives two separate genes, one from each parent, to control each characteristic. If one gene carries instructions to make the coat black and the other to make it tabby you would think that the kitten would be halfway between black and tabby. However, because some genes, like the tabby one, are more "pushy" than others this isn't the case. These "pushy" genes are known as dominant, and the more "retiring" types, like the black gene, are recessive. So all tabby/black crosses are tabby, but because they carry recessive black genes if they are mated amongst themselves they will produce tabbies and blacks on a three-to-one ratio.

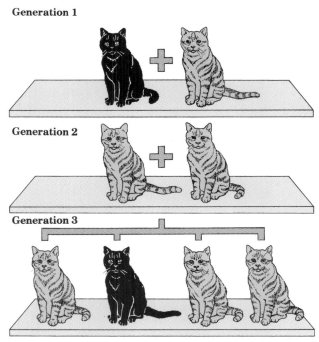

Generation 1

Generation 2

Generation 3

varying distribution of white areas in a piebald-spotted coat.

Linked genes

Although in general genes are distributed widely among the 19 pairs of chromosomes, and are "reshuffled" each time germ cells meet, there are some genes that stick together in pairs during sexual reproduction. They pass from generation to generation, and remain side-by-side on the same chromosome.

Sex-linkage

Some of these linked genes are carried on only one of the chromosomes. The best example of sex-linkage in the cat is the fact that tortoiseshells are always female. The reason for this is that a tortoiseshell coat is produced by a combination of a dominant orange and a recessive non-orange gene, both of which are linked to the X chromosome. An XY male can't therefore inherit this combination.

"Mimic" genes

Occasionally, quite different, distinct genes can produce similar bodily effects; these are said to be "mimic" genes. There are two well-known feline mimic rex genes — the Cornish and the Devon. Although these two breeds look very similar, genetically they are independent and have developed separately.

"Masked" genes

A phenomenon known as *epistasis* or masking occurs when some genes have such an overwhelming effect that they swamp the characteristics produced by other genes. The best example of this is where the non-agouti gene masks the effects of the various tabby genes. This explains why a black cat with tabby genes usually has no tabby markings — the non-agouti gene has eliminated the agouti ticking of the hairs to produce a solid black appearance. Sometimes

partial masking occurs, explaining why a faint tabby pattern is often seen in the coat of young, solid-coloured kittens.

"Rogue" genes

Genes don't always exert their influence in a positive or benign way — some can produce bad or even lethal effects.

The white gene

The dominant white gene frequently induces withering of the inner ear structures. Thus, white cats, particularly ones with blue eyes, have a tendency to deafness.

The Siamese gene

Like the white gene, the Siamese gene also tends to produce a health defect; this time in the optic nerve connecting the eye to the brain. This bad "anatomical wiring" causes reduced binocular vision (see p. 30) and a degree of double vision which the cat tries to correct by squinting.

The Manx gene

The effect of the gene that causes tail-lessness is akin to the human spina bifida condition, which can run in families. The Manx gene has a further rogue quality in that when an egg containing it is fertilized by a sperm that also contains a Manx gene, the kittens die in the uterus. Manx therefore aren't true-breeding cats. The fact that they survive at all means that they can only be carrying one Manx gene in the appropriate pair.

Other "rogue" genes

Other gene-induced abnormalities include:
- A cleft in the forefeet (splitfoot)
- Extra toes (Polydactyly)
- Hairlessness (sometimes associated with Rex genes)
- Badly positioned ear flaps
- Undescended testicles

Planning a litter

Female cats (queens) reach sexual maturity between 7 and 12 months, males (toms) between 10 and 14 months. With most breeds, only one litter of kittens a year is advisable, but Foreign types (see p. 77) can give birth once every 7—8 months without suffering any ill-effects.

Finding a suitable stud

If your queen is a pedigree, and you are new to cat breeding, you should ask someone with experience for advice on choosing a stud tom of the right quality. Such experts can be contacted through a cat show, club or vet.

A reputable breeder will have well-designed accommodation with spacious, warm, hygenic, secure quarters for the tom and queen. All the animals in the stud should be free of Feline Leukaemia virus (see p. 259). Ask to see veterinary certificates, and provide similar proof of your queen's health. You will have to pay a fee to the breeder for the stud's services. If the first mating proves unfruitful, a second mating is generally provided free of charge.

When should the queen go to stud?

When you first discuss the mating with the stud owner arrange an approximate date (the onset of oestrus is often unpredictable). Once your queen starts to "call" (see p. 204), telephone the breeder and arrange to deliver her. She should be fully fit, with no ailments, however mild. Make sure you take her vaccination certificates with you.

At the stud

On arrival, the queen will be checked to make sure that she is fit. Provided that she is healthy, she will be placed in her own quarters, adjoining the tom's but

REPRODUCTIVE SYSTEM

Like all mammals, cats reproduce sexually — spermatazoa from the male fertilize eggs from the female. The reproductive cycle and method are described on pp. 204—5.

Female organs

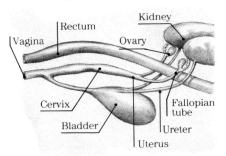

Beyond the cervix, the queen's narrow uterus is divided into two long arms or "horns". The left and right horns lead into the Fallopian tubes which run up towards the ovaries.

Male organs

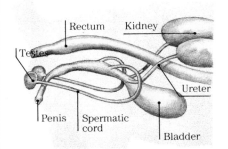

The tom's testes produce spermatozoa which pass down the spermatic cords to the urethra — the passage which links the bladder with the penis. When flaccid, the penis points back-wards. In the cat, the basal part of the glans (the head) is covered by horny spines, which stimulate ovulation in the female.

separated from his by wire mesh. When she begins to make advances to the tom, the breeder will allow her to enter his quarters. Once mating has been repeated three or four times, the cats may be left together for "ad-lib" mating over two to three days. After this, the queen will be returned to her own accommodation, and you will be able to collect her.

The return home

When your queen returns home she may still be in oestrus, so *don't* allow her out of the house. Local toms may add to the litter of developing embryos, producing a mixed bunch of kittens, some by the pedigree tom and some by neighbourhood mongrels. If she calls again, the mating hasn't taken, and you will have to return her to the stud.

What triggers ovulation?

The release of a mature egg from the ovary doesn't occur spontaneously, as in humans or dogs, but is triggered by the act of mating. It is probably the physical stimulation of the male's bony, spined penis which sends nerve impulses to the queen's brain, releasing a command hormone from the pituitary gland.

When is a queen ready to mate?

Just before oestrus a queen is unusually affectionate, rubbing and rolling far more intensely than usual. The signs of oestrus proper include: ☐ restlessness ☐ anxiety to seek out a mate ☐ howling and calling in a strident manner.

Courting behaviour

Although the queen may be ready for mating, she will often go through a ritual of non-acceptance of the tom, repelling his advances by spitting and clawing. The male usually takes such rejection passively: he doesn't retaliate, but withdraws, renewing his overtures a few moments later with a vocal appeal — an "entreaty" cry imploring a more reasonable response on her part. After several advances and repulses, the queen relents by purring and rolling in front of her suitor. This is the signal for mating to begin (see below).

MATING BEHAVIOUR

The queen's signal
When a queen finally permits mating, she goes into a characteristic posture, raising her hind quarters provocatively, and making "peddling" movements with her feet.

The tom's response
The moment that he gets the "green light" from the queen, the tom mounts her and grasps the scruff of her neck between his teeth.

THE QUEEN'S CYCLE

If your queen becomes pregnant, the cycle from oestrus through gestation, birth and lactation to the resumption of oestrus lasts on average 20 weeks.

When is a queen fertile?

Feline heat cycles are seasonal, and tend to start in January, peaking in March or April, June and September. Normally, the queen has no cycles between October and December, but there are exceptions. This seems to be governed by reduced light levels; consequently, cats kept indoors are less likely to have an inactive period. Within any phase, two to three two-week cycles occur. Each oestrus lasts two to four days.

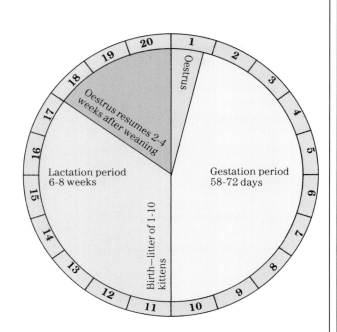

Oestrus

Oestrus resumes 2-4 weeks after weaning

Lactation period
6-8 weeks

Gestation period
58-72 days

Birth—litter of 1-10 kittens

Coitus

As soon as the tom's penis is introduced, ejaculation is immediate, and may be accompanied by a short, sharp howl from the queen. Then the tom separates from the queen, taking up a position some distance away, where he waits and watches her.

The female's post-coital behaviour

Once the tom has withdrawn, the queen goes into a display of rolling, rubbing and stretching, with her toes spread and her claws extended voluptuously. Five to 15 minutes later, the mating sequence begins again, and may occur many times a day during the oestrus period.

Pregnancy

If the mating has been successful, your queen won't come back into oestrus, and will soon show signs of pregnancy. However, if she hasn't conceived, oestrus will recur two to three weeks later. The length of gestation (pregnancy) is around nine weeks.

SIGNS OF PREGNANCY

● Reddening nipples — this is known as "pinking-up", and occurs about the third week of pregnancy
● Gradual weight gain — 1—2 kgs, depending on the number of kittens
● Swollen abdomen (*Don't* prod the abdomen to feel the foetuses — you could cause serious damage)
● Behaviour changes — becomes "maternal"

Consulting the vet

During your cat's pregnancy you should discuss preparing her for kittening with your vet, and get a prescription for safe worming drugs.

Caring for your pregnant queen

Provide a good well-balanced diet (see pp. 158—9), and give vitamin and mineral supplements (particularly calcium). The growing foetuses will exert pressure on the large intestine, and constipation may occur as a result. To correct this, mix a few drops of paraffin with her food.

Estimating the delivery date

Where the date of mating isn't known, judging the kittening date isn't easy. As a rough guide, allow six weeks after the first "pinking-up".

PREPARING A KITTENING BOX

When the queen is within two weeks of giving birth, keep her indoors and prepare a kittening box. The box should be put in a warm place, out of the main "traffic", and lined with cotton sheeting or news-paper (a good insulator, and easy to change when soiled). Ideally, you should suspend an infra-red lamp no lower than 1 m above the box. Once the box is ready, introduce the queen to it. If she selects an alternative site, move the box there. If she shuns your construction, put down disposable bedding in her chosen spot and fix an infra-red lamp above it.

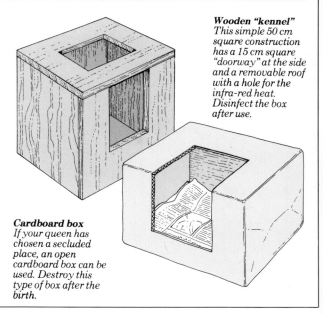

Wooden "kennel"
This simple 50 cm square construction has a 15 cm square "doorway" at the side and a removable roof with a hole for the infra-red heat. Disinfect the box after use.

Cardboard box
If your queen has chosen a secluded place, an open cardboard box can be used. Destroy this type of box after the birth.

The birth

When the time to give birth arrives, some undiscovered "clock" in the queen's body signals the hormone-producing glands to begin the process of ejecting the kittens from the uterus.

How long is the average pregnancy?

Although the average length of a cat's pregnancy is 65 days, birth may commence any time from one week before to one week after this date. Kittens born earlier than 58 days tend to be delivered dead or very weak, and should be regarded as miscarriages. Kittens born later than 71 days are likely to be bigger than normal, and may be dead. A queen may well have problems in giving birth to such late arrivals, so it is important to consult your vet if the 71st day of pregnancy arrives with no sign that the labour is about to start.

How easy is the birth?

The vast majority of queens have no difficulty in giving birth, and assistance by the owner or a vet is seldom required. Up to one-third of all kittens are born tail-end first; this is normal, it is *not* a breech birth. That term applies when a kitten's hind quarters enter the vagina first, with its hind feet pointing towards the mother's head. But even in such a case, queens generally manage to give birth unaided. For information on labour problems, see p. 210.

The first stage of labour

This stage may last up to six hours, and begins when the cervix opens up and a "wedge" of foetal membranes from the uterus enters it. As this happens, the involuntary contractions of the uterine muscles begin the new kitten's journey to the outside world. When these contractions begin, the queen will probably

FOETAL POSITION

During development, each foetus lies in one or other of the two "horns" or divisions of the feline uterus. Like a human baby, it is surrounded by two membranous bags of "water", and is attached to the uterine wall, from which it draws sustenance, by an umbilical cord. Where identical twin kittens occur, the two foetuses may share one set of membranes and a single placenta.

The pregnant uterus

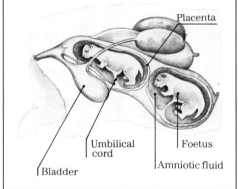

Placenta

Umbilical cord | Foetus

Bladder | Amniotic fluid

go to her kittening bed. She may start breathing more rapidly, panting and purring, but not in distress. Also, a clear vaginal discharge may be seen, and at the end of the first stage clear or slightly cloudy water and/or a little blood is sometimes released.

The second stage of labour

The next stage of the birth should last around 10–30 minutes, and no longer than 90 minutes. It starts when the emerging foetus and its membranes stimulate the mother to aid the involuntary uterine contractions with voluntary abdominal muscle contractions or straining ("bearing down"). At first, bearing down occurs once every 15—30 minutes. The queen starts licking at her vulva and she won't move from her kittening bed. Soon, a cloudy grey bleb — the first sign of the membrane that surrounds the kitten — appears at the vulval opening. The interval between bouts of bearing down decreases, until straining occurs once every 15—30 seconds. The membrane protrusion increases in size, and part of the kitten may be glimpsed within it. With a number of final contractions, the queen pushes out the kitten.

The third stage of labour
Once the kitten has emerged, the expulsion of the membranes and placenta usually follows very quickly. The birth of each kitten is a separate labour, with its own three stages. Each kitten has its own membranes and placenta, except in the case of identical twins, where they may share one set.

After a kitten is born
As soon as a kitten is born, the queen starts licking it, and she bites off the umbilical cord 2—4 cms from its navel. She may attempt to eat the placenta when this appears — this behaviour is instinctive in many mammals (the reason is probably to remove any material that might attract scavenging or predatory animals). Try to remove it before she eats it as it may give her diarrhoea or indigestion. But if she does eat it, don't worry — it won't harm her.

Coping with a weak kitten
If a kitten is very cold and feeble at birth, immerse it up to its neck in a bowl of water heated to feline blood temperature (38°C). Keep hold of the kitten by the head, and stroke and massage its body gently under the water. After two to three minutes it should become more vigorous. When it does, take it out of the water and dry it carefully with warm towelling. Place it in a warm box.

The third stage of labour
The queen shown above is in the final stage of a labour. Her contractions are pushing out a kitten (still surrounded by the membranes).

After the kittening
Once all the kittens are born (right), the queen will allow them to start suckling, so that they receive the important nutrient-rich first milk (known as the colostrum).

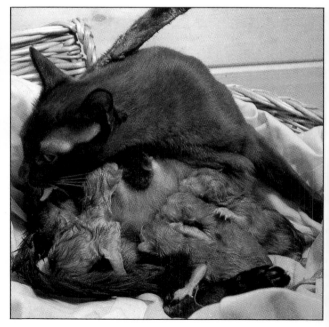

HELPING AN INEXPERIENCED QUEEN

Sometimes a first-time mother won't lick the kitten, break open the membranes where necessary, or sever the umbilical cord. In such a case, you will have to intervene immediately or the kitten may die.

1 If the membranes are still covering the new-born kitten, simply rip them off.

2 Next, rub the kitten dry with some warm towelling, paying particular attention to the nostrils as they must be cleared of any mucus blockage.

3 Once the kitten is breathing, making faint squeaking cries and wriggling, you can attend to the umbilical cord. Begin by immersing some strong cotton and a pair of scissors in antiseptic. Tie the cotton tightly around the umbilical cord about 3 cm from the navel.

4 Knot the cotton, then cut the cord 0.5 cm beyond the cotton on the *placental* side of the knot.

5 Finally, place the kitten in a box under an infra-red lamp.

The total length of kittening

The time between the birth of successive kittens varies — it can be as little as five minutes or as much as two hours. Sometimes a queen will deliver half a litter, then suspend operations for 12—24 hours before delivering the rest. If this happens, you may be worried. Should you call the vet? If the first group of kittens were delivered normally and at short intervals, and the queen appears content, suckles her kittens and accepts food, there may be no need to worry. But a delay can be confused with "uterine inertia", where the muscular contractions of the uterus weaken and fade, and the queen tires of bearing down, eventually giving up. This condition is *not* normal, and needs veterinary attention. An affected queen usually appears more fatigued and disinterested than a resting cat, but the difference can be difficult to judge. Therefore, if your queen clearly hasn't finished giving birth and two hours have elapsed since the last kitten was born, call the vet.

Suckling

With the births complete, all the kittens should be ready to suckle. Make sure that they latch firmly onto a teat and receive the first milk (colostrum) as it is packed with nutrients and protective antibodies.

POST-NATAL CHECKLIST

- As soon as kittening is over, change the bedding
- Provide a high-quality, balanced diet (see pp. 158—9)
- Give 200 mg calcium lactate, calcium gluconate or sterilized bone meal daily
- Add a pet or human baby multi-vitamin tonic to the food daily
- Keep her indoors for 3—4 days, but keep the kittens inside until weaned

Labour problems

In general, cats rarely have any problems in giving birth. However, if your queen is one of the few unfortunate cases where difficulty is experienced, keep her in a warm (22–4°C) room and put a heating pad or hot water bottle in the kittening box. Contact the vet for a house call or arrange to take her to the surgery immediately (transport her in a warm, well-bedded box in a heated car). The vet may have to perform an emergency Caesarian, manually manipulate jammed kittens, or give drugs for uterine inertia, and therefore time is of the essence.

Difficult labour

A kitten can occasionally jam in the birth canal: it may be an awkward presentation, or the kitten may be abnormally large, or the queen abnormally small. If a kitten is partly out of the vulva and the queen is obviously having difficulty getting it any further, wash your hands, then lubricate the kitten and vulval entrance with liquid paraffin, petroleum jelly or soap flakes in a little warm water. Firmly but gently grasp as much of the kitten as possible and try to ease it out, co-ordinating your help with the cat's "bearing down". Don't jerk or pull hard on the kitten, though twisting it slightly as you pull may help.

When is a Caesarian section necessary?

If a queen is known to have an anatomical defect like a very narrow pelvis which could interfere with the birth, the vet may decide on an elective Caesarian about 63 days into the pregnancy or when the queen enters the first stage of labour. Such a Caesarian is quick, low-risk, and doesn't interfere with the mother's ability to rear her young or have subsequent litters.

An off-colour queen

Giving birth to a large litter of kittens can take a lot out of a queen; she will need to rest after her labours, and may seem quite weak for a while. But by the following day she should start settling down to rearing her kittens, and resume normal eating and drinking. If this isn't the case, and she displays some of the signs shown below, you *must* contact the vet immediately as she may have a serious health problem.

WHEN TO CONTACT THE VET DURING THE BIRTH

- Where a queen has been bearing down for two hours without delivering a kitten
- Where no bearing down at all has been seen six hours after blood or any other coloured discharge appeared from the vulva
- Where bearing down has stopped for more than two hours, although the queen is obviously still carrying a kitten or kittens

WHEN TO CONTACT THE VET AFTER THE BIRTH

- If the queen bleeds significantly from the vagina (more than 2 tsp)
- If a coloured, white, or foul-smelling vaginal discharge appears
- If the queen seems lethargic or dull
- If normal eating isn't resumed after the first 12 hours
- When the queen is still straining
- If the queen seems very restless
- If the queen is feverish
- If the queen shows no interest in her new kittens

Preventing pregnancy

If your cat is a "mongrel" you should only breed from her if you are sure that you can find good homes for all the kittens. And if she is a pedigree, make sure that you are prepared for the initial work — and cost — of choosing a good stud so that you produce a saleable litter of pedigree offspring.

Neutering tom cats

Unless you are setting up a breeding stud, all pet toms should be castrated. This practice reduces fighting, unplanned litters, straying, and eliminates the pungent smells of sprayed tom-cat urine. The safe, painless operation is carried out under general anaesthetic after the cat is nine months old. Neutering a younger kitten is inadvisable as his penis won't be fully developed and an operation at this age might cause a urinary blockage later.

Spaying queens

If you definitely don't want kittens, then when your queen is between four and nine months old arrange for a vet to spay her. Leaving her unmated isn't the answer as virgin queens have a tendency to develop ovarian cysts and uterine problems when they are older. The operation involves the removal of both ovaries and much of the uterus under general anaesthetic. It is irreversible, and has no after-effects.

The neutering procedure

You will have to make an appointment with a vet to take your cat to the surgery for the operation. Because a general anaesthetic is used, you will be asked to keep the animal off food and drink for about 12 hours prior to admission. In most cases, cats will be ready for collection later the same day, although

---

FACTORS WHICH PREVENT SPAYING

● Don't spay a kitten less than 3 months old
● Avoid spaying during oestrus — the high level of sex hormones circulating in the blood will increase bleeding
● No queen more than 4 weeks pregnant should be spayed. Many vets refuse to spay pregnant queens unless there is a sound medical reason such as a congenitally deformed pelvis

---

some queens may be kept in overnight. When you get your cat home provide rest, warmth, light meals and affection. A spayed queen will have non-dissolvable stitches in her small skin wound, which the vet will remove 5—10 days later.

Putting queens on "the pill"

There is an alternative to spaying queens — the use of a contraceptive pill to prevent or postpone oestrus. This comes in the form of long-acting "depot" injections or as tablets, and is prescribed by the vet. However, except for a few short-term reasons, spaying is preferable to using a contraceptive. These reasons are: to give a pedigree breeding queen a rest between litters, to avoid oestrus at certain times, or to plan the arrival time of litters. There are several disadvantages to the contraceptive pill: □ it can't be given to diabetic animals □ if given over a long period, it may increase a tendency to uterine disease □ it may produce side-effects (sluggish behaviour, increased appetite, and undesirable weight gain).

HEALTH CARE

The cat's elegant, tough body design goes some way towards confirming the traditional belief that cats have nine lives. However, the cat's natural inquisitiveness, closeness to the ground and ability to explore most nooks and crannies expose it to a broad spectrum of germs. And its size predisposes it to certain types of accident, especially when it is a city dweller. Also, stress or poor condition can lower your cat's resistance to illness, giving disease a chance to attack. You can take precautions to keep your cat healthy, but if it does succumb to illness, you should consult a vet as soon as possible. This chapter provides information on the degree of urgency required in consulting a vet, and the likely diagnosis of your cat's condition. For information on what action to take in an emergency, consult the *First Aid* chapter (see pp. 276–83).

How to use this chapter

The chapter begins with information that helps you to decide whether or not your cat is ill, including instructions on *Taking a cat's temperature and pulse,* and *Diagnosis charts* that cover the major signs of ill-health in the cat. This is followed by the *Ailments and disorders* section, which is divided into areas of the body and systems within it. Finally, the *Care and nursing* section provides information on veterinary care, looking after an ill or elderly cat at home, and keeping your cat healthy.

Is my cat ill?
Strictly speaking, animals can't display symptoms, as these are sensations and phenomena which can be described *by the patient*. However, a sick or injured cat will show observable phenomena; these are termed "signs".

Is my cat healthy?
A healthy cat's fur is sleek and unbroken, its eyes are clear and bright, and its nostrils are clean and dry (not parched or moist). It has a hearty appetite, and its excretory systems function regularly. It walks fluidly, and moves with purpose and self-possession. It grooms itself regularly with its tongue, purrs at appropriate moments, and shows no sudden flashes of irritation or bizarre behaviour. And handling by humans produces no signs of pain or discomfort.

AILMENTS SECTION

System diagrams
Annotated diagrams show the composition of each of the body's systems.

"See also" boxes
These reference boxes lead you to relevant information in other sections of the book.

Quick-reference boxes help you to make decisions when you spot signs of illness.

Urgency advice
Crosses indicate how quickly you should contact a vet.

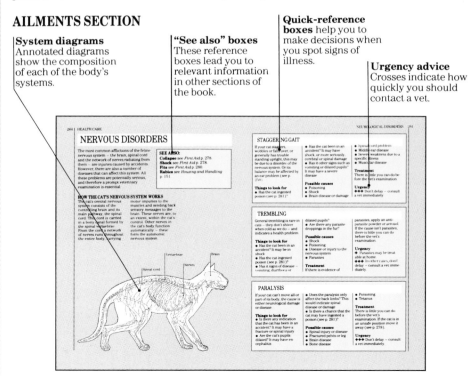

SIGNS OF ILLNESS

The first signs of ill-health you will probably notice in your cat usually involve behaviour: it becomes duller, more introverted and less active. Also, its appetite is often affected — it may decrease or increase.

Warning — acute signs: If your cat displays any of the following signs consult a vet immediately: ☐ collapse ☐ vomiting repeatedly for more than 24 hours ☐ diarrhoea for longer than 24 hours ☐ troubled breathing ☐ bleeding from an orifice ☐ dilated pupils.
Major signs: Looking off colour, Vomiting, Diarrhoea, Abnormal breathing, Bleeding, Scratching (see pp. 217–23).

Other common signs of illness

On close examination, you may be able to detect other signs:
Respiratory signs ☐ Sneezing (see p. 227) ☐ Nasal discharge (see p. 229) ☐ Coughing (see p. 226)
Oral/appetite signs ☐ Drooling (see pp. 230, 234) ☐ Over/undereating (see p. 233) ☐ Increased thirst (see p. 232)
Eye signs ☐ Discharge (see p. 244) ☐ Cloudiness (see p. 245) ☐ Closed lids (see p. 245)
Ear signs ☐ Discharge (see p. 246)
Body signs ☐ Pain when touched ☐ Limping (see p. 264)
Bowel/urinary signs ☐ Constipation (see p. 232) ☐ Frequent urination (see p. 252) ☐ Straining (see p. 252)

Back-up information

Following the quick-reference boxes, you will find more detailed information on specific problems.

Prevention boxes

Where relevant, preventative measures are given.

DIAGNOSIS CHARTS

Answer the questions and follow the arrows to an endpoint that suggests a likely veterinary diagnosis.

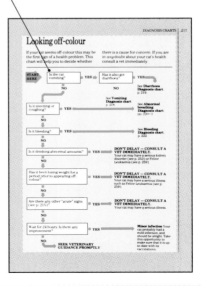

TAKING A CAT'S TEMPERATURE

If you suspect that your cat is ill, taking its temperature can be useful in assessing its condition. The normal level is about 38.6° C, but this may well fluctuate slightly. However, I don't consider a cat feverish until its temperature is over 39.2° C.

Method
Ask a helper to hold the cat firmly (see below). Using a stubby-ended glass clinical therm-ometer, shake down the mercury with several sharp flicks of your wrist. Lubricate the glass bulb with liquid paraffin or vegetable oil, lift the cat's tail and insert the thermometer slowly into the anus, until about 2 cms of it is inside the cat. Gently angle the thermometer so that the bulb comes into contact with the wall of the rectum. Hold it in position for about one minute, then with-draw, wipe and read it against the scale.

Holding the cat
Get your helper to grasp the cat by its scruff with one hand so that you are free to lift the tail and insert the thermometer.

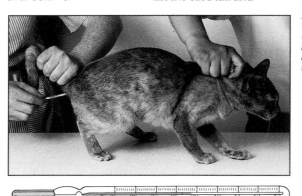

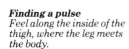

Temperature reading
A healthy cat's temperature is around 38.6°C.

TAKING A CAT'S PULSE

Most cats have a pulse rate of 110—40 beats per minute when at rest. You can detect it by feeling the femoral artery in the groin (see right) and counting the beats. The pulse should be strong and regular.

Finding a pulse
Feel along the inside of the thigh, where the leg meets the body.

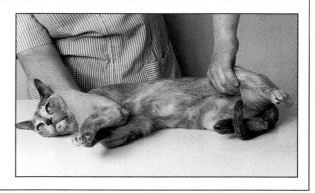

Looking off-colour

If your cat seems off-colour this may be the first sign of a health problem. This chart will help you to decide whether there is a cause for concern. If you are in *any* doubt about your cat's health consult a vet immediately.

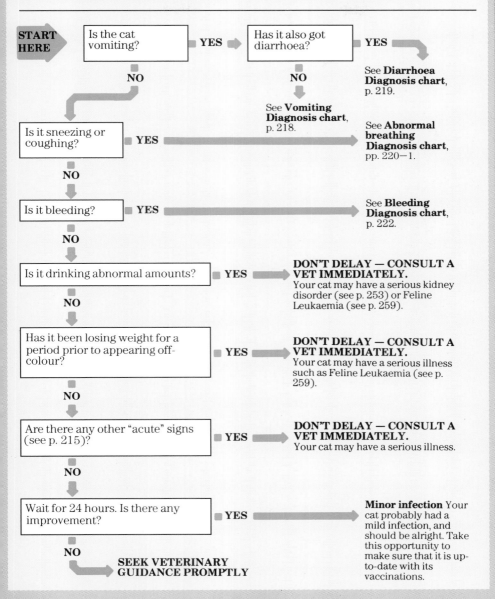

START HERE

Is the cat vomiting? — **YES** → Has it also got diarrhoea? — **YES** → See **Diarrhoea Diagnosis chart**, p. 219.

NO (diarrhoea) → See **Vomiting Diagnosis chart**, p. 218.

NO (vomiting)

Is it sneezing or coughing? — **YES** → See **Abnormal breathing Diagnosis chart**, pp. 220–1.

NO

Is it bleeding? — **YES** → See **Bleeding Diagnosis chart**, p. 222.

NO

Is it drinking abnormal amounts? — **YES** → **DON'T DELAY — CONSULT A VET IMMEDIATELY.** Your cat may have a serious kidney disorder (see p. 253) or Feline Leukaemia (see p. 259).

NO

Has it been losing weight for a period prior to appearing off-colour? — **YES** → **DON'T DELAY — CONSULT A VET IMMEDIATELY.** Your cat may have a serious illness such as Feline Leukaemia (see p. 259).

NO

Are there any other "acute" signs (see p. 215)? — **YES** → **DON'T DELAY — CONSULT A VET IMMEDIATELY.** Your cat may have a serious illness.

NO

Wait for 24 hours. Is there any improvement? — **YES** → **Minor infection** Your cat probably had a mild infection, and should be alright. Take this opportunity to make sure that it is up-to-date with its vaccinations.

NO → **SEEK VETERINARY GUIDANCE PROMPTLY**

Vomiting

There are many causes of vomiting in the cat, ranging from the mild to the very serious. If you are in *any* doubt about your cat's health you should telephone your vet or visit the veterinary surgery immediately.

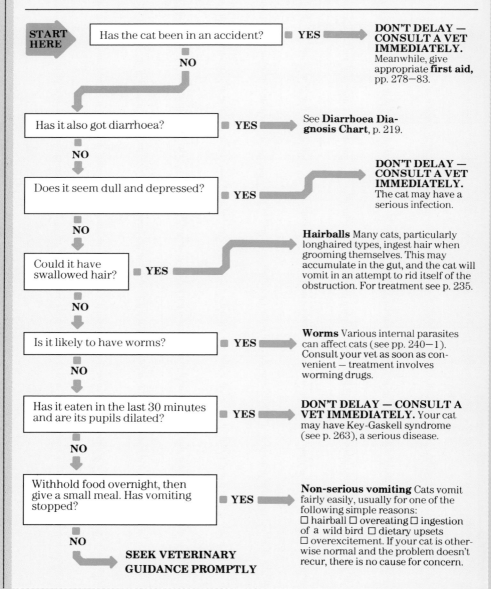

START HERE

Has the cat been in an accident? ■ **YES** ➜ **DON'T DELAY — CONSULT A VET IMMEDIATELY.** Meanwhile, give appropriate **first aid,** pp. 278–83.

■ **NO**

Has it also got diarrhoea? ■ **YES** ➜ See **Diarrhoea Diagnosis Chart**, p. 219.

■ **NO**

Does it seem dull and depressed? ■ **YES** ➜ **DON'T DELAY — CONSULT A VET IMMEDIATELY.** The cat may have a serious infection.

■ **NO**

Could it have swallowed hair? ■ **YES** ➜ **Hairballs** Many cats, particularly longhaired types, ingest hair when grooming themselves. This may accumulate in the gut, and the cat will vomit in an attempt to rid itself of the obstruction. For treatment see p. 235.

■ **NO**

Is it likely to have worms? ■ **YES** ➜ **Worms** Various internal parasites can affect cats (see pp. 240–1). Consult your vet as soon as convenient — treatment involves worming drugs.

■ **NO**

Has it eaten in the last 30 minutes and are its pupils dilated? ■ **YES** ➜ **DON'T DELAY — CONSULT A VET IMMEDIATELY.** Your cat may have Key-Gaskell syndrome (see p. 263), a serious disease.

■ **NO**

Withhold food overnight, then give a small meal. Has vomiting stopped? ■ **YES** ➜ **Non-serious vomiting** Cats vomit fairly easily, usually for one of the following simple reasons: ☐ hairball ☐ overeating ☐ ingestion of a wild bird ☐ dietary upsets ☐ overexcitement. If your cat is otherwise normal and the problem doesn't recur, there is no cause for concern.

■ **NO**

➜ **SEEK VETERINARY GUIDANCE PROMPTLY**

Diarrhoea

If your cat passes frequent liquid or semi-liquid motions it probably has a minor infection, but there is a possibility of something more serious. If you are in *any* doubt about its health telephone or visit your vet immediately.

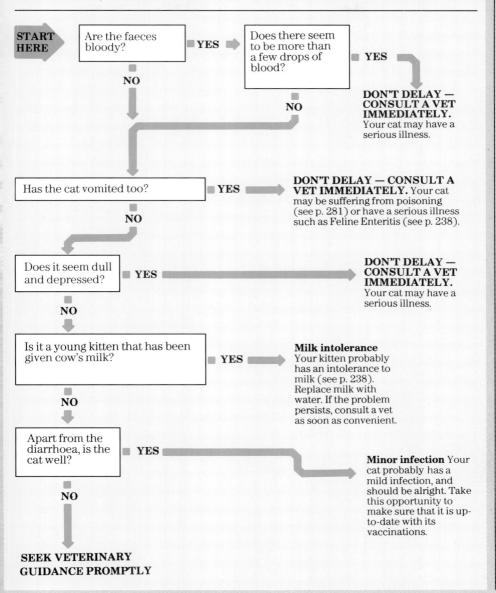

START HERE

Are the faeces bloody? ■ **YES** ➡ Does there seem to be more than a few drops of blood? ■ **YES**

NO

NO

DON'T DELAY — CONSULT A VET IMMEDIATELY. Your cat may have a serious illness.

Has the cat vomited too? ■ **YES**

NO

DON'T DELAY — CONSULT A VET IMMEDIATELY. Your cat may be suffering from poisoning (see p. 281) or have a serious illness such as Feline Enteritis (see p. 238).

Does it seem dull and depressed? ■ **YES**

NO

DON'T DELAY — CONSULT A VET IMMEDIATELY. Your cat may have a serious illness.

Is it a young kitten that has been given cow's milk? ■ **YES**

NO

Milk intolerance Your kitten probably has an intolerance to milk (see p. 238). Replace milk with water. If the problem persists, consult a vet as soon as convenient.

Apart from the diarrhoea, is the cat well? ■ **YES**

NO

Minor infection Your cat probably has a mild infection, and should be alright. Take this opportunity to make sure that it is up-to-date with its vaccinations.

SEEK VETERINARY GUIDANCE PROMPTLY

Abnormal breathing

A healthy cat's breathing is quiet and even, and consists of 25—30 breaths per minute. If your cat's breathing doesn't seem normal, it may have a health problem or merely be resting or affected by hot weather or exertion. To ascertain the cause follow this chart. If you are in any doubt about your cat's health you should telephone your vet or visit the veterinary surgery immediately.

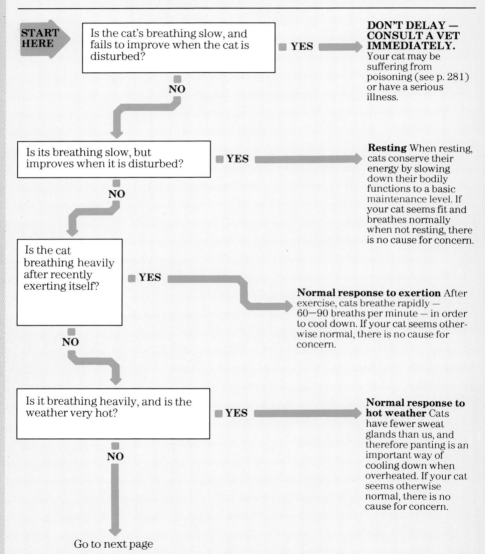

START HERE

Is the cat's breathing slow, and fails to improve when the cat is disturbed?

YES

DON'T DELAY — CONSULT A VET IMMEDIATELY. Your cat may be suffering from poisoning (see p. 281) or have a serious illness.

NO

Is its breathing slow, but improves when it is disturbed?

YES

Resting When resting, cats conserve their energy by slowing down their bodily functions to a basic maintenance level. If your cat seems fit and breathes normally when not resting, there is no cause for concern.

NO

Is the cat breathing heavily after recently exerting itself?

YES

Normal response to exertion After exercise, cats breathe rapidly — 60—90 breaths per minute — in order to cool down. If your cat seems otherwise normal, there is no cause for concern.

NO

Is it breathing heavily, and is the weather very hot?

YES

Normal response to hot weather Cats have fewer sweat glands than us, and therefore panting is an important way of cooling down when overheated. If your cat seems otherwise normal, there is no cause for concern.

NO

Go to next page

continued from previous page

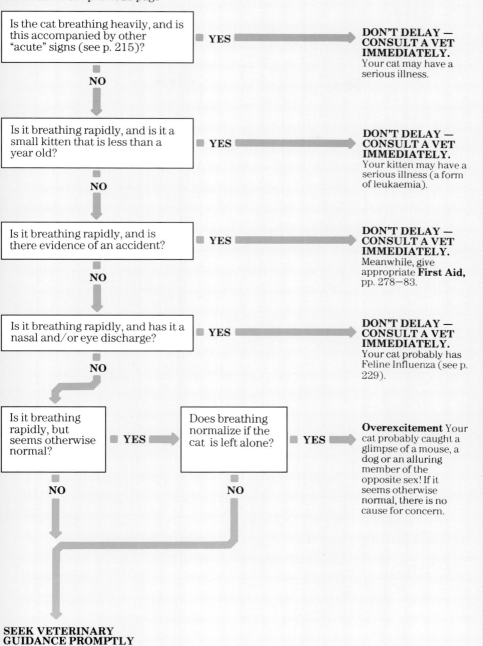

Is the cat breathing heavily, and is this accompanied by other "acute" signs (see p. 215)?

YES

DON'T DELAY — CONSULT A VET IMMEDIATELY. Your cat may have a serious illness.

NO

Is it breathing rapidly, and is it a small kitten that is less than a year old?

YES

DON'T DELAY — CONSULT A VET IMMEDIATELY. Your kitten may have a serious illness (a form of leukaemia).

NO

Is it breathing rapidly, and is there evidence of an accident?

YES

DON'T DELAY — CONSULT A VET IMMEDIATELY. Meanwhile, give appropriate **First Aid,** pp. 278–83.

NO

Is it breathing rapidly, and has it a nasal and/or eye discharge?

YES

DON'T DELAY — CONSULT A VET IMMEDIATELY. Your cat probably has Feline Influenza (see p. 229).

NO

Is it breathing rapidly, but seems otherwise normal?

YES

Does breathing normalize if the cat is left alone?

YES

Overexcitement Your cat probably caught a glimpse of a mouse, a dog or an alluring member of the opposite sex! If it seems otherwise normal, there is no cause for concern.

NO

NO

SEEK VETERINARY GUIDANCE PROMPTLY

Bleeding

If your cat is bleeding you must investigate the source and take immediate action as it may need urgent veterinary attention. Advice on applying bandages is given in the *First Aid* chapter, pp. 278–83.

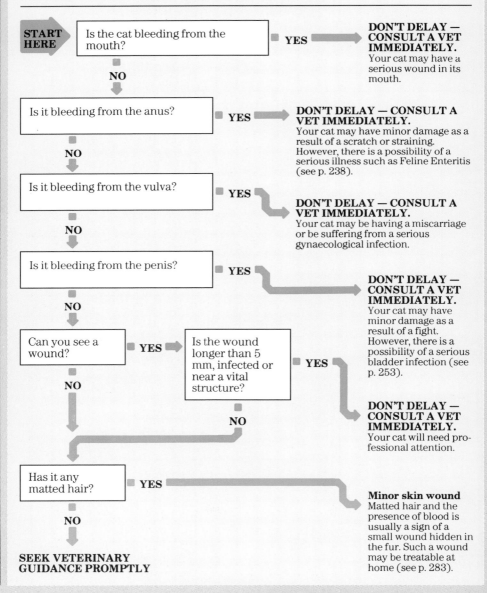

START HERE

Is the cat bleeding from the mouth?

NO

YES — **DON'T DELAY — CONSULT A VET IMMEDIATELY.** Your cat may have a serious wound in its mouth.

Is it bleeding from the anus?

NO

YES — **DON'T DELAY — CONSULT A VET IMMEDIATELY.** Your cat may have minor damage as a result of a scratch or straining. However, there is a possibility of a serious illness such as Feline Enteritis (see p. 238).

Is it bleeding from the vulva?

NO

YES — **DON'T DELAY — CONSULT A VET IMMEDIATELY.** Your cat may be having a miscarriage or be suffering from a serious gynaecological infection.

Is it bleeding from the penis?

NO

YES — **DON'T DELAY — CONSULT A VET IMMEDIATELY.** Your cat may have minor damage as a result of a fight. However, there is a possibility of a serious bladder infection (see p. 253).

Can you see a wound?

NO

YES — Is the wound longer than 5 mm, infected or near a vital structure?

NO

YES — **DON'T DELAY — CONSULT A VET IMMEDIATELY.** Your cat will need professional attention.

Has it any matted hair?

NO

YES — **Minor skin wound** Matted hair and the presence of blood is usually a sign of a small wound hidden in the fur. Such a wound may be treatable at home (see p. 283).

SEEK VETERINARY GUIDANCE PROMPTLY

Scratching

If your cat scratches itself persistently it probably has a skin problem or a parasitic infestation. In general, these problems aren't serious, but prompt attention is important for your cat's comfort.

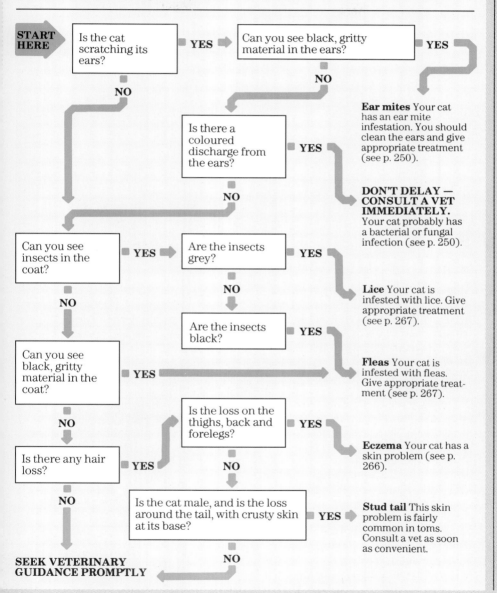

START HERE Is the cat scratching its ears?

YES → Can you see black, gritty material in the ears?

YES → **Ear mites** Your cat has an ear mite infestation. You should clean the ears and give appropriate treatment (see p. 250).

NO → Is there a coloured discharge from the ears?

YES → **DON'T DELAY — CONSULT A VET IMMEDIATELY.** Your cat probably has a bacterial or fungal infection (see p. 250).

NO

NO → Can you see insects in the coat?

YES → Are the insects grey?

YES → **Lice** Your cat is infested with lice. Give appropriate treatment (see p. 267).

NO → Are the insects black?

YES → **Fleas** Your cat is infested with fleas. Give appropriate treatment (see p. 267).

NO → Can you see black, gritty material in the coat?

YES → **Fleas** Your cat is infested with fleas. Give appropriate treatment (see p. 267).

NO → Is there any hair loss?

YES → Is the loss on the thighs, back and forelegs?

YES → **Eczema** Your cat has a skin problem (see p. 266).

NO → Is the cat male, and is the loss around the tail, with crusty skin at its base?

YES → **Stud tail** This skin problem is fairly common in toms. Consult a vet as soon as convenient.

NO

NO → **SEEK VETERINARY GUIDANCE PROMPTLY**

DISORDERS AND AILMENTS

This section is divided into areas and systems of the body. Each system sub-section starts with an illustration and explanation of how that system works. Next, a series of quick-reference boxes give basic guidance to help you to make decisions when you spot signs of illness in your cat. Crosses are used to denote the likely degree of urgency with which you should seek expert attention (this ranges from one cross for "may be treatable at home", to two crosses for "consult a vet as soon as convenient", to three crosses for "don't delay — consult a vet immediately"). Following the quick-reference boxes, detailed descriptions of common problems, diseases and treatments are given. Where applicable, preventative measures such as vaccinations or hygiene precautions are also included.

This guide isn't intended to be a substitute for professional veterinary care as diagnosis depends on the particular circumstances of the individual cat, and can only be made by a qualified veterinarian. The aim of this chapter is to inform you of the degree of urgency necessary in consulting a vet, and to help you to understand what is wrong with your cat after the vet's diagnosis has been made. Information included in this section represents an understanding of veterinary knowledge at the date of publication.

RESPIRATORY DISORDERS

The nasal passages, throat, voice box, windpipe, bronchial tubes and lungs make up the respiratory system of a cat, as shown below. The most common respiratory problems in cats are due to infection. Although most illnesses turn out to be mild "colds", some cat influenzas can be life-threatening, especially in unvaccinated animals. A prompt veterinary examination is therefore essential in order to assess the seriousness of the condition.

SEE ALSO:
Abnormal breathing see *Diagnosis Charts* pp. 220—1.
Handling a sick cat see *Home Nursing* p. 270.
Choking see *First Aid* p. 280.
Obstruction in throat see *First Aid* p. 280.

HOW THE CAT'S RESPIRATORY SYSTEM WORKS

Air enters through the cat's nasal passages, and travels down its windpipe and bronchi to the lungs, where the ribs and chest muscles act as bellows, pumping fresh, oxygenated air in and stale, carbon dioxide-filled air out. From the lungs vital oxygen is carried to the rest of the body by the blood, and unwanted carbon dioxide is carried back in the same way.

A resting cat takes 25—30 breaths per minute, compared to our 10—15.

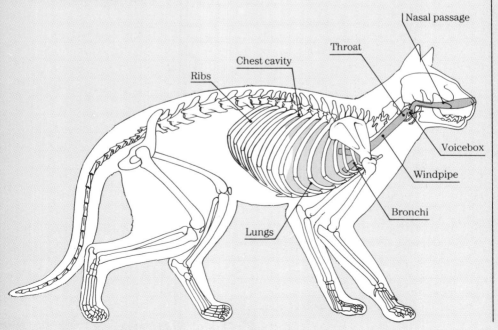

Nasal passage

Throat

Chest cavity

Ribs

Voicebox

Windpipe

Bronchi

Lungs

COUGHING

Generally associated with respiratory infections, a cough is a reflex action brought on by irritation of the air passages. Its purpose is to clear the airways of the irritant.

Things to look for
● Has the cat swallowed something that has stuck in its throat? If so, administer first aid (see p. 280)
● Are there any typical cold or flu signs present: fever, breathing problems, nasal or eye discharges, sneezing?
● Is the cat bringing up phlegm? If so, it may have an acute chest infection
● Does the cough sound "bubbly"? If so, fluid may have built up on the chest from an infection
● Does the cough sound dry and hacking? If so, the cat may have acute bronchitis
● Are there any pollutants such as cigarette smoke or aerosol insecticides in the atmosphere?

Possible causes
● Obstruction in the throat
● Viral respiratory disease
● Bronchitis
● Allergic reaction
● Reaction to pollutants

Treatment
If the cough was caused by an obstruction administer first aid (see p. 280).

If it was caused by an atmospheric pollutant, open the windows to air the room.

If the cat has a known allergy, you may be able to give an anti-histamine drug previously prescribed by the vet.

In other cases, there is little you can do before the vet's examination except keep the cat indoors. Cough suppressant medicines aren't advisable.

Urgency
✚ If caused by a transient atmospheric pollutant such as smoke, the cough may be treatable at home.
✚✚ If caused by an allergic reaction, consult a vet as soon as convenient.
✚✚✚ In other cases, don't delay — consult a vet immediately.

PANTING

At rest, a cat takes 25—30 breaths a minute. After exercise this rises to 60—90. If you think that your cat is breathing too rapidly, count the rate.

Things to look for
● Is the weather very hot? The cat may simply be trying to cool down
● Are the cat's nostrils obstructed? A blockage may be preventing it from breathing correctly through its nose
● Is there any sign of an accident — the cat may have a chest or lung injury, and/or be in shock
● Has the cat been in a fight or confrontation with another animal? It may have a chest/lung injury, be in shock or merely frightened
● Are any signs of respiratory disease such as fever, coughing, nasal or eye discharges or sneezing present?

Possible causes
● Hot weather
● Blocked nostrils
● Chest or lung injury
● Shock
● Severe pain
● Fear or stress
● Viral respiratory disease

Treatment
There is little you can do before the vet's examination; keep the cat indoors and handle it as little as possible.

Urgency
✚ If obviously due to overheating, it may be treatable at home.
✚✚✚ In other cases, don't delay — consult a vet immediately.

SHALLOW BREATHING

A cat will breathe shallowly only if breathing more deeply is impossible or causes it pain.

Things to look for
● Has the cat been in an accident? Shallow breathing may be a sign of damage to the chest area
● Has the cat lost its appetite? It may have a severe viral infection
● Are the lips, tongue and gums grey or blue? This is *cyanosis*, and occurs when insufficient oxygen gets into the blood

Possible causes
● Damage to the chest area (the ribs, diaphragm or chest wall) as the result of an accident
● Respiratory infection
● Pleurisy
● Fluid or air in the chest cavity

Treatment
While you wait for the vet, keep the cat indoors in a warm room.

Urgency
+++ Don't delay — consult a vet immediately.

SNEEZING

Generally associated with respiratory infections, sneezing is a reflex action brought on by irritation in the nasal passages.

Things to look for
● Has the cat a nasal discharge? If so, it probably has an infection of the nostrils or sinuses
● Are any cold or flu signs present: fever, breathing problems, nasal/eye discharges, coughing?

Possible causes
● Bacterial or fungal infection of the nostrils or sinuses
● Viral disease
● Allergic reaction
● Nasal tumour

Treatment
There is little you can do before the vet's examination; keep the cat indoors in a warm, but well-ventilated room. Nasal drops aren't advisable.

Urgency
+ If no other signs are present, consult a vet when convenient.
+++ If accompanied by other signs don't delay — consult a vet immediately.

WHEEZING

A whistling sound made on exhalation or inhalation, wheezing is a result of a partial obstruction at some point between the larynx and bronchioles. This narrows the tube, producing the sound much in the same way that the reed of a wind instrument does.

Things to look for
● Are the cat's lips, tongue and gums grey or blue in colour? This occurs when insufficient oxygen gets into the blood. It may indicate a heart problem
● Coughing — this might indicate the presence of lungworms

Possible causes
● Asthma
● Lungworm
● Congestive heart failure
● Tumour in the air passages

Treatment
There is little you can do before the vet's examination; keep the cat indoors in a warm, but well-ventilated room.

Urgency
+++ Don't delay — consult a vet immediately.

Chest problems

There are several infections that can affect the cat's bronchi and lungs. Only a vet will be able to tell how serious the problem is, so you must arrange for an examination straight away.

Pneumonia
The main signs of pneumonia in a cat are laboured, rapid breathing, often accompanied by loss of appetite and general malaise. If your cat shows these signs don't automatically assume that it has pneumonia as similar signs can be produced by pleurisy. Pneumonia isn't very common in cats, and is generally a complication of severe cat flu. Other causes are: ☐ bacterial and fungal infections ☐ inhalation of liquids ☐ irritation by gases or vapours ☐ parasites such as lungworms.

What is the treatment?
The diagnosis of pneumonia may include taking X-rays, swabs and/or blood samples, and withdrawing a sample of fluid from the chest. Treatment will depend on the diagnosis.

Pleurisy
Fairly common in cats, pleurisy is a build-up of milky, often purulent fluid in the chest cavity that compresses the lung and makes breathing difficult. The cause is sometimes a blood-borne bacterial infection, but in a large number of cases the causative factor isn't known.

What is the treatment?
For diagnosis and treatment see Pneumonia.

Other chest conditions
Other conditions may produce similar signs to those of pneumonia and pleurisy. They are: ☐ rupture of the diaphragm ☐ penetrating wounds of the chest wall ☐ haemorrhage into the chest ☐ bruising of the lungs.

Bronchitis
This condition is usually indicated by a cough, and is caused by inflammation of the air tubes (bronchi) that link the windpipe to the lungs. Causes include: ☐ irritants such as gases or smoke ☐ foreign bodies ☐ infections.

What is the treatment?
Treatment of bronchitis depends on the cause, but in all cases will probably include drugs to dilate the bronchi and dissolve thick secretions.

Lungworms
These tiny parasites are often found in cats' lungs, particularly in country areas. Most cats don't show any signs of infestation, though a few may have a chronic, dry cough. In general, affected cats get rid of the lungworm parasite of their own accord, but in a severe case drug treatment may be necessary.

Asthma
Asthmatic attacks are characterized by heavy, distressed breathing, wheezing, and in severe cases the development of a blue tinge to the tongue, gums, and lips (often combined with the animal's collapse). As in humans, the cause of this condition isn't fully understood, but an allergic sensitivity is a major factor.

What is the treatment?
Attacks can be relieved by drugs which open up the bronchial tubes to ease breathing.

Upper respiratory problems

Cats often seem to have identical respiratory problems to humans: coughing, sneezing, watery eyes, and runny nose. Often, these problems are signs of a mild illness, and will clear up in a few days with careful nursing. However, they can be signs of a more severe, even fatal infection, that requires prompt veterinary treatment. Only a vet will be able to tell how serious the infection is, so you must arrange for an immediate examination.

Viral diseases

Cats don't suffer from human viruses; they have their own range of respiratory germs, some mild and some dangerous. Just as human "flu" can appear in a strain that causes more fatalities than usual, so too can feline viruses. At least three viruses and one other germ (*rickettsia*) can produce inflammation of the cat's upper respiratory system – a condition known as Feline Influenza or "Cat Flu". Of these viruses, the two most important are *feline viral rhinotracheitis virus* or *herpesvirus* (FVRV) and *feline calicivirus* (FCV).

Feline viral rhinotracheitis virus
FVRV is the more serious of the two major viruses. After a 2–10 day incubation period it produces inflammation of the eye, nose and windpipe, with resultant discharges. The cat becomes apathetic and feverish,

---

PREVENTING CAT FLU

The main way of preventing feline influenza lies in the use of vaccines. These are very reliable, though they don't give 100 percent protection – very virulent strains of flu can sometimes break through their defences to produce mild signs of disease, and very occasionally a cat will fail to become immune when injected with the vaccine.

As well as having your cat vaccinated, you should try to avoid taking it to places where the risk of infection is high. In my view, catteries are the biggest danger spots. If you can't get a helpful neighbour to visit your cat at home while you are away, and you have to use a cattery, choose carefully. First and foremost, you must make sure that you pick one that insists on feline guests having been vaccinated before they arrive, and demands certificates as proof.

Getting your cat vaccinated
Ask your vet at what age your kitten should be vaccinated. Normally, kittens don't receive their first flu shot until they are about nine weeks old. This is followed by a second shot 3–4 weeks later. Kittens under nine weeks old will still retain maternal flu antibody in their blood, and this would interfere with the development of immunity. However, when there is a high risk of infection your vet may recommend that a younger kitten is vaccinated. Some vaccines protect against flu and other diseases.

Vaccine checklist
To keep your cat healthy, remember the following:
● All cats need an annual booster dose.
● If your cat is pregnant, she must be given dead or inactivated vaccine, never the live sort.
● Only healthy cats should be vaccinated.
● No animal is protected by vaccine until one week after its second dose.

loses its appetite, and sneezes continually. As the secondary bacteria move in, the discharges from the eyes and nostrils become thicker and purulent, and sometimes the cat develops painful ulcers on its tongue. Pneumonia, pleurisy and miscarriage of pregnant queens may also follow. The mortality rate for affected kittens and elderly cats is high.

Feline calici virus
The FCV germ produces signs that can range from a state that is almost as severe as that of an FVRV-infected cat, to a very mild infection indeed, with just a runny nose and moderate sneezing for a few days. It produces tongue ulcers which cause excess salivation, interfere with eating and cause a marked loss of weight and condition. FCV tends not to affect the eyes or nose very dramatically, though some strains are associated with pneumonia.

Reovirus
This third virus is much less serious than the first two. It causes a very mild "cold", and is very rarely fatal.

How cat flu is transmitted
Respiratory viruses come from other cats, and unlike some viruses (such as foot and mouth disease), they can't live long outside the body. FVRV can live for a day away from feline cells, and FCV for about three days. The main way that a virus is transmitted is by contact with an infected cat. Cat shows, catteries, and vets' surgeries are particularly risky places. Apart from the chance of a "carrier" being there, because of the large numbers of cats present, there is also the possibility that a high concentration of virus particles exists, shed by cats passing through. And because a strange environment is more than likely

to cause stress, your cat's resistance to viruses will be lowered.

Cats which have recovered completely from cat flu can become carriers, and pass on the virus virtually indefinitely. Others may be left with chronic catarrh of the nasal cavities. In the main, these "snuffles" cases suffer from a recurrent secondary bacterial infection, but they too may be able to pass on the virus.

What is the professional treatment?
The vet will prescribe antibiotics for secondary bacterial infections, and anti-inflammatory drugs for any inflammation. In addition, the cat may be given vitamin and/or hormone injections to boost its recuperative abilities.

What is the home treatment?
Once the cat has been seen by the vet and appropriate treatment given, its successful recovery relies on careful home nursing (see pp. 272−3).

Clearing the nose and eyes
Cats find breathing through their mouths unnatural and troublesome, and since they can't blow into a handkerchief, they rely on you to keep their nostrils clear. Wipe around the nose several times a day, using a damp cotton pad. If necessary, ask the vet to prescribe a nasal decongestant. After cleansing, grease the nose tip with petroleum jelly. And don't allow the cat's eyes to "gum up"; clean them with warm water on damp cotton wool. If the cat's eyes are very inflamed, ask the vet for eye drops.

DIGESTIVE DISORDERS

A cat's digestive system comprises the passageway from mouth to anus, the liver, pancreas, stomach and intestines, as shown below. The most common problems affecting this system are vomiting, diarrhoea, constipation, loss of appetite, loss of weight and swelling of the abdomen. These have a number of potential causes, some unimportant, some life-threatening, so examination by a vet is essential. Nutritional problems are unusual, and when they do occur they are generally allergic reactions to food. The most common allergy in cats is to cow's milk.

SEE ALSO:
The teeth see *Anatomy* p. 25.
The gullet and intestines see *Anatomy* pp. 34—5.
Nutritional requirements see *Feeding* pp. 156—9.
Diarrhoea see *Diagnosis Charts* p. 219.
Vomiting see *Diagnosis Charts* p. 218.
Obstruction in the mouth or gullet see *First Aid* p. 280.
Poisoning see *First Aid* p. 281.

HOW THE CAT'S DIGESTIVE SYSTEM WORKS

Food enters the cat's mouth, is cut up by its teeth, mixed with saliva and then passed down its oesophagus into its stomach. Here, digestive juices turn the food into pulp. From the stomach the pulp travels to the duodenum and upper small intestine where enzymes from the pancreas and small bowel and bile from the gall bladder go to work to digest nutrients. The dissolved nutrients pass through the bowel wall into the blood stream, which carries them to the liver where they are converted into stored energy. Undigested waste matter continues the journey through the intestine to the large bowel, leaving the body through the anus.

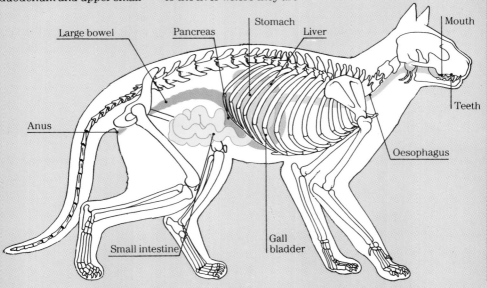

Large bowel · Pancreas · Stomach · Liver · Mouth · Teeth · Oesophagus · Anus · Small intestine · Gall bladder

BAD BREATH

A healthy cat's breath doesn't smell, although a temporary scent of meat or fish immediately after eating isn't abnormal.

Things to look for
● Is the cat drooling? If so, it may have a mouth infection or gum disease
● Are its teeth stained?

Tartar may be the cause
● Has it any mouth ulcers? It may have an infection
● Has it vomited? It may have a gastric problem
● Does it have fits? It may have vitamin B deficiency

Possible causes
● Mouth infection
● Tooth decay
● Ulcers
● Digestive upset
● Vitamin B deficiency

Treatment
If necessary, clean its teeth (see p. 234).

Urgency
✚✚ Consult a vet as soon as convenient.

CONSTIPATION

A healthy cat usually opens its bowels once or twice a day. Difficulty in passing stools occurs for one of two reasons: the passage is obstructed or the stool is too hard.

Things to look for
● Are stools hard and dark? This indicates insufficient fluid present
● Is the cat straining, but not passing stools? If normal stools are present, it may have a urinary tract problem (see p. 252)

● Is the cat lethargic? This indicates lack of condition due to poor diet
● Is the cat longhaired? Its intestines may be blocked by a hairball
● Is the cat vomiting? It may have a serious intestinal blockage

Possible causes
● Low water intake
● Incorrect diet
● Lack of exercise
● Old age (weaker abdominal muscles)
● Hairballs
● Intestinal blockage

Treatment
Add dry cat food or bran to the diet to increase the fibre content.

Urgency
✚ If the problem is due to diet, it may be treatable at home.
✚✚ If a diet change has little effect, consult a vet as soon as convenient.
✚✚✚ If the cat is vomiting, don't delay – consult a vet immediately.

EXCESSIVE THIRST

If you notice your cat drinking markedly more water than usual it may have a serious health problem.

Things to look for
● Has the cat's appetite increased too? It may be diabetic
● Has the cat lost weight? This is a serious sign

● Is the cat being treated with cortisone drugs?
● Is the cat vomiting too? This is a serious sign
● In a queen, has she had kittens? If not, she may have a uterine abscess

Possible causes
● Diabetes
● Corticosteroid therapy
● Kidney or liver disease
● Hormone disease
● Certain toxic conditions
● Uterine pus (Pyometra)

Treatment
Don't restrict liquids.

Urgency
✚✚✚ Don't delay – consult a vet immediately.

FLATULENCE

This condition is caused by undigested carbohydrates which, when fermented by bacteria in the colon produce gas.

Things to look for
- Is the cat's diet rich in protein food or liver?
- Is the problem recurrent? If so, it is likely to be caused by one diet item
- Is the problem constantly present? If so, it is likely to be caused by an absorption problem
- Are the droppings of a normal colour and consistency? If not, it may have an intestinal disorder

Possible causes
- Diet
- Malabsorption in the gut
- Intestinal disorder

Treatment
Add fibre to the diet, and cut out liver and raw meat. In addition, give the cat ½ tsp charcoal powder or 2 tablets of activated charcoal daily, mixed in with its food.

Urgency
✚ If the stools are normal, the condition may be treatable at home.
✚✚ If the stools are abnormal, consult a vet as soon as convenient.

LACK OF APPETITE

There are a number of reasons why your cat might ignore its food: disease, hot weather, or disapproval of the menu are the likeliest.

Things to look for
- Are there any other signs such as vomiting, diarrhoea or constipation? If there are, check these entries

Possible causes
- Loss of appetite can be a sign of many different disorders

Treatment
Don't force-feed the cat – instead try to tempt it with a variety of foods. And make glucose-water (see p. 272) available.

Urgency
✚✚✚ If the cat's appetite is greatly reduced for 3–4 days, or it doesn't eat at all for more than 1 day, or if other signs are present, don't delay – consult a vet immediately.

OVEREATING

If your cat suddenly demands extra rations a parasitic infection is the most likely cause, but it may have a metabolic problem.

Things to look for
- Has the cat been ill or pregnant? It may simply need building up
- Has the cat been wormed?
- Has the cat's thirst increased? If so, see *Excessive thirst*, opposite
- Is the cat losing weight? If so, it may have parasites, leukaemia or diabetes
- Is the cat gaining weight? If so it may have a metabolic disorder

Possible causes
- Recovery from an illness
- Recovery from a birth
- Internal parasites
- Diabetes
- Pancreatic disease
- Glandular disease

Treatment
Don't restrict the food

Urgency
✚✚ If the cat overeats for more than two weeks, or if other signs appear, consult a vet as soon as convenient
✚✚✚ If other signs indicate diabetes, don't delay – consult a vet immediately.

Problems in the mouth

Health troubles in your cat's mouth will probably come to your notice when one or more of the following signs are exhibited: □ bad breath □ pawing at the mouth □ chattering teeth when attempting to bite □ excessive salivation □ difficulty in eating.

Pain or discomfort in the teeth, gums or tongue are responsible, and can be caused by a number of abnormalities.

Tooth decay

The modern cat's diet of minced, tinned food may have a detrimental effect on its teeth. Wild cats clean and polish their teeth as they cut through the skin and gristle of fresh carcasses, but giving your cat bones won't have the same effect. Although the sort of decay (caries) we suffer from is rare in felines, they do have a tendency to accumulate tartar or scale around their teeth. Soft at first and hardening later, this deposit has a high calcium content and is mainly due to the milk and cereal elements of a cat's diet. The main effect of an accumulation of tartar is on the gums, encouraging inflammation (gingevitis), and enabling germs to enter the socket. Slowly, the infection creeps down the socket creating peridontal disease. As a result, the tooth may become loose, the nerve will die and extraction will be necessary.

Gingevitis

There are several causes of gum inflammation: □ tartar □ licking of irritant chemicals □ kidney disease □ vitamin B deficiency □ Leukaemia. At first, the only sign may be a dark red line bordering the teeth. Later, more extensive areas of gum become sore, tender, and a dirty reddish colour. Ulceration may occur.

PREVENTING TOOTH DECAY

To prevent a build-up of tartar a cat's teeth must be kept clean. Many cats will let you clean their teeth once a week with a soft toothbrush, salt and water. If the cat resists, take it to the vet yearly to have its teeth "descaled".

Cleaning your cat's teeth

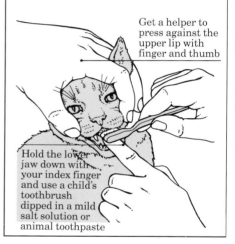

Get a helper to press against the upper lip with finger and thumb

Hold the lower jaw down with your index finger and use a child's toothbrush dipped in a mild salt solution or animal toothpaste

---

Swelling of the tongue or lip

A translucent swelling beneath one or both sides of the tongue is known as a *ranula*, and is usually noticed when a cat exhibits temporary difficulty in eating. This condition is caused by a blockage of saliva ducts. And a chronic, gradually expanding slow-to-heal ulcer or swelling on a cat's lip is usually an *eosinophilic granuloma* (a "rodent ulcer"), the cause of which isn't understood. Both these problems can be successfully treated by your vet.

Gullet and stomach problems

The most common health problems affecting the gullet and stomach are obstruction by foreign bodies (see p. 280), and balls of swallowed hair in the stomach.

Problems of the gullet

Inflammation of the gullet is induced by the passage of a foreign body, an irritant poison, or, more rarely, a tumour. Signs are pain and difficulty in swallowing. An affected cat will need immediate veterinary attention as it will gradually become seriously dehydrated.

What is the treatment?
One of the first aims of treatment will be to replace the body's lost fluids, probably by injection. The vet will take steps to neutralize and/or eliminate any poisons or remove any foreign body (see pp. 280–1), and repair any damage to the gullet. Oesophagal tumours are very serious, and euthanasia (see. 271) is usually advisable.

Gastritis

Vomiting, thirst, a miserable expression, and little else in the way of signs is often diagnosed as gastritis. Pure gastritis – inflammation limited to the wall of the stomach – is rare, and usually caused by the ingestion of poisons or irritant chemicals. A milder form, where the cat seems healthy except for a tendency to regurgitate food after eating, is often referred to as "indigestion". This problem may well be caused by hairballs. In the Southern U.S., the presence of *Spirocerca* worms in the stomach wall may be a factor.

What is the treatment for severe cases?
If the vomiting, thirst and malaise are severe, immediate veterinary help is essential. While you wait for the vet, withdraw solid food and milk. If the cat is thirsty, provide small, frequent "doses" of sweetened, warm water. Also, spoon in ½ tsp of a human anti-acid.

What is the treatment for mild cases?
If your cat has mild indigestion, give it frequent small meals made from fresh, high-quality ingredients. Dose it with one tsp of liquid paraffin daily for three days, and groom it at least once a day. Human anti-acid tablets may be effective – give the cat ½–1 tablet three times a day.

Hairball blockage

Cats who groom themselves very frequently are prone to swallow hairs which gradually build up into a soggy, dark-coloured mass in the stomach. If the furball isn't regurgitated or passed through the intestine certain signs may develop. First, the cat becomes constantly hungry, but is easily filled – no sooner has it taken a mouthful than it walks off apparently replete, but it soon returns again, looking peckish. Eventually, poor condition and weight loss are apparent.

What is the treatment?
Although surgical intervention is necessary in a few cases, the vast majority of cats can be treated at home. Dosing with liquid paraffin will result in the mass either being regurgitated or passed in the faeces. Give three tsp the first day, two tsp the second day and one the third day. Don't add liquid paraffin to the diet of a furball-collecting cat permanently as it will reduce its absorption of some vitamins.

Abdominal problems

Besides containing important organs which can succumb to disease, the abdominal cavity can become infected.

Peritonitis

The lining of the abdominal cavity and the covering of the contained organs is known as the peritoneum. This can become inflamed for several reasons: □ infection enters via a rupture in the abdominal wall or intestines □ infection spreads from other abdominal organs □ the presence of tumours □ germs arrive through the blood or lymphatic system.

What are the signs?
The signs include: □ persistent pain in the abdomen □ it sits in a "tucked-up" posture □ vomiting □ diarrhoea or constipation □ fever □ no appetite.

What is the treatment?
Prompt veterinary attention is essential. Diagnosis may involve blood tests and even an exploratory operation. Drugs can fight infections, and reduce the chances of internal adhesions forming.

Feline Infectious Peritonitis

This infection of the cat's abdominal cavity is caused by a virus, and mainly attacks cats under three years of age. It affects the peritoneum and attacks several organs including the liver, kidneys and brain. Most infected cats die after a few weeks of illness.

What are the signs?
Signs include: □ fever □ chronic loss of weight and condition □ dropsical swelling of the abdomen □ vomiting □ diarrhoea. Also but less frequently: □ jaundice □ respiratory signs □ abnormalities in the nervous system.

What is the treatment?
There isn't a vaccine available to protect cats against this disease. Treatment consists of combatting dehydration by replacing fluids, giving vitamin and hormone supplements, draining off fluid and fighting secondary infections with antibiotics. Keep your cat warm and give it plenty of liquids (see p. 272).

Feline Immunodeficiency virus

This disease, sometimes called Feline AIDS or "FAIDS", is caused by a virus in the same family as the human AIDS virus, but there is no evidence that people can be infected from cats. It is becoming increasingly common in cat populations, and because it suppresses the cat's immune systems, symptoms include weight loss, inappetance, fever, chronic diarrhoea, chronic respiratory disease, skin disease and neurological disturbances. It is probable that spread of the disease is through bites, though close and prolonged contact is thought also to be required. Infected cats can carry the virus, without showing any signs of illness, for years. Diagnosis is by blood test. As yet, there is no specific treatment or protective vaccine.

The tucked-up posture
A cat with abdominal pain due to peritonitis may assume this characteristic stance.

Nutritional problems

Dietary problems shouldn't occur if your cat is given a good-quality, well-balanced menu (see pp. 156-9).

Obesity
Cats shouldn't weigh more than eight kg; persistent overfeeding will result in gross obesity which will put a strain on the heart, liver and joints.

Excess fats in the diet
Cats need a high percentage of fat in their diet, particularly as they get older. But too much fatty fish or fish oil can produce heart and fat tissue disease. The signs include: □dullness □ stiffness □ soreness on being handled □ circulatory abnormalities □ fever. Vitamin E is used for treatment.

Calcium deficiency
The most important mineral to a cat, calcium is essential for pregnant and nursing queens and growing kittens. In kittens skeletal deformities can occur, and in adults brittle bones and lactation tatany (see p. 256) may result. Lean meat is low in calcium, so include milk, fish (with the bones), and balanced proprietary foods in your cat's diet. Treatment consists of calcium supplements or sterilized bone flour.

Deficiencies of other minerals
Many other minerals are essential to cats (see p.157), but deficiencies rarely occur as sufficient quantities are obtained from meat and fish.

Because cats eat a high-protein diet, they require a relatively large amount of iodine. Signs are: □ sluggishness □ alopecia □ scurfy, dry skin □ infertility. Iodine has to be given very carefully to avoid overdosing. Season home-cooked food with iodized household salt or give proprietary multi-vitamin/trace element tablets.

Vitamin A deficiency
Cats on a purely lean meat diet are sometimes deficient in vitamin A. Signs include: □ infertility □ abortion □ poor condition □ bone, skin and eye disease. Feeding liver or cod liver oil corrects the problem . But don't give too much fish oil – an overdose can lead to bone disease.

Vitamin B deficiency
There are several vitamins in the B group, all of which are essential for the cat. Deficiency of vitamin B1 can occur if too much overprocessed food or raw fish is given. Signs include convulsions and strokes. Vitamin B6 can be destroyed by overprocessing, leading to weight loss, anaemia and convulsions. Commercial cat foods have extra B vitamins added. Treatment for deficiency involves B-complex injections, yeast or multi-B tablets.

Vitamin D deficiency
A shortage of vitamin D, leading to bone disease, is uncommon in cats, and is caused by a diet of purely lean meat. Treatment is vitamin injections, feeding cod liver oil and a balanced diet.

PREVENTING NUTRITIONAL PROBLEMS
● Feed a well-balanced diet (see p. 156–9)
● Lightly season food with salt or give multi-vitamin/trace element tablets designed for small animals
● Never overfeed (see p. 165)

Problems of the intestinal tract

The most common health problems encountered with the feline intestinal tract are diarrhoea and constipation.

Milk sensitivity diarrhoea

Chronic diarrhoea may be due to a deficiency of the milk-sugar-digesting enzyme, lactase, or to an allergy to milk protein.

What is the treatment?
In severe cases, the diet should be modified to exclude milk, milk products and most cereal products. Calcium supplements may be necessary. In mild cases, just dilute milk with water.

Enteritis and colitis

Inflammation of the small intestine alone is known as enteritis. Colitis is an inflammation of both the colon and rectum. Inflammation is caused by: □ bacterial or viral infections □ ingestion of irritant chemicals or poisons □ abdominal tumour □ chronic kidney disease □ parasites. Signs of intestinal inflammation may include fresh blood and mucus in the stools.

What is the treatment?
Get as much fluid as possible into the cat to combat the risk of dehydration. The vet will give antibiotics.

Feline Infectious Enteritis

Also known as *Feline Panleucopenia*, this highly contagious viral disease is resistant to many antiseptics, and can be transmitted by direct or indirect contact, even via fleas. With a 2—9 day incubation period, it invades the cells of the small intestine wall, the liver, spleen, bone marrow, some lymph nodes and, in unborn or newly born kittens, the brain. Cats may die within minutes of first showing signs of the disease. Less acute cases show signs that include: □ depression □ persistent vomiting □ diarrhoea □ rapid dehydration □ sitting in a typical "hunched-up" posture □ wailing pitifully when touched.

What is the treatment?
The vet will give fluids and stimulant drugs, also antibiotics to tackle any secondary bacterial infection. After seeing the vet, keep your sick cat warm and give it small, frequent helpings of warm glucose and water (see p. 272).

PREVENTING FELINE ENTERITIS

This fatal disease can be prevented by a vaccination given along with the "Cat Flu" vaccine (see p. 229) at 8—9 weeks of age. A second injection is given 3—4 weeks later, with boosters every 12 months. Dead vaccines are available, so a pregnant queen can be boosted to ensure high levels of antibodies in the colostrum and thus protect newly born kittens.

Constipation

Older cats, particularly longhaired, fastidious self-groomers, are the most likely to develop impaction of the large intestine and rectum.

What are the signs?
The cat may: □ strain hard to pass the faecal mass □ often show signs of pain □ gradually become dull □ crouch miserably □ show no interest in food or the world about it.
   It is important to differentiate between straining caused by bowel

impaction and straining due to urinary obstruction (see p. 252) as the two can resemble one another closely.

What is the treatment?
Start by giving liquid paraffin by mouth (see p. 275). If this doesn't work, the vet may give a softening enema. A disposable enema kit suitable for home use is available which your vet may prescribe, and instruct you on its use. Alternatively, you can give docusate sodium tablets by mouth; this chemical softens and draws water into hardened, impacted faeces.

If these measures fail, the vet will anaesthesize the cat and break up the mass directly. In a few cases, an operation may be necessary.

Obstruction of the rectum
The terminal portion of the intestinal tract is the most common site for a foreign body to jam, producing pain on defecation, irritation, constipation and sometimes straining.

What is the treatment?
Grease the anus gently with salad oil or liquid paraffin, or, if there is room, insert a glycerine suppository. If the obstruction doesn't clear as a result, consult the vet, who will remove it under anaesthetic. *Never* pull at any thread protruding from a cat's anus — it may run around bends in the intestinal canal, and you could easily lacerate the delicate lining. In such a case, consult the vet immediately.

Rectal prolapse
Persistent diarrhoea and straining may result in a short length of bowel turning inside out and protruding from the anus. Once out, this prolapse acts as an irritant, giving rise to more straining and, often, more prolapse.

PREVENTING INTESTINAL PROBLEMS
- Don't feed chicken bones
- Don't let the cat hunt and eat any wild food
- Groom the cat regularly to reduce loose hair
- Add a bulk-acting laxative as directed to the cat's diet

What is the treatment?
If your cat has a prolapse you *must* seek urgent veterinary attention. Before you see the vet, clean the exposed rectum with warm water on cotton swabs, then grease it liberally with liquid paraffin. The vet will push the prolapse back into place under anaesthetic and insert retaining sutures. Whatever caused the problem — often chronic diarrhoea — must be treated concurrently.

Anal irritation
In cats, irritation is usually due to the presence of wriggling tapeworm segments or matted hair following diarrhoea. Matted hair provides perfect conditions for the development of wet dermatitis (skin inflammation accompanied by a discharge), the moisture from which may attract blowflies to lay their eggs which hatch into maggots. An affected cat may turn round to spit at its tail, hold its tail pulled beneath it or make sudden little forward dashes.

What is the treatment?
Clip away all long, matted hair. Then wash the area with soap and water, rinse and dry it. Apply a human nappy cream. Where infection is present, an antibiotic ointment may be prescribed by the vet. If necessary, lightly dust with a proprietary powder (available from the vet) to kill maggots.

Problems with internal parasites

Found in virtually any of the cat's tissues, including the eye, lung and heart, the most common feline parasites are worms, and the most important group of these parasites are those which infect the gastro-intestinal tract: roundworms, tapeworms and flukes.

Roundworms

Two kinds of roundworms of the *Ascarid* family are commonly found in cats: *Toxocara* and *Toxascaris*. They don't suck blood, but feed on the digesting food in the cat's intestinal canal. Eggs are laid which pass out in the stools, and are then eaten by another cat, either directly, or after passing through mice, rats or beetles. Larval worms can penetrate the placenta to infest the foetus in the womb, and they are sometimes present in the mother's milk. Once in a kitten's body, the worms migrate through liver, heart and lungs to the intestine. Kittens are thus much more seriously affected than adults, and may develop: □ either diarrhoea or constipation □ anaemia □ pot-bellies □ poor condition.

Whipworms and threadworms

Smaller than *Ascarids*, these parasites are rarer in cats. Like roundworms, they have a direct lifecycle, the eggs and larvae requiring no intermediate host. The threadworm larvae inhabit the small intestine, where they burrow into the wall and may cause haemorrhages, whilst whipworms prefer the large intestine. Both parasites cause signs including: □ diarrhoea □ loss of weight □ anaemia.

Hookworms

These serious blood-sucking worms are more common in the U.S. than the U.K. They enter their host via the mouth or by burrowing through the skin, and then migrate to the small intestine. And they can pass to unborn kittens via the placenta. These worms produce signs of: □ diarrhoea (often blood-streaked) □ weakness □ anaemia.

Tapeworms

Not as dangerous as roundworms or flukes, tapeworms live in the small and large intestine and share the cat's

COMMON PARASITES

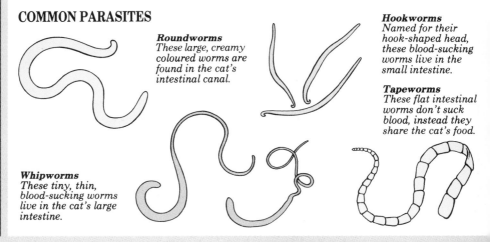

Roundworms
These large, creamy coloured worms are found in the cat's intestinal canal.

Hookworms
Named for their hook-shaped head, these blood-sucking worms live in the small intestine.

Tapeworms
These flat intestinal worms don't suck blood, instead they share the cat's food.

Whipworms
These tiny, thin, blood-sucking worms live in the cat's large intestine.

digesting food without sucking blood. Their presence may cause irritation and flatulence, but little else. When segments are passed through the anus they can cause irritation (see p. 239). The tiny, round eggs also pass out of the cat's anus, and these "rice grains" stuck to a cat's rear end are often the only sign of a tapeworm infestation. Once they have left the cat, the tapeworm's eggs must be eaten by an intermediate host such as a mouse or flea (one common U.S. tapeworm has *two* intermediate hosts, first a tiny crustacean, and then a fish). In this host's body they develop into a larval stage. Only when the intermediate host has been eaten by another cat will the larva be able to develop into another adult tapeworm.

Flukes
Found in the small intestine, pancreas and bile ducts, though rare in the U.K., flukes are fairly common in Asia, Europe and Canada. The intermediate hosts are a snail and a freshwater fish. Signs are: ☐ digestive upsets ☐ jaundice ☐ diarrhoea ☐ anaemia.

Other parasites
Cats can be infested with microscopic *Protozoa* parasites: *Amoeba, Trichomonas, Coccidia* and *Giardia*. All of these may produce diarrhoea and other gastro-intestinal signs, but are uncommon as causes of disease.

More important is *Toxoplasma*, which can invade various tissues of the cat's body, including the intestine, and is generally contracted through eating raw meat. Acute attacks, with signs that are easily confused with other diseases, may occur; these can be fatal. Chronic cases also exist. A common sign in both forms is diarrhoea. The cat sheds the parasites in its stools, and these can be passed on to humans. Although this disease is rare, it is a risk to pregnant women, who may pass it on to their unborn baby.

What is the treatment for parasites?
Ask your vet for advice on safe, effective deworming drugs. In most cases, your vet will recommend worming only healthy cats, unless the worms themselves are the cause of illness. It is generally advisable to worm queens before they become pregnant, and they can be safely treated when pregnant too. Two doses of worming drugs are usually given, with the second dose intended to catch immature parasites.

PREVENTING TOXOPLASMOSIS AFFECTING HUMANS
Careful hygienic precautions are important:
● Use disinfectant to clean the litter tray and surrounding area
● Change the litter daily
● Wear rubber gloves when handling litter (essential if you are pregnant)
● Cook all food for your cat thoroughly
● Keep children's sandpits covered
● Wear gardening gloves to avoid contact with infected soil

PREVENTING PARASITIC INFESTATION
● Stop your cat eating wild life
● Groom it regularly and use anti-parasitic powders to keep it free of larvae-carrying fleas
● Change bedding regularly to avoid the conditions that attract skin-burrowing worms
● Dispose of litter by burning, deep-burial or placing it in the dustbin
● Regular worming against tapeworms every 4 months and roundworms every 6 months is advisable

Liver and pancreatic problems

The liver and pancreas are employed in the process of digesting and metabolizing food and are therefore very important to a cat's well-being.

Liver problems

This important organ can be damaged by: □ poisons □ parasites (e.g. flukes or migrating worms) □ direct infections (Toxoplasmosis) □ indirectly when other organs are affected (e.g. by fevers or Feline Infectious Peritonitis) □ malnutrition □ tumours □ physical trauma.

What are the signs?
The signs of liver malfunction vary, and can range from the very dramatic (the cat may even die suddenly) to the very mild, and include □ jaundice □ collapse □ coma □ vomiting □ diarrhoea or constipation □ changes in stool colour □ increased thirst □ excitation (due to accumulation of waste products in the brain) □ swollen abdomen (due to an accumulation of fluid) □ depression □ dullness.

What is the professional treatment?
Only a vet can diagnose liver disease, generally by blood, urine and fecal sample analysis. The treatment is likely to include vitamin B complex, liver extract, glucose and corticosteroid treatment to raise the blood sugar level, increase the liver function and protect the cells.

What is the home treatment?
You should keep your sick cat warm and provide it with plenty of liquids at all times. Glucose and water (see p. 272) is preferable. You should also give it low-fat, high-protein diet (see p. 157).

Acute inflammation of the pancreas

Occasionally, a cat's pancreas becomes severely inflamed. This is usually very serious, and the cat may well die within hours or a few days. The signs include: □ vomiting □ tenseness and pain in the abdomen □ fever □ shock □ collapse.

What is the treatment?
Veterinary treatment *must* be given very quickly. It may include an intravenous injection of fluids, analgesics and anti-inflammatory drugs. The outlook isn't generally very good.

Chronic inflammation of the pancreas

Long-term inflammation will damage the pancreas. In such cases, the output of enzymes needed for the digestion of food and absorption of fat is lowered.

What are the signs?
This condition produces changes in the stools, which become clay-coloured, pale and fatty. With its ability to digest food efficiently markedly reduced, the cat develops a prodigious appetite, but loses weight and condition.

What is the treatment?
Following laboratory tests on the stools to confirm the malfunctioning pancreas, treatment involves providing a low-fat diet and adding substitute pancreatic enzymes to the food.

Diabetes

Diabetes mellitus or sugar diabetes is fairly common in cats, particularly in older, fatter individuals. And there seems to be a tendency to diabetes in some feline breeding lines.

GIVING YOUR CAT AN INJECTION

If your cat suffers from diabetes or certain other ailments, daily injections may be necessary. In the case of a diabetic cat, these will be of insulin. Your vet will supply you with the bottles of insulin at varying strengths, and with disposable, sterile needles and syringes. Insulin injections should always be given first thing in the morning.

1 Test the urine to determine insulin needed, and prepare the syringe. Grasp your cat firmly by its scruff.

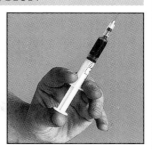

2 Point the syringe at the ceiling and press the plunger to force air out of it. Swab the site with alcohol on cotton wool.

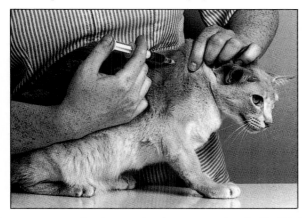

3 Push the needle through the skin into the layer of fat close to your "scruffing" hand. Don't worry about hurting your cat as most injections are painless, and the more relaxed you and your pet are, the easier it will be to administer the injection.

What are the signs?
The signs include: □ great thirst □ increased appetite □ a progressive loss of weight □ cataracts may develop in the eye □ in advanced cases, vomiting may occur. Diagnosis depends on the analysis of sugar levels in the blood and urine.

What is the treatment?
First, make sure that all carbohydrates, including any sugary treats, are eliminated from the diet. And cut out cat food that contains cereal such as barley. Your vet will instruct you how to give daily insulin injections — a relatively painless, simple procedure — and will also give you guidance on estimating dosage using the urine testing strips (these are dipped into a puddle of urine and change colour when sugar is present). The dosage may vary from time to time because of stress, illness or changes in diet.

EYE AND EAR DISORDERS

Of the number of eye and ear problems found in cats, the most serious are blindness and deafness. However, the chances of a sighted or hearing cat going blind or deaf are small, and the most common problem you are likely to encounter is obstruction — foreign matter in the eye or wax in the ear. When treating a cat's eyes or ears, you may find that you need to restrain it (see p. 270). Once it is held still, use a torch and a magnifying glass for the examination.

SEE ALSO:
The structure of the eye see *Anatomy* p. 22.
Foreign body in the eye see *First Aid* p. 280.
The structure of the ear see *Anatomy* p. 23.
Restraining a cat see *Health Care* p. 270.
Bleeding and wounds see *First Aid* p. 282.

BULGING EYE

Swelling of the tissue behind the eye will push the cat's eyeball forward, making it protrude out of the socket.

Things to look for
- Protruding eyeball
- Staring look
- Eyelid won't close
- Dilated pupil — due to stretched nerves to eye

Possible causes
- Accidental blow
- Infection spread from sinus
- Tumour behind eyeball
- Glaucoma

Treatment
There is very little you can do before the vet's examination; just keep the cat indoors.

Urgency
+++ Don't delay — consult a vet immediately. To reduce the swelling, drugs, or perhaps surgery, will be needed.

DISCHARGE FROM THE EYES

A clear discharge is often caused by blocked tear ducts, and is fairly common, particularly in Longhairs. Less common but more serious is a cloudy discharge, probably due to an infection.

Things to look for
- Is the discharge clear? If so, the cat probably has blocked tear ducts

- Is the discharge cloudy? If so, the cat may well have a bacterial or viral infection
- Are the cat's eyes also causing it pain? If so, see *Painful eye* (right)

Possible causes
- Blocked tear ducts
- Conjunctivitis
- Viral respiratory illness
- Eye disease such as glaucoma

Treatment
Don't let the discharge mat into the cat's fur — bathe the area around its eye with warm water on cotton.

Urgency
++ If clear, seek veterinary advice as soon as convenient.
+++ If purulent or painful, don't delay — consult a vet immediately.

FAILING SIGHT

This condition can't be detected from looking at the eye; you are more likely to suspect it from observing the cat's behaviour. If you think that your cat might have vision problems, try the test on the right, testing one eye at a time.

Things to look for
● Is the cat's coordination impaired?
● Is the cat bumping into furniture?
● Does the cat's eye(s) look cloudy? If so, it may have a serious infection of the eye
● Does the cat respond to a moving object?

Testing sight
Cover one eye and move your finger towards the other, as if you were going to touch it. If the cat blinks, it has some sight in that eye.

Possible causes
● Diseases such as retinal disease, cataract, keratitis or glaucoma

● Processes affecting the brain such as encephalitis caused by an infection, a stroke, a tumour, or an inherited neurological disease

Treatment
Prompt veterinary attention is important. Meanwhile, keep the cat indoors in familar surroundings, and put a guard in front of fires.

Urgency
+++ Don't delay — consult a vet immediately. Total or partial loss of sight may be reversible with prompt treatment.

PAINFUL EYE

A foreign body in the eye, accidental injury or disease can affect a cat's eyes. The main sign of these problems is usually pain or discomfort.

Things to look for
● Does the cat keep its eyelid closed? It may have an irritant infection or a corneal abrasion
● Is the cat pawing at its eye? It may have an irritant infection or a foreign body in its eye
● Is there a blue or white opacity in or on the eye? This may indicate that the cat has a cataract
● Is there any discharge? If so, see *Discharge from the eyes* (left)

Possible causes
● Foreign body in the eye
● Conjunctivitis
● Severe infection such as glaucoma
● Cataract
● Accidental abrasion
● Tumour
● Congenital disease

Treatment
In all cases, you can help the cat by gently flooding or bathing its eyes with a soothing liquid solution. The best way to do this is to soak a pad of cotton in cold tea or a solution of 1 tsp of boracic acid in 1 cup of warm water, and squeeze the liquid into the cat's eye.
  If the eye is bleeding, you should hold a pad of cotton wool soaked in iced water onto it until the vet can examine it.

Bathing a cat's eye
Use a cotton pad to gently squeeze a suitably soothing liquid onto the eye.

Urgency
+++ Don't delay — consult a vet immediately.

DEAFNESS

A hearing cat turns its head to look in the direction of a sound, moving its ears around to locate the exact position of a noise. If your cat doesn't do this, it may well be deaf. This condition may be either temporary or permanent, depending on the cause. Hereditary or degenerative factors and inner ear disease generally produce permanent deafness, whilst deafness brought on by outer and middle ear infections, wax or parasites may be temporary. Cats generally cope well with deafness.

Things to look for
● Are there signs of a build-up of wax in the ear? If so, the ear canal may be blocked
● Is there any sign of irritation, soreness or discharge (see below)? This would indicate an outer or middle ear infection
● Is the cat holding its head to one side? This would indicate a middle or inner ear infection
● Is the cat white in colour? It may have hereditary deafness
● Is it old? It may have a degenerative problem

Possible causes
● Wax blockage
● Outer ear infection
● Middle ear infection
● Inner ear infection
● Hereditary factor
● Old age

Treatment
There is little you can do before the vet's examination.

Urgency
✚✚ Seek veterinary advice as soon as convenient. The vet will check the ears for the presence of wax, infection, tumours or parasites.

DISCHARGE FROM THE EARS

This common problem is generally a sign of a bacterial infection or a parasitic infestation. Often, such problems can be prevented by regularly inspecting and cleaning your cat's outer ear area (see p. 250).

Things to look for
● Is the discharge dark and waxy? If so, the cat may have an ear mite or fungal infestation
● Is the discharge purulent? If so, the cat may have a bacterial infection
● Is the cat shaking its head? This would indicate an ear mite infestation

Possible causes
● Ear mites
● Bacterial infection
● Fungal infection

Treatment
Gently clean the outer ear area, using a twist of cotton wool soaked in warm olive oil (see below). Don't let the discharge mat into the cat's fur — bathe the surrounding area with warm water, then dry it carefully.

Discourage the cat from scratching its ear — it may develop a large blood blister known as a haemotoma (see p. 250). *Don't* probe down into the ear canal with any object, not even your fingers.

Urgency
✚✚ Seek veterinary advice as soon as convenient.

Cleaning the ear
Wipe the outer ear area clean with a gentle, circular motion.

Eye problems

There are several signs which indicate an eye disorder: ☐ partial or total closure of the eye ☐ swelling and inflammation of the eyelid ☐ covering of part or all of the eye by the third eyelid ☐ profuse watering or discharge ☐ cloudiness or blueness of the normally transparent cornea ☐ changes of colour deeper in the eye ☐ swelling of the eyeball ☐ blood in the eye itself ☐ blood oozing from the eyelid ☐ signs of blindness (see p. 245). If you observe any of these signs, singly or in combination, apply first aid and don't delay in contacting a vet as expert treatment is essential for *all* eye problems.

Scratched eyelid or eye

The most common cause of damage to the eyelids or eye itself is a scratch from another cat. At first, the cat will display: ☐ soreness ☐ watering ☐ blinking ☐ closure of the eyelids. This may lead to an infection, resulting in: ☐ swollen eyelids ☐ purulent discharge. And, if the eyeball is affected: ☐ ulceration or inflammation of the cornea.

Conjunctivitis

Inflammation of the lining of the eyelids and the thin layer of tissue covering the visible white of the eyeball is known as conjunctivitis. Signs include: ☐ redness ☐ watering or discharge ☐ soreness ☐ blinking ☐ closure of the lids. Conjunctivitis can be caused by: ☐ bacterial infection ☐ upper respiratory viruses (see p. 229) ☐ congenitally inturned eyelids ☐ allergic reaction ☐ a foreign body ☐ irritant gases, vapours, smoke or liquids ☐ an eye worm known as *Thelazia*.

Conjunctivitis
There are several possible causes for the inflammation and discharge affecting this cat's eye. In all such cases prompt veterinary attention is essential.

Corneal problems

The normally transparent "window" of the eye may be damaged by a blow or infected by bacteria, becoming cloudy and bluish, and later white and opaque. This is *not* the same thing as a cataract. Simple, non-infected corneal wounds heal quickly, but where infection is present, ulceration or further inflammation deeper in the eye may follow.

Ulcers on the cornea can be caused by wounds, particularly in breeds like Longhairs which have prominent eyes. Alternatively, they can be caused by an infection, such as the FVRV virus (see p. 229).

A black area of dead cells in the centre of the cornea, the cause of which is unknown, occasionally occurs in Longhairs, producing watering and associated conjunctivitis.

Conditions of the inner eye

Inflammation of the iris itself, the choroid and its associated muscles can be due to a number of causes, including: ☐ penetrating wounds ☐ corneal ulcerations ☐ infections such as Feline Infectious Peritonitis or Toxoplasmosis.

Retinal inflammation also has many causes, from tuberculosis to Toxoplasmosis. And a blow can detach part of the retina, leading to partial blindness.

Glaucoma

This serious condition involves enlargement of the eye, often with attendant corneal cloudiness, and occurs when the fluid within the eye can't circulate as a result of internal bleeding, inflammation of the iris and associated structures, or a tumour.

Cataracts

Opacity of the pupil of a cat's eye is often due to the development of a cataract in the lens, and generally occurs in elderly or diabetic cats. Apparent opacity of the lens in elderly cats isn't necessarily a cataract — it may be merely a change in the refractive index of the lens due to age. This doesn't interfere with normal vision.

Third eyelid problems

The "haw", nictating membrane or "third eyelid" is a little triangle of pink or white tissue that peeps out from the inner corner of each eye. Sometimes one of these "eyelids" is damaged in a fight. Once swollen and inflamed, it protrudes at the corner of the eye, and in such cases it is best dealt with by the vet under anaesthetic.

Often a worried owner will take a cat to the vet because it has suddenly developed "white sheets" over its eyes. What has happened is that the third eyelid has moved over a portion of the cornea. The cat is *not* blind as a result, but it certainly makes the cat look very odd. The cause of this common complaint isn't fully understood. It is likely that a debilitating factor such as a virus either makes the eyeball muscles contract into the socket or the pad of fat behind the eye shrink in size so that the eyeball settles back, pushing the third eyelid forward. Often a generalized condition lies behind it: incipient cat flu, diarrhoea or a parasitic infestation.

Eyeball abnormalities

A tumour or a foreign body in the eye can cause a non-congenital squint in any breed of cat, whilst a congenital squint is generally seen in Siamese. Another eye problem peculiar to Siamese produces a rhythmic oscillation of the eyeball. This may be congenital, or the result of an ear

Glaucoma
An opaque, cloudy look to the eye, often accompanied by protrusion, is the most common sign of this disorder.

Cataract
Opacity restricted to the pupil is usually a sign of a cataract on the lens. Surgery is only recommended if cataracts affect both eyes.

Protruding third eyelids
This cat's third eyelids or nictating membranes are clearly visible protruding across the eyeballs from the inner corners of its eyes.

APPLYING OINTMENT TO A CAT'S EYELID

Hold your cat's head still with one hand and use the other to apply the ointment. Only use a proprietary ointment for cats that has been prescribed by your vet.

And don't apply any form of eye ointment to your cat's eyes before visiting the vet as it may interfere with the examination.

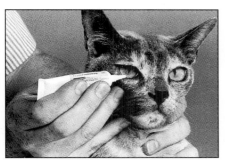

1 Hold the tube parallel with the eye, *not* pointing towards it. Squeeze it, allowing a line of ointment to fall across and into contact with the eyeball.

2 Hold the eyelids gently together for a few moments to allow the ointment to melt onto the eye.

disorder such as middle ear disease or a brain condition like a stroke.

Blindness

Severe eye conditions such as infected ulcers on both corneas will drastically affect vision. However, evidence of blindness (see p. 245) is sometimes seen in a cat which displays no obvious signs of eye disease or damage. Such cases are caused by changes in the deep structure of the eye, in the visual centre of the brain or the nerves linking eye to brain. Expert examination is urgently needed as some cases respond to speedy treatment.

Gradually developing blindness in a cat which knows its own home can be coped with. The cat has time to adjust to its loss of sight, and still enjoy life. Though obviously, it can't be allowed outdoors. However, a cat that turns blind suddenly can become very disturbed. In such a case, if the vet advises that the condition is irreversible, euthanasia is the most humane course.

What is the treatment for eye problems?

When you notice any signs of eye trouble in your cat *don't* delay — contact a vet immediately. Meanwhile, you can help your pet by removing matted discharges and bathing "gummed-up" eyelids. Swab the affected area gently and repeatedly with warm human eye wash or tea. Don't apply any form of eye ointment before visiting the vet as it may interfere with the examination. And don't use eyedrops prescribed for humans without your vet's permission. Some problems such as infections require drug therapy; others, like cataracts, require an operation.

Ear problems

If your cat is suffering from pain or irritation in the ear examine it carefully. Look for red-brown wax, and if present, clean the ears as shown below. If there is no sign of this wax, soothe the ear by flooding it with warm olive oil or liquid paraffin, stand back and let the cat shake out any excess. Then don't delay — contact a vet immediately.

Canker

This common outer ear inflammation is caused by the presence of foreign bodies such as grass seeds, mange mites, bacteria or fungi. An affected cat will show signs of irritation and sometimes discharge, it will scratch its ears and shake its head. Mange mites are present in most cats' ears. They irritate the ear canal, resulting in the secretion of a protective red-brown wax. As the wax builds up, infection may set in.

Middle ear disease

Deeper ear infections can produce problems in the middle ear. This condition is characterized by: ☐ tilting of the head towards the affected side ☐ staggering ☐ circling ☐ loss of balance ☐ some deafness. Prompt veterinary attention is important. Treatment consists of drugs, and, in some cases, surgical drainage.

Puffy ear

Cats which scratch violently at their ears often burst blood vessels in the ear flap, producing a large blood blister or *haematoma*. While this isn't particularly painful, it will irritate the cat, who will carry on scratching, and may tilt its head to the affected side. If left untreated, it will form a "cauliflower" ear. The vet will treat the cause and drain off the blood.

PREVENTING EAR PROBLEMS

Regular visual inspection of your cat's ears is essential. But don't poke inside with cotton buds, tweezers or fingers. A normal outer ear canal looks clean and clear. If your cat has any red-brown wax treat it before it can lead to an infection.

 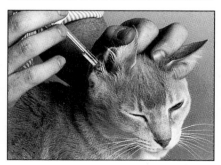

1 Lightly moisten small pads of cotton wool with warm olive oil. Then insert the oiled cotton into the outer ear with a gentle, twisting motion.

2 Apply proprietary ear drops (available from your vet) using the dropper provided. Massage the ear afterwards to spread the effect.

DISORDERS OF THE URINARY TRACT

The kidneys, bladder and connecting passages are the route that various toxic wastes travel through to the outside world. Normally this waste takes the form of clear, yellow urine, but infection can affect its colour. The most common problem in this system is inflammation of the bladder and urethra. All urinary tract disorders are potentially serious, so a veterinary examination is essential.

SEE ALSO:
Liquids see *Feeding* p. 163.
Lack of water see *Feeding* p. 156.

HOW THE CAT'S URINARY SYSTEM WORKS

Waste products from the blood are filtered by the kidneys. They form urine, and drain into the ureters via the renal funnels. From the ureters, urine flows into the bladder. And from the bladder urine is carried out of the body by the urethra, which ends at the tip of the penis in the male and between the folds of the vulva in the female. Voiding is controlled by the central nervous system.

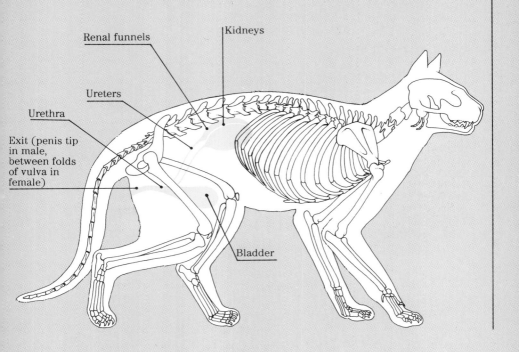

Renal funnels

Kidneys

Ureters

Urethra

Exit (penis tip in male, between folds of vulva in female)

Bladder

INCONTINENCE

The natural place for a cat to urinate is at one of its territorial marks. With appropriate training (see p. 133), its litter tray soon becomes one of these. If your cat urinates elsewhere, clean the area scrupulously with a strong disinfectant to avoid a repetition of the soiling.

Things to look for
● Is the cat a new arrival? It may simply be nervous or unfamiliar with the location of the litter tray
● Is the cat an unneutered tom? If so, he may be marking his territory
● Has the cat's thirst increased? If so, it may have diabetes (see p. 242)
● Are there any other signs such as straining (see below), vomiting or diarrhoea? If so, the cat may have an infection

Possible causes
● Territorial marking
● Diabetes
● Bladder inflammation
● Urethral inflammation
● Damage to the bladder

Treatment
If your cat is a tom and is spraying, either arrange to have him neutered, or build a tom's run (see p. 142) and keep him out of the house. If your cat isn't a tom and there are no other signs (such as straining, increased thirst, vomiting or diarrhoea), give it a 250 mg hexamine tablet 2—3 times a day.

Don't restrict the supply of liquids available to your cat. Don't rub your cat's nose in the urine — this practice only encourages it to re-use the spot as the area then becomes one of its territorial marks.

Giving liquids
Cutting back on your cat's liquid intake won't solve its incontinence problem and may harm its kidneys.

Urgency
✚ If there are no other signs, consult a vet as soon as convenient
✚✚✚ If there are other signs (such as straining, increased thirst, vomiting or diarrhoea) don't delay — consult a vet immediately.

STRAINING

If the cat appears to be straining (see the diagram opposite) and it isn't constipated (see p. 232), then it probably has a urinary blockage.

Things to look for
● Has the cat passed any faeces in the last 24 hours? If not, it may be constipated or have an intestinal blockage (see p. 238)
● Is the cat passing urine normally? If not, there is a possibility of a blockage
● Does the cat seem to be in pain? It may have a urinary infection
● Is the cat a queen due to go into labour? If she is, her labour contractions may be starting (see p. 207)

Possible causes
● Constipation
● Intestinal blockage
● Cystitis
● Urinary "stones"
● Onset of labour

Treatment
There is little you can do before the vet's examination.

Urgency
✚✚✚ Don't delay — consult a vet immediately.

Problems of the urinary tract

Problems in this system are generally caused by infections. Kidney disorders are rare, but inflammation of the feline urinary tract is quite common. If you suspect a urinary problem, contact the vet immediately.

Acute kidney problems

Nephritis, or acute kidney infection, doesn't occur very often. Signs are: ☐ vomiting (may be blood-tinged) ☐ thirst ☐ inflammation of the mouth (often with difficulty in swallowing) ☐ severe dullness ☐ convulsions ☐ coma.

What is the treatment?
If the cause is a poison, the vet will try to get rid of the toxin. And in all cases, fluids are given to combat dehydration.

Chronic kidney problems

Old cats frequently show signs of chronic disease, starting with: ☐ great thirst ☐ increased urinary output ☐ loss of weight and condition. In advanced cases more signs develop: ☐ uraemia (retention of waste products in the blood) ☐ vomiting ☐ bad breath ☐ a sore, ulcerated mouth ☐ anaemia ☐ dehydration. In terminal cases death is preceded by: ☐ vomiting of blood ☐ convulsions ☐ coma.

What is the treatment?
Destroyed kidney tissue can't be replaced, so the load on the remaining kidney must be kept to a minimum. Give your cat a good-quality low-protein, high-carbohydrate diet: glucose, honey and sugar are useful energy sources. The vet may prescribe fluid injections, vitamin supplements, and suitable drugs.

Straining
A cat with a urinary blockage will crouch uncomfortably over the litter tray.

The bladder and urethra

At first, a cat with urinary trouble will strain to pass a little bloodstained urine. In more advanced cases this straining may be fruitless, the cat crouches in an awkward position (see above) and develops a distended abdomen. Do *not* squeeze the tummy — this is painful for the cat and may even burst its bladder. Most often found in neutered males, this condition is due to a gritty sludge in the urine blocking the passage. Causes are: ☐ too-early neutering ☐ low fluid intake ☐ dry foods ☐ old age ☐ obesity ☐ lack of exercise.

What is the treatment?
A blocked urethra needs immediate veterinary attention — the vet will free the blockage under anaesthetic.

PREVENTING URINARY BLOCKAGE

● Don't have males neutered until they are at least nine months old
● Provide plenty of water to drink
● Don't give too much dried food
● Add a little salt to your cat's meals to encourage it to drink

REPRODUCTIVE DISORDERS

This section is mostly concerned with problems of the female cat's reproductive tract as there are no special problems of the male feline genitalia. The most common condition in males is a bite wound inflicted by another tom, which should be treated like other wounds (see p. 282). If the injury is extensive or infected, consult the vet.

> **SEE ALSO:**
> **The structure of the reproductive system** see *Breeding* p. 203.
> **Labour problems** see *Breeding* p. 210.
> **Bleeding** see *Diagnosis charts* p. 222.
> **Wounds** see *First Aid* p. 282.

MISCARRIAGE

Premature onset of labour is uncommon in the cat. However, if a pregnant queen begins straining and the birth isn't due, suspect an imminent miscarriage.

Things to look for
● Is there blood or other discharge at the vulva?
● Are there any other signs of illness such as vomiting or diarrhoea? She may have an infection which has induced a premature birth
● Are you sure that she isn't going into labour at the normal time (nine weeks after season)?

Possible causes
● Accident
● Infection
● Foetal abnormality

Treatment
Keep the cat in a quiet place until the vet arrives.

Urgency
+++ If you are sure that the labour is premature, don't delay — contact the vet immediately. If in doubt, wait three hours, then contact the vet if no kittens have been born.

INFERTILITY

The failure of your queen to produce kittens may be the result of an unsuccessful mating or a physical defect in either her or the tom concerned. If the mating was concluded normally, the most likely cause is an infection in the queen's reproductive system.

Things to look for
● Has your cat been in an accident? If so, she may have had an early undetected miscarriage
● Is your queen exhibiting any signs of sickness or poor condition?
● Have her heat periods been regular? Frequent or permanent oestrus is a sign of ovarian cysts
● Did the queen show the usual signs of pregnancy following mating? A false pregnancy may have developed

Possible causes
● Undetected miscarriage
● Uterine or vaginal infection
● Pyrometra
● Ovarian cysts
● Congenital absence or abnormality of reproductive organs
● False pregnancy
● Blocked fallopian tubes
● Failure to ovulate

Treatment
There is little you can do before the vet's examination.

Urgency
+++ Don't delay — consult a vet immediately.

Problems in the queen

Disorders of the female cat's reproductive tract won't affect a neutered cat. However, if you have an unneutered female (queen) she may suffer from one of these problems.

Ovarian cysts
When ovarian follicles don't ripen, but instead enlarge into cysts and turn out large quantities of female sex hormone, this interferes with the normal sexual cycle. Signs include: □ infertility □ frequent or permanent heat periods □ loss of condition and weight □ nervousness □ a generally discontented temperament.

What is the treatment?
The vet may use hormones to encourage the cyst to ripen and dissolve, or if that is likely to be ineffective, operate to remove the ovaries. Occasionally, surgery doesn't solve the problem, however treatment with the male hormone, testosterone, generally helps such cases.

Metritis
Infection and inflammation of the uterus (womb) may follow a difficult birth, particularly in a debilitated or older queen, or where placental material has been retained, or where a dead kitten was born or removed by forceps or Caesarian section. Signs may include: □ dullness □ lack of appetite □ fever □ pain in the abdomen □ unpleasant, smelly, bloody or purulent vulval discharge □ excess thirst □ vomiting.

What is the treatment?
The vet will give antibiotic injections, and may use a hormone to shrink down the uterus. Where dehydration has become evident, fluid replacement is essential; provide your cat with nourishing liquids such as beef tea, honey-water and protein hydrolysate.

Pyometra
Although this term strictly means "pus in the womb", it is used in veterinary medicine to describe a hormonal condition that occurs in the uterus. Structural changes, probably due to ovarian cysts, lead to thickening of the uterine wall, and the development of microscopic cysts. Inflammation then develops, and the uterus eventually fills with a sticky, pus-like fluid. Signs include □ vulval discharge □ dullness □ enlargement of the abdomen □ thirst □ loss of appetite □ vomiting □ poor body condition. Treatment involves removal of uterus and ovaries.

Prolapse of the uterus
Occasionally, following a difficult birth, some or most of the uterus will prolapse through the vagina, presenting itself as a bulging, red mass. Once the delicate lining membrane is exposed, it can easily be damaged.

What is the treatment?
Urgent veterinary attention is required. While you wait, keep the prolapse clean and moist, sponging it with warm water on cotton wool. Apply liquid paraffin or petroleum jelly to it, and cover it with clean cloth. If attended to quickly, the vet may be able to replace the uterus under sedative or anaesthetic. If time has elapsed or the case is severe, an abdominal operation will be necessary to fix the uterus back into place.

TREATING MASTITIS

This problem is generally caused by kittens scrabbling at the breast as they suckle, producing shallow lacerations through which bacteria can enter. You can relieve the swelling by applying a saturated solution of magnesium sulphate and warm water several times a day.

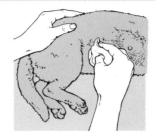

1 Swab the swollen gland with the magnesium sulphate solution on cotton wool.

2 Dry the area gently and thoroughly, then lightly dust it with an antiseptic powder.

Post-partum haemorrhage

After a difficult labour a queen may sometimes haemorrhage from the uterus. In serious cases, shock, collapse and even death can result, so if this happens to your cat you *must* take her to the vet at once. Signs are:
□ a flow of blood from the vagina
□ constant licking of the vulva
□ weakness □ pale mouth and eye membranes □ rapid, gasping breathing
□ as shock sets in, the cat will feel cold and the pale membranes may turn blue.

What is the treatment?
Drugs will be administered by the vet to contract down the uterus and speed up clotting. If blood loss is severe, and the queen is in shock, a blood transfusion will be required, and the cat will probably be hospitalized for some time.

Mammary gland problems

Inflammation of a queen's mammary glands (mastitis) sometimes occurs during lactation. The signs are: □ swelling □ redness □ tenderness □ feverishness □ dullness

□ disinterest in food □ refusing to let the kittens suckle.

Chronic mastitis, cysts and tumours frequently occur in older cats. Only a vet will be able to differentiate between them.

What is the treatment?
The vet will prescribe antibiotics. You can help by swabbing the swollen glands (see above). In the case of a tumour, surgery is performed at once.

Lactation tatany

Sometimes called eclampsia or "milk fever", this syndrome is caused by a fall in the calcium level in the blood, usually during lactation or, very rarely, during pregnancy. Signs vary, but include: □ muscular twitching
□ tremors □ spasms □ staggering
□ paralysis □ panting □ vomiting.

What is the treatment?
Urgent veterinary attention is essential; an injection of a calcium salt will be administered, and calcium supplements prescribed. This condition responds to treatment very quickly.

CIRCULATORY DISORDERS

The circulatory system has two main functions: transporting oxygen and other vital materials around the body, and combatting infection. Unlike us, cats aren't prone to heart disease, and blood problems are the major health threat to the feline circulatory system. All these problems are potentially serious and therefore require immediate veterinary attention.

SEE ALSO:
Taking the pulse see *Health Care* p. 216.
Bleeding see *First Aid* p. 282.
Collapse see *First Aid* p. 278.
Feeling for a heartbeat see *First Aid* p. 278.

HOW THE CAT'S CIRCULATORY SYSTEM WORKS

The heart is a muscular pump divided into four chambers: left and right auricles, and left and right ventricles. Blood is pumped out from the left ventricle through arteries to reach the network of capillaries that permeates all the body's tissues. The blood returns to the heart through veins, passes through the right auricle and ventricle, and proceeds via the pulmonary arteries to the lungs where it recharges with fresh oxygen and discharges carbon dioxide. The rejuvenated blood returns once again to the heart via pulmonary veins, passing through the left auricle and left ventricle before it sets out round the tissues again.

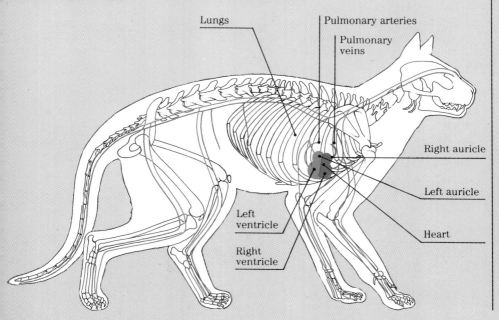

Lungs

Pulmonary arteries

Pulmonary veins

Right auricle

Left auricle

Heart

Left ventricle

Right ventricle

Blood and heart problems

Simple blood disorders such as anaemia are fairly common in cats, but heart conditions such as thrombosis are rare.

The heart

Several different kinds of heart problems are found in cats: kittens may be born with holes in the heart walls, infections such as septicaemia and feline influenza (see p. 229) can cause damage; and tumours, pneumonia and pleurisy (p. 228) can also affect the heart. And as cats get older, the heart valves may get weaker or become blocked. Signs of heart disease include: □ a tendency to tire easily □ breathlessness or heavy breathing □ a lilac tinge to the gums □ coughing □ wheezing □ gasping and respiratory malfunction □ intestinal upsets □ nervous signs.

What is the treatment?
The vet will listen to your cat's heart with a stethoscope, and may take an electrocardiogram, X-ray and/or blood samples in order to make the diagnosis. The treatment varies – certain drugs used on humans such as digitalis can be given to cats under strict veterinary supervision. Feline cardiac patients must be kept indoors, and taken for regular check-ups with the vet.

Illiac thrombosis

Thrombosis sometimes occurs in the main artery (the aorta). It is probably caused by a section of inflammatory tissue on a diseased heart valve breaking away, and being carried along by the blood stream until it jams in the aorta. Signs are dramatic and develop suddenly, they include: □ shock □ pain □ collapse □ partial or complete hind leg paralysis □ the hind legs feel *extremely* cold to the touch □ the femoral pulse (see p. 126) is absent in both hind legs.

What is the treatment?
Urgent surgery or drug treatment is necessary, and careful nursing is essential. Unfortunately, the recovery rate is low, and animals that do recover often suffer a second attack.

Heart worm

A round worm called *Dirofilaria immitis* is sometimes found in the right ventricle and pulmonary artery. This parasite affects cats in Southern Europe, the U.S., Far East and Australia. Larvae are transmitted to other animals by blood-sucking mosquitos or fleas. Signs aren't always produced, but when evident, they resemble those of heart disease.

If you live in a high-risk area control fleas and protect cats from mosquitos at night by keeping them indoors in mosquito-proof quarters.

What is the treatment?
Drugs are available which kill the worms, but the presence of the dead worms in the heart can in itself result in thrombosis or shock as the cat's body may react to the protein substances released by the dead parasites. However, larvae can be removed safely from the blood by drug treatment.

Feline Infectious Anaemia

This disease is caused by a parasite, *Haemobartonella felis*, which can infest feline red blood cells. It is probably transmitted by blood-sucking insects such as fleas and mosquitos. It may live in the red cells without causing much damage, but at times (for example, when a cat's resistance is lowered), it can destroy cells, resulting in anaemia. Signs are: □ dullness □ weakness □ loss of weight and condition □ pale eye and mouth membranes.

What is the treatment?
The vet will take blood samples to look for the parasite and estimate the degree of anaemia. FIA often occurs where there is a concurrent Feline Leukaemia condition. When a cat has both diseases the outlook is very poor, but where it exists alone the prognosis is good. Treatment consists of antibiotics, anti-anaemic therapy and, in severe cases, blood transfusion.

Anaemia

A reduction in number of circulating red blood cells and/or the amount of oxygen-carrying haemoglobin within those cells is known as anaemia. There are three main reasons why this happens:

1 The destruction of red cells by: □ parasites (as in FIA) □ a poison (for example, lead) □ a bacterial toxin □ an immunity reaction (as in an incompatible blood transfusion).

2 Loss of blood as a result of: □ an accident □ ingestion of an anti-coagulant chemical (such as the rodent poison, warfarin) □ a constantly bleeding ulcer, tumour or lesion □ the presence of blood-sucking parasites.

3 Reduced or abnormal production of new red blood cells in the bone marrow as a result of: □ a tumour □ a poison □ an acute infection □ a chronic septic condition □ chronic kidney disease □ tuberculosis □ deficiency of essential substances in the diet.

What are the signs?
The basic signs of anaemia are pale eye and mouth membranes. In advanced cases indications of "oxygen hunger" –

weakness, breathlessness, fatigue and restlessness – may occur.

What is the treatment?
The vet will take blood samples to determine the cause and profundity of the condition. Anaemia isn't a disease in itself, merely a sign of an underlying illness. Therapy will include specific treatment for the cause, combined with iron supplements, drugs and, in some cases, a blood transfusion.

Leukaemia

This cancerous, uncontrolled multiplication of white cells in the blood and lymphatic system is common in cats. Caused by a virus, Feline Leukaemia is contagious and is spread by direct contact. It can't live long outside the cat's body and is easily destroyed by disinfectants. Some cats are naturally resistant whilst others develop immunity to it without showing any signs of illness. The unlucky remainder, once infected, develop signs which may include: □ eye disease □ kidney failure □ anaemia □ vomiting □ diarrhoea □ loss of weight □ weakness □ respiratory problems.

What is the treatment?
There is no cure and an infected cat should be euthanased to prevent the disease spreading to other animals. A blood test for the presence of the virus is available. Although cats that are positive to the test may not show signs of the disease, they may well be shedding the virus and will be a source of infection. If they aren't euthanased they must be isolated from other animals. Cats can be vaccinated against Feline Leukaemia, along with the Feline Influenza and Feline Enteritis "shots" from 9 weeks of age. Booster vaccinations are necessary annually.

NERVOUS DISORDERS

The most common afflictions of the feline nervous system — the brain, spinal cord and the network of nerves radiating from them — are injuries caused by accidents. However, there are also a number of diseases that can affect this system. All these problems are potentially serious, and therefore a prompt veterinary examination is essential.

SEE ALSO:
Collapse see *First Aid* p. 278.
Shock see *First Aid* p. 278.
Fits see *First Aid* p. 280.
Rabies see *Housing and Handling* p. 151.

HOW THE CAT'S NERVOUS SYSTEM WORKS

The cat's central nervous system consists of the controlling brain and its main pathway, the spinal cord. This cord is carried in a bony canal formed by the spinal vertebrae. From the cord a network of nerves runs throughout the entire body, carrying motor impulses to the muscles and sending back sensory messages to the brain. These nerves are, to an extent, within the cat's control. Other nerves in the cat's body function automatically — these form the autonomic nervous system.

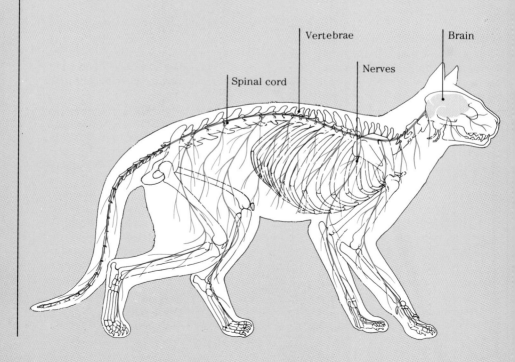

Spinal cord   Vertebrae   Nerves   Brain

STAGGERING GAIT

If your cat staggers, wobbles or falls over, or generally has trouble standing upright, this may be due to a disorder of the nervous system. Or its balance may be affected by an ear problem (see p. 250).

Things to look for
● Has the cat ingested poison (see p. 281)?
● Has the cat been in an accident? It may have shock, or more seriously, cerebral or spinal damage
● Has it other signs such as vomiting or dilated pupils? It may have a severe disease

Possible causes
● Poisoning
● Shock
● Brain disease or damage
● Spinal cord problem
● Middle ear disease
● Severe weakness due to a specific illness
● Muscular disease

Treatment
There is little you can do before the vet's examination.

Urgency
✚✚✚ Don't delay — consult a vet immediately.

TREMBLING

General trembling is rare in cats — they don't shiver when cold as we do — and indicates a health problem.

Things to look for
● Has the cat been in an accident? It may be in shock
● Has the cat ingested poison (see p. 281)?
● Has it signs of disease — vomiting, diarrhoea or dilated pupils?
● Are there any parasite droppings in the fur?

Possible causes
● Shock
● Poisoning
● Disease or injury to the nervous system
● Parasites

Treatment
If there is evidence of parasites, apply an anti-parasite powder or aerosol. If the cause isn't parasites, there is little you can do before the vet's examination.

Urgency
✚ Parasites may be treatable at home.
✚✚✚ In other cases, don't delay — consult a vet immediately.

PARALYSIS

If your cat can't move all or part of its body, the cause is either neurological damage or disease.

Things to look for
● Is there any indication that the cat has been in an accident? It may have a fracture or spinal injury
● Are the cat's pupils dilated? It may have encephalitis
● Does the paralysis only affect the back limbs? This would indicate spinal disease or damage
● Is there a chance that the cat may have ingested a poison (see p. 281)?

Possible causes
● Spinal injury or disease
● Fractured pelvis or leg
● Brain disease
● Bone disease
● Poisoning
● Tetanus

Treatment
There is little you can do before the vet's examination. If the cat is in an unsafe position move it away (see p. 278).

Urgency
✚✚✚ Don't delay — consult a vet immediately.

Neurological problems

Health problems which can affect the brain and spinal cord of a cat range from mild concussion following a fall to serious infections such as meningitis.

Meningitis
This uncommon disease affects the membranes covering the brain and spinal cord, and is usually caused by the spread of infection from some other parts of the body. Signs include: □ dullness □ depression □ loss of appetite □ fever □ convulsions □ dilated pupils. Swift veterinary attention is essential. The vet will tap the spine with a hypodermic to take specimens of the cerebro-spinal fluid. Therapy consists of antibiotics and corticosteroids.

Encephalitis
Inflammation of the brain can be caused by: □ bacteria following septicaemia □ bacteria spreading from an infected middle or inner ear □ viruses such as Rabies □ fungi □ protozoans (*Toxoplasma*) □ some poisons.
   Signs include: □ dullness □ fever □ dilated pupils □ staggering gait □ paralysis epilepsy □ coma. In many cases, the vet may find it difficult to pinpoint the cause. Where the cause is known, drugs are given. The cat should be confined to quiet surroundings.

B.S.E ("Mad Cow Disease") and cats
A strange, incurable disease – bovine spongiform encephalopathy (B.S.E.), appeared in Britain in 1986. It attacks the brain and spinal cord of cattle and seems to be caused by a maverick speck of protein smaller than a virus. Within 8 years 140,000 cattle were dead as well as a small number of domestic cats, a puma, an ocelot and some cheetahs. All had eaten cow meat before the government introduced measures to remove nervous tissue from carcases in 1986. Due to the long incubation period of the disease there may be odd cases in the future in cats born before 1986. The symptoms, unsteadiness and loss of orientation resemble those in other far more common diseases of cats such as Middle Ear Disease, which, if caught early, can be treated by the vet.

Epilepsy
This is a disturbance in the brain. Often obscure, the causes may be related to parasites, a tumour or an injury.

What are the signs?
The signs resemble "fits": the cat keels over, frothing at the mouth, chattering its jaws and paddling with its paws. Faeces and urine are often passed. After a few minutes, the cat quietens, getting to its feet as if nothing had happened.

What is the treatment?
For immediate action see First Aid on p. 280. If your cat has frequent attacks (more than once a month), consult the vet, who will administer a drug.

Concussion
An accidental blow to the head affects the brain, resulting in concussion. The animal is unconscious for a period, then may show signs of brain damage such as paralysis, a staggering gait or blindness. In most cases, signs are temporary and last at most five days. Treatment may include drug and vitamin injections.

Myelitis and spinal cord damage
Damage to the spinal cord ranges from bruising to laceration or even severing,

and generally occurs as a result of an accident. Myelitis is inflammation of the spinal cord, and can be caused by bacteria spreading from infected tissues nearby (often a septic bite wound in the back), viruses (for example, Rabies), parasites (such as *Toxoplasma*) and poisons. Signs vary, but include limb paralysis and back pain.

What is the treament?
Treatment begins with indentification of the cause and the use of specific drugs aimed at this. In some cases drainage of the spinal canal is necessary, and if paralysis is present, physiotherapy is advised. Good nursing and control of secondary infections are essential, particularly where paralysis renders bowel and bladder control impossible. If after a month the paralysis has shown no definite signs of improvement, recovery isn't likely to occur. If the cat has improved, a full return to health will still take several months.

The Key-Gaskell syndrome
This mysterious disease has only been recognized recently, and the cause hasn't yet been identified. It usually affects only one cat in a group, and is as likely to strike a domestic cat as a free-ranging feline. The signs are: □ dullness □ loss of appetite □ vomiting and regurgitation of food □ constipation □ dilated pupils □ paralytic dilation of the gullet.

What is the treatment?
The vet will prescribe liquid paraffin as a laxative and give drugs to strengthen control of the nervous system. The mortality rate is around 70 percent.

Local nerve paralysis
Sometimes a nerve supplying part of the body ceases to function and the area becomes paralyzed. Usually the result of an accident, this generally happens to the tail or a limb. Unable to control the appendage, the cat drags it about, and friction from the ground produces ulceration. As the animal usually can't feel any pain, further damage can occur.

What is the treatment?
In cases where paralysis has existed for over a month without any perceptible sign of improvement despite treatment, it is best to have the leg or tail amputated (see below).

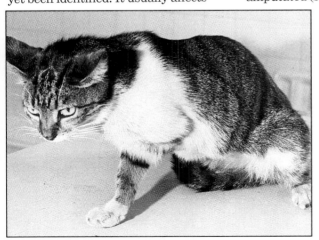

A feline amputee
Three-legged cats like the one shown here get around very well indeed, and recover rapidly from the operation. This treatment isn't in any way cruel, and the animal isn't turned into a cripple.

MUSCLE AND BONE DISORDERS

Diseases which affect the muscles, bones or joints are rare in cats, and the main health problems are due to injuries sustained in accidents or fights. Minor injuries such as sprains may be treatable at home, but if the cat seems to be in pain a veterinary examination is advisable.

Never give aspirin or use human linament; if you want to treat your cat before the vet's examination swab the area with an infusion of comfrey leaves in water.

SEE ALSO:
The skeletal anatomy see *Anatomy* p. 19.
The muscles see *Anatomy* p. 20.
Caring for an elderly cat see *Care and nursing* p. 274.
Fractures see *First Aid* p. 283.

LIMPING

There are a wide range of reasons why a cat drags its leg or finds it difficult to put its full weight on it.

Things to look for
● Does the cat seem in pain if you touch the affected limb? This would indicate an injury or infection
● Is a single limb affected? If so, is it thicker than the other one? It may be fractured or sprained
● Is there any blood on the limb? The cat may have been in an accident
● Is there a swelling on the limb? A tumour may be the cause

Possible causes
● Bone infection
● Accidental injury
● Fracture
● Sprain
● Wound
● Tumour

Treatment
Apply first aid if necessary (see p. 282). Never give human or dog analgesics. Keep the cat indoors until the vet's examination.

Urgency
+++ Don't delay – consult a vet immediately.

SWOLLEN LEGS AND FEET

A sudden swelling of your cat's legs and/or feet is most likely to be the result of an infection.

Things to look for
● Has your cat been in a fight? A bite may have caused an infection
● Is a single limb affected? It may be fractured or have a tumour
● Does the cat look pot-bellied? Circulatory or kidney problems may have caused dropsy
● Does your pet seem stiff or have difficulty moving around, especially after a period of rest? It may have arthritis or another bone disease

Possible causes
● Bone infection
● Fracture
● Tumour
● Dropsy
● Arthritis

Treatment
Apply first aid if necessary (see p. 282). Keep the cat indoors until the vet's examination.

Urgency
+++ Don't delay – consult a vet immediately.

Problems with muscles, bones and joints

Always consult a vet if your cat shows signs of pain or stiffness, or if it is limping. *Never* give aspirin to a cat, even if it seems in pain, as this drug is toxic to cats.

Bone disease

Cats' bones lie fairly close to the surface of the body and are, in general, less protected by layers of soft tissue than those of humans or dogs. During a fight, the sharp teeth of a feline adversary can easily penetrate to the bone, and therefore limb or tail-bone infections are quite common. A pocket of infection, producing pus, is set up on or within the bone. If the marrow is involved a very serious infection known as osteomyelitis may develop. Wounds must therefore be treated before this serious infection can gain hold in the bone.

What is the treatment?
All bite wounds must receive veterinary attention — antibiotics will be prescribed to prevent the infection spreading to the bone. Treatment of osteomyelitis includes surgery to cut away areas of diseased bone.

Arthritis and joint disease

Inflammation of the feline joints is very rare, and chronic arthritis of the type suffered by humans or dogs seldom affects cats. However, occasionally an elderly cat may develop lameness due to the degeneration of a joint. If this happens to your cat, consult a vet who will prescribe anti-inflammatory drugs.

TREATING A SPRAIN

Sprains seldom occur in the lithe, light cat. When they do, signs are pain and diminished function of the affected part. Wrenched or crushed muscle fibres may be torn or bruised. Treat with hot and cold compresses and then support the affected part with a loosely wrapped bandage (see p. 282).

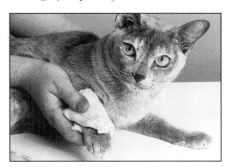

1 Immediately after the accident make a cold compress by soaking clean cotton wool or cloth in chilled water.

2 Apply a fresh cold compress every 30 minutes. After a few hours, change to a hot compress (water as hot as the back of your hand can bear).

DISORDERS OF THE SKIN AND COAT

The signs of skin disease in cats aren't specific to any one ailment: loss of hair, changes in the underlying skin, inflammation and irritation are common to a variety of skin conditions. Diagnosis requires professional examination, often aided by laboratory analysis of skin scrapings. Skin problems aren't always caused by disease or infestation — in some cases they are simply battle scars from fighting.

SEE ALSO:
The coat's function see *Anatomy* p. 26.
Coat care see *Grooming* pp.170—5.
Scratching see *Diagnosis Charts* p. 223.

ECZEMA

There are many types of skin problem categorized under this name.

Things to look for
● Is the cat's diet broad? If not, it may have a vitamin deficiency
● Does the condition recur at regular intervals? If so, it may be an allergy
● Has it dry scaliness, redness, pimples, wet oozing, matted hair or hair loss? It may have a skin disease
● Are there any parasites such as fleas in the fur?
● Is the cat neutered? If so, it may have a hormone deficiency

Possible causes
● Nutritional problems
● Allergy
● Microbe attack
● Parasitic infection
● Hormone upset

Treatment
Clip matted hair, bathe in weak antiseptic, then dry. Apply cetrimide cream.

Clipping hair
Work carefully, making sure that you don't cut the skin.

Urgency
++ Consult a vet as soon as convenient.

HAIR LOSS

If patches of your cat's hair fall out and it isn't the moulting season, a health problem is the likely cause.

Things to look for
● Is the skin reddened, broken, weeping or bumpy? If so, the cat may have fungal dermatitis
● Can you see insects or fine, black "coal dust" flea droppings in the coat?
● Is the cat's diet broad? If not, it may have a vitamin deficiency

Possible causes
● Fungal dermatitis
● Parasites
● Vitamin deficiency

Treatment
If the skin is affected, bathe it in weak disinfectant, then apply liquid paraffin. For parasites, use a proprietary powder. If necessary, correct the diet (see p. 237).

Urgency
++ Consult a vet as soon as convenient.

Skin and coat problems

There are two main kinds of skin disease — parasitic and non-parasitic. Both are quite common in cats, and should be checked for at your regular grooming sessions.

Flea infestation

A cat can become infested with feline, dog or human fleas, the presence of which makes the cat scratch, twitch or lick itself frenziedly. Wherever fleas exist, what looks like coal dust can be found in the cat's coat. These particles are flea droppings. Reddish pimples with a darker, crumbly centre can develop, particularly along the spine as this area is sensitive to the protein in flea saliva. Fleas may carry tapeworm larvae, and can also spread certain viral diseases.

Lice infestation

Two kinds of louse are found on cats: one sucking type, one biting type. The most common site is on the head, but they can make their home anywhere on the body. A heavily infested cat will be run-down and anaemic.

Tick infestation

Country-dwelling cats can pick up sheep ticks. These parasites suck

Signs of fleas
A black "coal-dust" powder found in a cat's fur is actually flea droppings. To check this, wipe them on a moist tissue — if they are droppings they will leave a dark red smudge (blood).

blood, swelling up so that they resemble blackcurrants. You may mistake them for a tumour or a cyst. They don't move around as their mouth parts are buried securely in the cat's skin. For this reason, you mustn't pull them off as the mouthpart may be left behind, causing an abcess.

Mange mite infestation

These minute creatures burrow into a cat's skin, causing chronic inflammation, hair loss and irritation. The most common species is *Notoedres*, which affects the head and ear area, producing baldness, scurfiness and dermatitis.

Other mite infestation

During the autumn harvest mites or chiggers (*Trombicula autumnale*) can cause irritation and areas of dermatitis on a cat's skin. And the Fur mite

EXTERNAL CAT PARASITES

Flea (*Ctenocephalides felis*)
Dark brown and the size of a pinhead, these insects can cause skin problems.

Louse (*Felicola*)
This pinhead-size, grey creature can cause poor health and anaemia.

Sheep tick (*Ixodes*)
This large, round, blood-sucking parasite affects country cats and can cause anaemia.

Mange mite (*Notoedres*)
This mite can cause inflammation and hair loss.

Signs of ringworm
This small, circular area with a bald centre and crusty outer edge is characteristic of ringworm, a common form of fungal dermatitis.

(which can affect humans as well as furry pets) causes excessive dandruff in the coat.

What is the treatment for infestation?
Seek your vet's advice on the best form of treatment for flea or mite infestation as there are many different types of anti-parasitic preparations on the market.

Remove ticks by applying a drop of chloroform or ether to them, waiting until the mouthparts relax, and then picking them off with tweezers. Once you have removed the tick, you should treat the cat with the appropriate anti-parasitic preparation.

PREVENTING HUMAN INFECTION

Humans can contract fungal dermatitis and some forms of mange mite, so take precautions to make sure the infection doesn't spread from the cat to the family. Burn all bedding and litter, and sterilize equipment such as boxes and utensils in a hot, cat-safe disinfectant.

Cat fleas and lice may bite you, but they can't live on you and therefore preventive precautions aren't necessary.

Fungal dermatitis
Caused by a fungus (*Microsporon* or *Trichophytes*), this skin problem takes the form of small, circular areas with bald centres and weeping or crusty outer edges or a general area of scaly, powdery skin.

After tests, the disease is treated either with an antibiotic given by mouth or an anti-fungal lotion or wash applied to the affected area.

Non-parasitic disease
Dermatitis and inflamed sores can be the result of: ☐ a bacterial infection ☐ a food allergy ☐ contact with irritant chemicals ☐ sunburn ☐ vitamin deficiencies ☐ hormonal problems.

What is the treatment?
Don't apply any ointment without veterinary advice — the cat may lick it off and suffer ill effects. Instead, clip away hair from the area, clean the skin with warm water and weak antiseptic and dry it carefully. Then contact the vet. If your cat licks or bites the area, fit an Elizabethan collar.

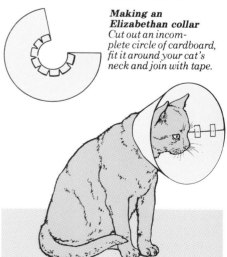

Making an Elizabethan collar
Cut out an incomplete circle of cardboard, fit it around your cat's neck and join with tape.

NURSING AND CARE

Keeping your cat healthy is basically a matter of common sense, and the principles of caring for it are much the same as those used in looking after a human baby. Since your cat can't tell you if it is feeling under the weather, it is up to you to keep a close check on it, and to investigate any abnormalities immediately.

In the course of its life even a normally healthy cat may be involved in an accident and require veterinary attention, and once it becomes elderly it will certainly need regular checks by the vet. Aside from professional care, your pet will occasionally need to be nursed at home. You may be able to deal effectively with some minor ailments, but you should always consult your vet if a condition persists or you can't detect what is wrong.

The domestic cat can be a difficult patient, and the quality of nursing provided by the owner is often as important to a full and speedy recovery as any sophisticated drug treatment or life-saving surgical operation. A sick cat needs a quiet, clean, warm and comfortable environment. This can be provided at the veterinary hospital or in the home. However, over and above these requirements, it also needs love. An ailing cat will make a better recovery if it is ministered to by someone who really cares for it, so in the majority of cases I find it more beneficial to have a cat nursed by its owner in its own home than in the most modern, highly equipped veterinary hospital.

Veterinary care

If your cat is unwell or injured, you will most likely have to take it to the vet's surgery or request a home visit. In all cases, telephone first and follow the vet's advice. In most instances, it is best to take your pet to the vet's, but for mini-epidemics among more than one cat in a household, difficulties while giving birth, if a badly injured cat is in an awkward spot, or if you are infirm and can't arrange transport, the vet may make a house call. You should withhold food and water before the examination in case an anaesthetic is needed.

The vet's examination

In the consulting room, the vet will ask for details of your pet's problem, and its past medical history. (If you have seen the vet previously your pet's medical record will be on file.) Be clear, concise and objective in giving information, and don't anticipate the diagnosis.

MOVING A SICK CAT

If the cat is in pain or agitated, hold its scruff firmly with one hand, with the other under its hindquarters. Wrap it in a blanket and place it in a carrying basket (see p. 149). A calm cat can travel on someone's lap.

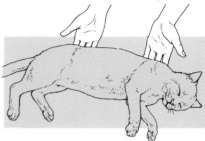

Moving a calm or unconscious cat
Gently turn the cat onto its side and lift it with two hands placed palms uppermost beneath the chest and the pelvis.

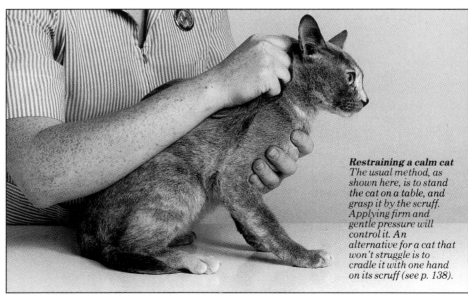

Restraining a calm cat
The usual method, as shown here, is to stand the cat on a table, and grasp it by the scruff. Applying firm and gentle pressure will control it. An alternative for a cat that won't struggle is to cradle it with one hand on its scruff (see p. 138).

EXAMINING AN AGITATED OR NERVOUS CAT

There are various ways of presenting an agitated cat for examination, depending on the form of the inspection and the state of the animal. In extreme cases, the vet may have to give it a tranquilizer. In all instances, the vet will handle the cat with your assistance or that of a veterinary nurse. You may find that wrapping your cat in a blanket (see below) for a while will calm it, and the vet will then be able to examine it unwrapped. Or the vet may prefer to immobilize the cat by holding its legs while carrying out the inspection.

Restraining for a head examination
The cat is wrapped in a cloth or blanket, with only its head sticking out. This will enable the vet to inspect its eyes, ears, mouth or nose.

Preventing the cat from clawing
The cat is placed prone on the table with its legs held by the assistant. The animal is unharmed, but can't use its claws.

After the diagnosis
Your vet will tell you whether home nursing (see p. 272) will be possible, or whether your pet should be left at the surgery for hospitalization so that further diagnostic or therapeutic measures can be carried out. Some new developments in small-animal medicine are best performed "in hospital", where the staff can monitor your pet. In other cases, home care in familiar surroundings may be preferable.

Death

If you are fortunate, your cat will die in its sleep when its time comes. However, if a cat is in pain that isn't likely to be relieved, or if the animal is diseased and obviously unhappy, then as a humane owner, you will have to make a difficult decision. I feel it is irresponsible to deny the creature a dignified end.

Euthanasia
This merciful procedure is an extension of deep general anaesthesia. The vet injects an overdose of an anaesthetic either intravenously or into the chest. Rapid, painful poisons are never used, and the only pain is that of a needle prick. You may ask to watch the procedure, if you wish. Most vets can arrange cremation or burial for your pet, or you may prefer to bury it yourself or take it to a pet cemetery.

If your vet suggests that a post-mortem examination is of value, I recommend you agree as your pet won't feel anything, but may contribute to the advancement of pet health.

Home nursing

If your cat should become ill, you will need to provide it with a comfortable, hygienic rest area, and a nutritious, tempting diet. And you may have to administer drugs prescribed by the vet.

Providing a suitable "sick-room"
The main requirements of a sick cat are rest and warmth. It should be provided with a clean, heated, airy environment and snug bedding. Good draught-free ventilation is particularly important if your cat has a respiratory ailment. Warmth can be provided by central heating or by a fan heater, infra-red lamp, hot water bottle or blankets. But take care when using infra-red lamps and hot water bottles, as they can cause burns if placed too close to a cat. Set up and turn on the lamp, wait a minute or two, then test the distance (usually a minimum of 60 cm) by placing your hand where the cat will lie. Hot water bottles are best wrapped in a cloth cover before being put in contact with the cat. Don't allow a sick, convalescent or injured cat to go out of doors. It must remain under your round-the-clock control until it has completely recovered.

Feeding a sick cat
Loss of appetite is a common feature of many feline illnesses, but cats rarely die from starvation. But dehydration caused by a drastic reduction in the fluid intake can be aggravated by vomiting and/or diarrhoea, and can kill a cat very quickly. You should provide nourishing liquid food and, if necessary, spoonfeed your cat. Give it 1–3 tsp regularly.

Invalid foods
Unless the vet advises giving a special diet, feed your pet a variety of tempting, high-value, tissue-building foods – those that are rich in protein, minerals and vitamins – and give energy-rich, easily digested items to provide calories.

SPOONFEEDING A CAT

Grasp it by the scruff, and twist your wrist so that the head is flexed backwards and the mouth opened. Then spoon in the liquid, drop by drop, letting it run down the tongue.

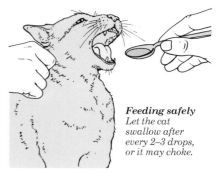

Feeding safely
Let the cat swallow after every 2–3 drops, or it may choke.

Liquids
- Dilute glucose (2 tsp : 1 cup of water)
- Dilute honey (2 tsp : 1 cup of water)
- Beeftea
- Warmed, liquified calf's foot jelly
- Proprietary liquid invalid foods
- Fish and meat soups
- Feline instant diets (proprietary concentrated powders made up with water)

Solids
- Fresh fish and shellfish
- Best quality minced meat
- Cheese and eggs
- Cooked poultry, lamb or pig's liver
- Meat- and fish-based baby foods

Administering Drugs

You should be able to serve pills, tablets or liquid medicines yourself. However, if your cat requires an injection, the vet will give this, unless the cat is diabetic, when you will be instructed in the method (see p. 243).

Pills and tablets

Follow the instructions below. Don't crush the tablet and sprinkle the resulting powder onto the tongue as many drugs have an unpleasant or bitter taste which will cause the cat to produce copious, foamy saliva and to become agitated.

Liquid medicines

The easiest way of giving cats these is by spoonfeeding (see opposite). Very bitter liquids and some tablets crushed and mixed with water may produce salivation in the cat. Most cats can detect drugs mixed in their food and will refuse to eat.

Injections

For these, you may need to make regular, possibly daily, visits to the vet, but in some cases a continous thera-peutic action over several weeks can be obtained with a single injection.

Sick-room hygiene

During illness, it is especially important to continue with the regular hygiene, grooming and inspection of your pet (see p. 168). Also disinfectants should be used to clean the "sick-room" area.

Warning: Many commonly used household disinfectants – the phenolic, coaltar and woodtar, hexachlorophene and iodine preparations – are dangerous for cats. Other disinfectants are safe for general use if diluted as indicated on the containers. These include cetrimide, quaternary ammonium compounds, and the safest and most effective, dodecine. To find out whether a disinfectant is suitable, study the list of ingredients on the label.

GIVING YOUR CAT A PILL OR TABLET

Generally two people are required, one to immobilize the cat by pressing it down firmly onto a flat surface with one hand on its scruff, while the other person acts as the "pill pusher". You can use your fingers, the blunt end of a pencil or a "pill gun" to push the pill further into the cat's mouth. Smearing the pill with butter may help its passage. Once you have pushed the pill down the cat's throat, close its mouth and stroke its throat until it swallows.

1 With forefinger and thumb, grasp the head from above where the jaws meet, and tip it back. Press finger and thumb in.

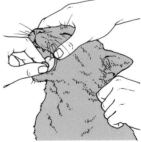

2 Push on the lower jaw with the other index finger. Drop the pill far back on the middle of the tongue. Push it quickly so it moves over the back of the tongue.

Looking after an elderly cat

A cat that survives beyond 17 years of age is doing very well. Very few pets reach 20 years old (see p. 35).

As cats age, they change physically, frequently becoming thinner, and their appetite often alters. These changes may be caused by failing liver and kidneys, conditions which, in the absence of other signs, are difficult for the vet to diagnose. All elderly cats should receive regular check-ups with a vet every 3—4 months.

SEE ALSO:

Intestinal problems see *Ailments* pp. 238—9.
Urinary tract problems see *Ailments* pp. 251—2.
Eye problems see *Ailments* pp. 247—8.
Ear problems see *Ailments* p. 250.
Bones and joints see *Ailments* pp. 264—5.

FEEDING TIPS

● If your cat's appetite increases, give more food at each meal or more meals
● Provide high-quality protein food — fish, meat and poultry — and a variety of vegetables and fruit
● Give warm water or milk when required as denying increased thirst is dangerous
● Mix 1 tsp of lard with food to provide the extra calories needed by an old lean animal who can't absorb nutrients very well and no longer has the underskin layer of insulating fat
● Add liquid paraffin to the diet occasionally to combat constipation
● Bran and oily fish can aid constipation problems

Bowel problems and soiling
Many old cats suffer from bowel sluggishness and constipation. Others occasionally lose control of their bowels or bladder. If the problem becomes troublesome, ask your vet to check the cat. Involuntary "leaking" can be caused by cystitis, which should be treated.

Caring for the teeth
Regular veterinary attention throughout your cat's life should have stopped the build-up of tartar, but a sudden fondness for soft snacks may cause rapid tartar formation, gum damage, inflammation of the tooth sockets and loosening teeth. These in turn may contribute to kidney and liver rundown. Clean an elderly cat's teeth once or twice weekly (see p. 234).

Eye and ear problems
An elderly cat's hearing and eyesight may fail gradually. If this happens to your pet, remember that a deaf cat can't hear potential dangers such as a vacuum cleaner. With a blind cat, keep its feeding bowls in the same place, avoid rearranging familiar furniture, and protect it from dangers such as open fires.

Keeping your cat healthy

With a little care, it is possible to reduce your cat's chances of becoming ill. There are four basic ways you can do this: keeping it out of danger, taking appropriate hygiene precautions, registering it with a vet, and having it vaccinated regularly.

Safety precautions
As a general principle, it is best not to let your pet wander far and wide, especially in an urban area — restrict it to your own garden, supervise its outdoor expeditions or train it to walk on a lead (see p. 145). However, if it gets adequate exercise, I don't believe it is unhealthy or oppressive to keep a cat permanently indoors (see pp. 145—7).

Hygiene precautions
For good feline health, hygiene is most important so keep your cat's bedding and feeding utensils scrupulously clean (see p. 140). Also, inspect its ears, eyes, nostrils, mouth, feet, fur, genitalia and anal area regularly to check that they are free from dirt, discharge and abnormalities (see pp. 168—9).

Registering with a vet
As soon as you acquire a cat, register it with a vet. Ideally, you should choose one who specializes in the domestic cat or small animals. Such vets frequently have premises equipped with facilities for the most up-to-date medical and surgical techniques. A veterinary practice without such elaborate equipment may be capable of providing a high degree of medical care for cats, but it may refer complicated cases to other practices — ask to whom and where. Nevertheless, *all* vets are trained in feline diagnosis and treatment, and finding a vet who has a "feeling" for cats, who handles them with sympathy and interest, and who will explain the diagnoses clearly, is better than choosing a practice with advanced hardware and fancy surgical techniques.

Medical insurance
It is worth investigating a pet medical insurance scheme. This can ease the financial burden of unexpected disease and accidents.

Vaccinations
Make sure your cat receives preventive vaccinations against the major infectious diseases, and that it has regular booster doses (see pp. 229 and 238).

ZOONOSES

A few cat ailments, known as zoonoses, can affect humans. They are: ☐ Rabies (see p. 151) ☐ skin parasitism (see pp. 267—8) ☐ Toxoplasmosis (see p. 241). However, there are a number of precautions you can take to prevent infection:
- Always wash your hands after touching a pet
- Don't allow pregnant women and young children to touch cat's droppings
- Keep sandpits covered
- Clean all bite and scratch wounds and treat with antiseptic. If pain or swelling develops, seek medical advice as infected wounds can induce "cat scratch fever"
- Keep a cat with ringworm (see p. 268) "in quarantine" in a spare room

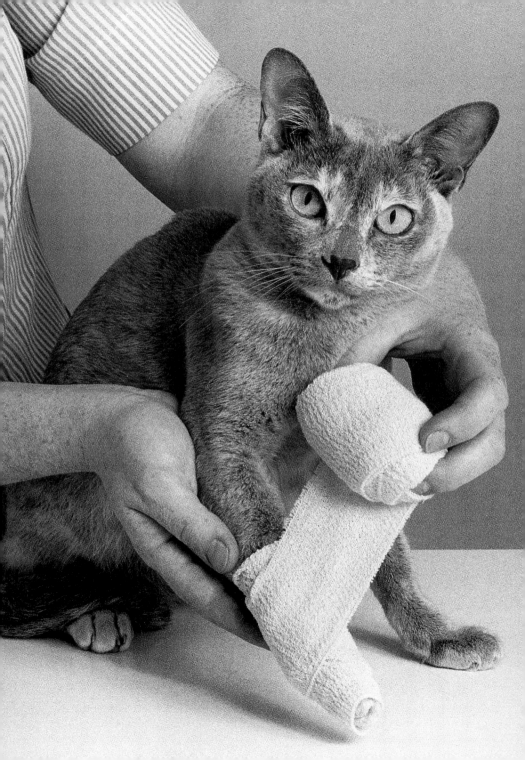

13

FIRST AID

Cats occasionally appear to have nine lives; their bodies are so
elastic and wiry that they often survive a minor fall or
encounter with a car without suffering fractures or serious
damage. Nevertheless, they don't always escape accidents
damage-free, and it is therefore important to be aware of the
emergency procedures outlined in this chapter that can save
an injured cat's life.

Collapse and accident

An injured or unconscious cat may need prompt first aid action — stopping bleeding, treating shock, clearing its airways and giving artificial respiration — in order to save its life. You should therefore familiarize yourself with the basic methods involved. If possible, get someone else to telephone the vet so that you can begin the emergency procedure straightaway.

> **SEE ALSO:**
> **Taking the pulse** see *Health Care* p. 216.
> **Wounds and burns** see *First Aid* p. 282.
> **Restraining a cat** see *Health Care* p. 270.
> **Convulsions** see *Health Care* p. 280.

DO NOT:

- Don't move the animal unless it is in danger (in the road, for example)
- Don't raise its head or prop it up because saliva, blood or vomit may run to the back of the throat and block the airway
- Don't give the animal anything — solid or liquid — by mouth

ACTION

1 Getting the cat out of danger
If you have to move an injured cat slip a sheet under it and carry it like a hammock. You may need to restrain it first (see p. 270). Lay the cat down in a quiet, warm place and cover it with a blanket. Place a hot water bottle next to it. Make sure it isn't scalding — it is safest to wrap the bottle in a cloth.

2 Check the pulse This can be felt on the inside of the cat's thigh, where the leg joins the body (see p. 216).

3 Check breathing If breathing is irregular or nonexistent: □ loosen the collar □ open the mouth □ pull the tongue forward □ remove any foreign body present (see p. 280) □ wipe away any saliva, blood or vomit □ give artificial respiration.

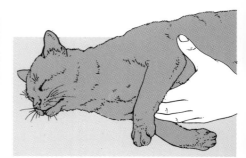

4 Check for heartbeat This can be felt by placing the fingertips on the lower part of the chest, just behind the front leg. Give heart massage if necessary — rub the area over the heart vigorously but carefully (it is easy to crush its ribs) with both hands. Also give artificial respiration (see opposite).

5 Treat bleeding Staunch any heavy blood flow (see p. 282).

6 Look for broken bones Give emergency treatment (see p. 283).

7 Treat shock Keep the cat warm with blankets or hot water bottles.

8 Contact the vet Arrange for an immediate examination.

Possible causes of collapse

□ Epileptic fit (see p. 280) □ Heart disease (see p. 258) □ Poisoning (see p. 281) □ Diabetes (see p. 242) □ Severe exposure □ Injury in an accident

A BASIC FIRST AID KIT

Keep a separate kit: **1** Safe disinfectant (p. 273) **2** Milk of magnesia **3** Human eye wash **4** Liquid paraffin **5** Antiseptic cream **6** Antiseptic wash **7** Round-ended scissors **8** Tweezers **9** Stubby thermometer **10** 5 and 10 cm bandages **11** 5 cm adhesive dressing **12** Cotton wool **13** Cotton buds **14** Lint gauze **15** Plastic bags to cover foot dressings

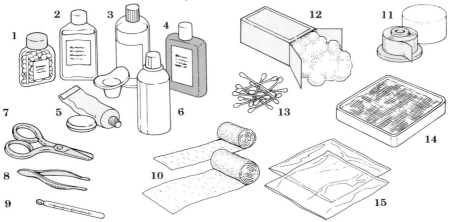

ARTIFICIAL RESPIRATION

Unless the cat is unconscious or there is a possibility that its back or hind legs are injured, it is best to start by swinging it (see p. 280). This will clear fluid and mucus from the airways. If this doesn't work, you will probably find the external method easiest. If the cat is unconscious or you suspect chest damage, the mouth-to-mouth method is best. With both methods, keep the cat horizontal during treatment.

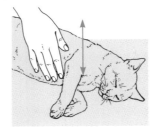

External method
Place both palms on the chest over the ribs and push down firmly to expel air from the lungs. Be careful not to press to firmly or you may damage the cat's ribs. Release pressure straightaway so that the chest expands and the lungs refill. Repeat at 5-second intervals.

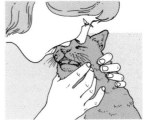

Mouth-to-mouth method
Check that the airway is clear, then apply your lips to the cat's nostrils and blow in air steadily for 3 seconds. Pause for 2 seconds, then repeat.

CONVULSIONS

Most fits, including epileptic types, start with uncharacteristic, bizarre behaviour which may include: □ Champing □ Chewing □ Foaming at the mouth □ Jerking of the limbs □ Incontinence □ Collapse. This is followed by loss of consciousness.

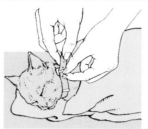

ACTION

1 Contact the vet immediately.

2 Make sure that the cat is in a safe place.

3 Leave the cat where it is, but try to make it as comfortable as possible by loosening its collar and covering it with a blanket to keep it warm. Once you have done this, try to avoid touching it until the fit is over.

4 Reduce external stimuli (dim the room lights, draw the curtains and turn off the radio or television).

5 The fit shouldn't last longer than five minutes. Once it is over, wipe the froth from the cat's mouth and clean up any urine and faeces.

6 Keep the animal indoors in a warm, quiet place until the vet arrives.

Foreign body in mouth
Grasping the cat's body firmly, open its mouth and push the lower jaw down with a pencil. Locate the object, using a torch if necessary, and remove it with fingers or fine pliers. If you can't dislodge the obstruction try the swinging method (right). Now contact the vet.

Foreign body in the eye
Don't allow the cat to paw at its eye. Grasping its body firmly, part the eyelid and examine the eye. If the foreign body is penetrating the surface don't attempt to remove it, go straight to the vet. If the object doesn't wash out, put 1–3 drops of olive oil in the eye. Contact the vet.

Foreign body in the nose
Don't try to remove the object. First apply a cold compress to soothe irritation and control bleeding. Now contact the vet.

Resuscitating a drowning cat
Pick it up by its back legs and whirl it round and round so that centrifugal force drives out the water blocking the airways.

Poisons

Cats are at risk from a number of poisons, ingested in two main ways: first, if a cat's coat becomes contaminated with a chemical it will lick it off in an attempt to clean itself, and second its hunting lifestyle means that a cat may eat, unwittingly, poisons used to kill pests. Don't try to make an accurate diagnosis of the kind of poison from its effect – many different types produce similar signs.

ACTION

1 Contact the vet Arrange for an immediate examination.

2 Wash the cat at once Use human hair shampoo or even soap. Rinse it well, and dry it thoroughly.

3 Visit the vet If you suspect a particular chemical causant, bring a sample of it and its container with the cat.

Treatment
If indicated (see below), or on your vet's advice give an emetic to make the cat vomit, a demulcent to protect its stomach and intestines, or a laxative.
Emetics Suitable substances are: □ a pea-sized piece of sodium carbonate given as a tablet □ a very strong solution of salt in water □ mustard in water.
Demulcents Suitable substances are: □ milk □ raw egg white □ milk of magnesia □ olive oil.
Laxatives Suitable substances are: □ liquid paraffin □ magnesium sulphate.

COMMON POISONS

Type	Source	Visible signs	Emergency action
Arsenic	● Horticultural sprays ● Rodent poisons	● Vomiting ● Diarrhoea ● Paralysis	● Wash coat ● Emetic ● Demulcent
Lead	● Paints	● Paralysis ● Nervous signs	● Wait for vet
Phosphorus, Thallium	● Rodent poison	● Vomiting ● Diarrhoea	● Emetic
Phenols, Cresols, Tar products, Turpentine	● Tar ● Wood preservative	● Burnt mouth ● Vomiting ● Convulsions ● Coma	● Wash coat ● Demulcents, particularly milk
Aspirin		● Vomiting ● Liver damage	● Emetic ● Demulcent
Chlorinated, carbons (DDT, Gamma BHC)	● Insecticides	● Nervousness ● Salivation ● Convulsions	● Wash coat ● Wait for vet
Warfarin	● Rodent poison	● Stiffness ● Diarrhoea ● Haemorrhages	● Wait for vet
Anti-freeze (ethylene glycol)	● Drips from car radiators	● Incoordination ● Depression ● Convulsions ● Coma	● Wait for vet

Wounds and burns

The most common causes of wounds are bites or scratches from other cats. If you notice blood on your cat's coat and can't find the source, run your fingers through its coat to locate the wound.

ACTION

1 **Clean the area** Clip surrounding hair if necessary (see p. 266).

2 **Control any bleeding** Bandage the wound (see below).

3 **Treat shock** Keep the cat warm with blankets or a hot water bottle.

4 **Contact the vet** Arrange for an immediate examination.

TREATING BURNS

Burns are usually caused by hot liquid spilt on a cat. However, chemicals, extreme cold and electric current can also be causes. Apply cold water or ice to the site. (If the cause is a burning chemical, wash it off with copious amounts of water.) Then apply a greasy ointment such as petroleum jelly to the burn. Now contact the vet.

White cats sometimes suffer from sunburn to the ears. Ask your vet for a healing ointment, and keep your cat indoors in sunny weather.

BANDAGING

Use hospital-quality bandages, making a two-thirds overlap every turn, and keeping the degree of tightness even. When bandaging a limb, take the bandage down to envelop the foot. This avoids a "tourniquet" effect where the circulation in the lower leg is adversely affected by the bandage.

1 Cover the wound with a pad (at least 1 cm thick) of absorbent material.

2 Secure the pad with a crepe bandage fixed with a safety pin.

PRESSURE POINTS THAT CONTROL BLEEDING

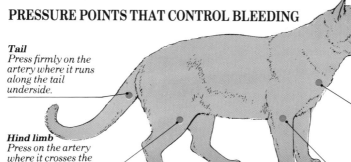

Tail
Press firmly on the artery where it runs along the tail underside.

Head and neck
Press on the artery (in a groove in the lower part of the neck where it meets the shoulder).

Hind limb
Press on the artery where it crosses the bone on the inner thigh.

Fore limb
Press firmly on the artery where it crosses the bone 2—5 cm above the inside of the elbow joint.

COMMON WOUNDS

Type	Emergency action	Degree of urgency
Minor wound with little or no blood	Wash with dilute anti-septic; apply ice-cold comp-ress; apply bandage	✚ May be treatable at home
Bleeding wound	Control bleeding; wash with dilute antiseptic; apply pressure bandage	✚✚✚ Don't delay — contact a vet immediately
Deep or long wound (over 2 cm)	Clean; apply antiseptic powder; clip hair; apply pressure bandage	✚✚✚ Don't delay — contact a vet immediately
Wound with skin missing	Cover with a damp cotton compress	✚✚✚ Don't delay — contact a vet immediately
Infected or bite wound	Clip hair; apply a saturated warm water/Epsom salt solution; leave uncovered	✚✚✚ Don't delay — contact a vet immediately

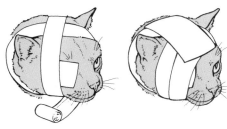

Bandaging an eye wound
Secure an absorbent pad with a crepe bandage, taking it round the head 4–5 times and fixing in place with tape.

Bandaging a torso wound
Secure a pad with a rectangular piece of linen. Cut the sides to make tails, and tie these together over the cat's back.

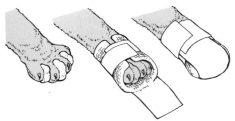

Bandaging a foot or leg wound
Insert cotton between the toes. Secure an absorbent pad with tape, looped under the foot, then across the top.

Applying a splint
Pad the site with gauze, then put two flat 1.5 cm wide pieces of wood either side of the limb and bind with a bandage.

Index

Acknowledgements

Author's Acknowledgements

I would like to thank the Dorling Kindersley team, particularly Judith More and Carole Ash, for their expertise, enthusiasm and many kindnesses. Thanks are also due to Diane Wilkins who typed the manuscript and whose family stoically endured my dictation tapes, to my daughter Lindsey for much help and to the members of my practice for wise advice. Lastly, I must mention my parents – it was as a result of their encouragement when I was a small boy that I became a veterinary surgeon. Their encouragement has continued – from my first patient, a cross-eyed old tom with bladder trouble, right up to the Atlas lion cub with eye disease that I treated yesterday.

Dorling Kindersley would like to thank:

Grace Pond for her advice on the cat fancy; Peter Scott for additional veterinary advice; Lesley Davy for picture research; Hilary Bird for the index; Bruce Fogle for the use of his surgery; Animal Fair of Kensington for the loan of equipment; Jenny Berry, Maxine Clark, Mr and Mrs Ash, Karen Fletcher, Neil Cousins, Richard Warner, Sal Marsh, Richard Ollet, Mr Klauf Defsauer, Spud, Tiger, Robin and Daisy for modelling; Ron Bagley, Mike Hearne and Ken Hone for photographic services.

Illustrators

Breeds chapter colour illustrations: John Francis of Linden Artists.
Other illustrations: Coral Mula, Chris Forsey, John Woodcock, Eugene Fleury, David Ashby.

Photography

Paddy Cutts, Karen Norquay, Thomas Dobbie, Vincent Oliver, Arthur Sidey.

Photographic credits

Agence Nature/NHPA: p. 24
Creszentia Allen: p. 125
Larry Allen/Image Bank: pp. 53, 98
Animal Health Trust: pp. 247, 248 c
Animals Unlimited/Paddy Cutts: pp. 25 t, 27, 46, 49 t l and r, 50 t and l, 52, 54, 56, 57, 59, 61 r, 64 b, 65, 66 r, 69, 71, 77, 83, 85 r, 94, 95 t and b, 97, 101, 105, 109 l, 144, 164, 180, 184, 185, 208 l and r
Ardea London: p. 191
Jane Burton/Bruce Coleman Ltd.: pp. 33, 126, 198
Chanan Photography: pp. 49 b, 55, 75, 90, 92, 106, 107, 111
Stephen Dalton/NHPA: pp. 163, 186
John Daniels/Ardea London: p. 28
Mary Evans Picture Library: p. 7 b l
Farming Press Ltd.: pp. 248 l, 263, 280
Jean Paul Ferrero/Ardea London: pp. 64 t, 81, 89
Joseph & Marna Fogarty: p. 185
Sonia Halliday: p. 74
Marc Henrie: pp. 62, 87, 100, 269
Michael Holford: p. 7 b r
Ed Holt/Vision International: pp. 11 r, 13 t, 128, 135
Howletts and Port Lympne Zoo Parks: p. 41 b
Peter Johnson/NHPA: p. 26
Lacz Lemoine/NHPA: pp. 61 l, 70, 72
Orbis: p. 15 t
Robert Pearcy/Animals Animals/OSF: p. 93
Francis Petter/Jacana: p. 36
Photoresources: p. 7 t
Hans Reinhard/Bruce Coleman Ltd.: pp. 23, 63, 103
Spectrum Colour Library: pp. 12, 134, 197
Solitaire: pp. 16, 66
Tony Stone Photolibrary – London: pp. 2, 10, 11 l, 13 b, 14, 15 b, 41 t, 51, 88, 118, 154, 168
Sally Anne Thompson: pp. 18, 58, 78, 84, 86, 99, 102, 109 r, 195
University of Glasgow Veterinary School: pp. 284 r, 267, 268
Albert Visage/Jacana: p. 40
John Visser/Bruce Coleman Ltd.: p. 41 c
Sam Zarember/Image Bank: p. 9
Zefa: pp. 8, 112
Brian Doyle, owner of "Book of the Cat" (1903) which was reproduced c/o J & P Reprographic, Birkenhead Merseyside: p. 178

Cover:

Colour illustrations John Francis
Line illustrations Coral Mula
Photographs Animals Unlimited

Typesetting by Gedset, Cheltenham
Reproduction by New Interlitho, Milan